THE NEW FOLGER LIBRARY SHAKESPEARE

Designed to make Shakespeare's great plays available to all readers, the New Folger Library edition of Shakespeare's plays provides accurate texts in modern spelling and punctuation, as well as scene-by-scene action summaries, full explanatory notes, many pictures clarifying Shakespeare's language, and notes recording all significant departures from the early printed versions. Each play is prefaced by a brief introduction, by a guide to reading Shakespeare's language, and by accounts of his life and theater. Each play is followed by an annotated list of further readings and by a "Modern Perspective" written by an expert on that particular play.

Barbara A. Mowat is Director of Academic Programs at the Folger Shakespeare Library, Executive Editor of *Shakespeare Quarterly,* Chair of the Folger Institute, and author of *The Dramaturgy of Shakespeare's Romances* and of essays on Shakespeare's plays and on the editing of the plays.

Paul Werstine is Professor of English at King's College and the Graduate School of the University of Western Ontario, Canada. He is general editor of the New Variorum Shakespeare and author of many papers and articles on the printing and editing of Shakespeare's plays.

The Folger Shakespeare Library

The Folger Shakespeare Library in Washington, D.C., a privately funded research library dedicated to Shakespeare and the civilization of early modern Europe, was founded in 1932 by Henry Clay and Emily Jordan Folger. In addition to its role as the world's preeminent Shakespeare collection and its emergence as a leading center for Renaissance studies, the Folger Library offers a wide array of cultural and educational programs and services for the general public.

EDITORS

BARBARA A. MOWAT
Director of Academic Programs
Folger Shakespeare Library

PAUL WERSTINE
Professor of English
King's College and the University of Western Ontario

For information regarding special discounts for bulk purchases, please contact Simon & Schuster Special Sales at 1-800-456-6798 or business@simonandschuster.com

.THE NEW.
FOLGER LIBRARY
SHAKESPEARE

MEASURE
FOR
MEASURE

BY

WILLIAM SHAKESPEARE

WASHINGTON SQUARE PRESS
PUBLISHED BY POCKET BOOKS

New York   London   Toronto   Sydney   Singapore

A WASHINGTON SQUARE PRESS *Original* Publication

WSP

A Washington Square Press Publication of
POCKET BOOKS, a division of Simon & Schuster Inc.
1230 Avenue of the Americas, New York, NY 10020

ISBN: 0-671-72276-X

Washington Square Press New Folger Edition December 1997

10 9 8 7 6

Cover art by Kinuko Y. Craft

Printed in the U.S.A.

From the Director of the Library

For over four decades, the Folger Library General Reader's Shakespeare provided accurate and accessible texts of the plays and poems to students, teachers, and millions of other interested readers. Today, in an age often impatient with the past, the passion for Shakespeare continues to grow. No author speaks more powerfully to the human condition, in all its variety, than this actor/playwright from a minor sixteenth-century English village.

Over the years vast changes have occurred in the way Shakespeare's works are edited, performed, studied, and taught. The New Folger Library Shakespeare replaces the earlier versions, bringing to bear the best and most current thinking concerning both the texts and their interpretation. Here is an edition which makes the plays and poems fully understandable for modern readers using uncompromising scholarship. Professors Barbara Mowat and Paul Werstine are uniquely qualified to produce this New Folger Shakespeare for a new generation of readers. The Library is grateful for the learning, clarity, and imagination they have brought to this ambitious project.

Werner Gundersheimer,
Director of the Folger Shakespeare
Library from 1984 to 2002

Contents

Editors' Preface

In recent years, ways of dealing with Shakespeare's texts and with the interpretation of his plays have been undergoing significant change. This edition, while retaining many of the features that have always made the Folger Shakespeare so attractive to the general reader, at the same time reflects these current ways of thinking about Shakespeare. For example, modern readers, actors, and teachers have become interested in the differences between, on the one hand, the early forms in which Shakespeare's plays were first published and, on the other hand, the forms in which editors through the centuries have presented them. In response to this interest, we have based our edition on what we consider the best early printed version of a particular play (explaining our rationale in a section called "An Introduction to This Text") and have marked our changes in the text—unobtrusively, we hope, but in such a way that the curious reader can be aware that a change has been made and can consult the "Textual Notes" to discover what appeared in the early printed version.

Current ways of looking at the plays are reflected in our brief prefaces, in many of the commentary notes, in the annotated lists of "Further Reading," and especially in each play's "Modern Perspective," an essay written by an outstanding scholar who brings to the reader his or her fresh assessment of the play in the light of today's interests and concerns.

As in the Folger Library General Reader's Shakespeare, which this edition replaces, we include explanatory notes designed to help make Shakespeare's language clearer to a modern reader, and we place the notes on the page facing the text that they explain. We also follow the earlier edition in including illustrations—of objects, of clothing, of mythological figures—from books and manuscripts in the Folger Library collection. We provide fresh accounts of the life of Shakespeare, of the publishing of his plays, and of the theaters in which his plays were performed, as well as an introduction to the text itself. We also include a section called "Reading Shakespeare's Language," in which we try to help readers learn to "break the code" of Elizabethan poetic language.

For each section of each volume, we are indebted to a host of generous experts and fellow scholars. The "Reading Shakespeare's Language" sections, for example, could not have been written had not Arthur King, of Brigham Young University, and Randall Robinson, author of *Unlocking Shakespeare's Language*, led the way in untangling Shakespearean language puzzles and shared their insights and methodologies generously with us. "Shakespeare's Life" profited by the careful reading given it by the late S. Schoenbaum, "Shakespeare's Theater" was read and strengthened by Andrew Gurr and John Astington, and "The Publication of Shakespeare's Plays" is indebted to the comments of Peter W. M. Blayney. We, as editors, take sole responsibility for any errors in our editions.

We are grateful to the authors of the "Modern Perspectives"; to Leeds Barroll and David Bevington for their generous encouragement; to the Huntington and Newberry Libraries for fellowship support; to King's College for the grants it has provided to Paul Werstine; to the Social Sciences and Humanities Research Council of Canada, which provided him with a Research Time Stipend for 1990–91; to R. J. Shroyer of the University of Western Ontario for essential computer support; to Jo Ann McNamara for generously sharing her expertise in the history of the religious life; and to the Folger

Institute's Center for Shakespeare Studies for its fortuitous sponsorship of a workshop on "Shakespeare's Texts for Students and Teachers" (funded by the National Endowment for the Humanities and led by Richard Knowles of the University of Wisconsin), a workshop from which we learned an enormous amount about what is wanted by college and high-school teachers of Shakespeare today; and especially to Steve Llano, our production editor at Pocket Books, whose expertise and attention to detail are essential to this project.

Our biggest debt is to the Folger Shakespeare Library—to Werner Gundersheimer, Director of the Library, who made possible our edition; to Deborah Curren-Aquino, who provides extensive editorial and production support; to Jean Miller, the Library's Art Curator, who combs the Library holdings for illustrations, and to Julie Ainsworth, Head of the Photography Department, who carefully photographs them; to Peggy O'Brien, former Director of Education at the Folger and now Director of Education Programs at the Corporation for Public Broadcasting, who gave us expert advice about the needs being expressed by Shakespeare teachers and students (and to Martha Christian and other "master teachers" who used our texts in manuscript in their classrooms); to Jessica Hymowitz and Wazir Shpoon for their expert computer support; to the staff of the Academic Programs Division, especially Amy Adler, Mary Tonkinson, Kathleen Lynch, Linda Johnson, Carol Brobeck, Mariann Payne, Toni Krieger, and Martha Fay; and, finally, to the generously supportive staff of the Library's Reading Room.

Barbara A. Mowat and Paul Werstine

Shakespeare's
Measure for Measure

Measure for Measure is a play rooted deeply in early seventeenth-century culture; at the same time, it retains a powerful hold on the imaginations of modern readers. In an attempt to suggest why *Measure for Measure* continues to be among the most passionately discussed of Shakespeare's plays, we might think about the ways that the seventeenth-century issues it dramatizes relate to present-day concerns.

Measure for Measure features a duke who is so anxious about the decline in the moral quality of his subjects' lives that he temporarily removes himself from the government of his city-state and deputizes a member of his administration, Angelo, to enforce existing laws more rigorously. Angelo, who has never before had the opportunity to exercise such power over others and who thus has never had to withstand the temptation to misuse it, experiences no qualms of conscience as he holds all in the city to the same idealized standard of moral behavior that he thinks he himself exemplifies. The man he chooses as his first victim is Claudio, who has impregnated Juliet before they have solemnized their marriage. For this crime, Angelo condemns Claudio to death.

At Claudio's request, Isabella, who is Claudio's sister, approaches Angelo to plead for her brother's life. Every bit as idealistic as Angelo, Isabella is in the process of entering the convent of the Order of Poor Clares, where she will vow lifelong obedience, poverty, and chastity. Her eloquence in addressing Angelo arouses in him the desire to possess her, a desire so strange to him that he immediately gives in to it and, renouncing integrity and morality, attempts to extort sex from her in return for her brother's life. Isabella, denied any opportunity to expose Angelo's corruption, is nonetheless resolute in her spiritual commitment to preserve her chastity, no matter the consequences. Meanwhile, the duke has disguised himself as a friar so as to discover the true nature of his subjects. After eavesdropping on Isabella's revelation to her brother about Angelo's attempted extortion, the duke (in his friar's disguise) offers to ally himself with Isabella against Angelo.

In view of the overriding importance of religion and the spiritual life in early seventeenth-century England, and in view of the control exerted over both religion and morality by the State in this era when Parliament actually debated the death penalty for pre-marital sex, it is easy to see how *Measure for Measure* might capture its audience's interest. In today's culture, however, in which religion exerts an influence on the lives of only part of the population, it would seem unlikely that *Measure for Measure* could engage audiences in anything like the same way it once did. Yet there are now other issues that have attached themselves to the play.

One such issue is the division of opinion about the role of government in shaping the morality of citizens. For those who regard such governmental action as intrusive, the duke may seem intolerably meddlesome in his interference in the lives of his people; for those who want government to act in the defense of conventional morality, the duke may be understood as properly exerting himself to impose standards of moral behavior on his people. Another issue that has become attached to the play is sexual harassment of women by men, with Angelo and Isabella's encounter presenting itself as a powerfully dramatic representation of this ongoing problem. Yet another current issue, the right of a woman to control her own body, has arisen for modern readers from the scenes in which Isabella is forced to choose between her virginity and her brother's life. Modern responses to *Measure for Measure* indicate how a play that is formed in a past culture can be transformed in its reception by present culture into a spectacle of continuing fascination.

After you have read the play, we invite you to turn to the essay printed after it, *"Measure for Measure:* A Modern Perspective" by Professor Christy Desmet of the University of Georgia.

Reading Shakespeare's Language: *Measure for Measure*

For many people today, reading Shakespeare's language can be a problem—but it is a problem that can be solved. Those who have studied Latin (or even French or German or Spanish) and those who are used to reading poetry will have little difficulty understanding the language of Shakespeare's poetic drama. Others, though, need to develop the skills of untangling unusual sentence structures and of recognizing and understanding poetic compressions, omissions, and wordplay. And even those skilled in reading unusual sentence structures may have occasional trouble with Shakespeare's words. Four hundred years of "static" intervene between his speaking and our hearing. Most of his immense vocabulary is still in use, but a few of his words are not, and, worse, some of his words now have meanings quite different from those they had in the sixteenth and seventeenth centuries. In the theater, most of these difficulties are solved for us by actors who study the language and articulate it for us so that the essential meaning is heard—or, when combined with stage action, is at least *felt*. When reading on one's own, one must do what each actor does: go over the lines (often with a dictionary close at hand) until the puzzles are solved and the lines yield up their poetry and the characters speak in words and phrases that are, suddenly, rewarding and wonderfully memorable.

Shakespeare's Words

As you begin to read the opening scenes of a play by Shakespeare, you may notice occasional unfamiliar words. Some are unfamiliar simply because we no longer use them. In the opening scenes of *Measure for Measure*, for example, you will find the words *kersey* (coarse cloth), *foppery* (foolishness, folly), *sith* (since), and *foison* (abundance). Words of this kind are explained in notes to the text and will become familiar the more of Shakespeare's plays you read.

In *Measure for Measure*, as in all of Shakespeare's writing, more problematic are the words that we still use but that we use with a different meaning. In the opening scenes of *Measure for Measure*, for example, the word *meat* has the meaning of "food" in general (rather than a particular kind of food), *owe* is used where we would say "own" or "possess," *straight* is used where we would say "immediately," *friends* where we would say "relatives," and *unhappy* where we would say "unfortunate." Such words are explained in the notes to the text, but they, too, will become familiar as you continue to read Shakespeare's language.

Some words are strange not because of the "static" introduced by changes in language over the past centuries but because these are words that Shakespeare is using to establish the multiple settings in which the fiction of his play is to be imagined as taking place. *Measure for Measure* brings together worlds that we in modern culture ordinarily regard as being widely separated from each other. The first of these is the highest level of public administration and of the justice system of Vienna, built up for us in the play's opening dialogue with reference to "terms of common justice," "deputation," and "secondary," or subordinate. By the play's second act, however—and repeatedly thereafter—the elevated language of this world is brought into connection with accounts of an underworld of organized prostitution, of a "hothouse," a "whoremaster," and a "trot." Thus *Measure for Measure* brings together, with some satiric effect, two language worlds that are conventionally regarded as far removed from each other in terms of respectability. Into these worlds comes Isabella, who is first presented to us in an altogether distinct setting, the convent, which becomes vivid to us with such terms as "votarists," "renouncement," and "Prioress." The collision of perspectives that makes for intense drama in *Measure for Measure* arises in part from the play's bringing together characters who come from such different settings.

Shakespeare's Sentences

In an English sentence, meaning is dependent on the place given each word. "The dog bit the boy" and "The boy bit the dog" mean very different things, even though the individual words are the same. Because English places such importance on the positions of words in sentences, on the way words are arranged, unusual arrangements can puzzle a reader. Shakespeare frequently shifts his sentences away from "normal" English arrangements—often to create the rhythm he seeks, sometimes to use a line's poetic rhythm to emphasize a particular word, sometimes to give a character his or her own speech pattern or to allow the character to speak in a special way. When we attend a good performance of the play, the actors will have worked out the sentence structures and will articulate the sentences so that the meaning is clear. In reading for yourself, do as the actor does. That is, when you become puzzled by a character's speech, check to see if words are being presented in an unusual sequence.

Look first for the placement of subject and verb. Shakespeare often rearranges verbs and subjects (e.g., instead of "He goes" we find "Goes he"). In *Measure for Measure*, when Lucio says "Upon his place . . . /*Governs Lord Angelo*," he is using such a construction. (The "normal" arrangement would be "Lord Angelo governs.") The duke also inverts subject and verb when he says "Then *was your sin* of heavier kind than his." Shakespeare frequently places the object before both the subject and the verb (e.g., instead of "I hit him," we might find "Him I hit") or between the subject and the verb ("I him hit"). Escalus's "A power I have" is an example of such an inversion, as is Isabella's "men their creation mar."

Inversions are not the only unusual sentence structures in Shakespeare's language. Often in his sentences words that would normally appear together are separated from each other. (Again, this is often done to create a particular rhythm or to stress a particular word.) Take, for example, the duke's "Old *Escalus*, /

Though first in question, *is* thy secondary"; here the phrase "Though first in question" separates the subject ("Escalus") from its verb ("is"). Or take the duke's lines *"We have* with a leavened and preparèd choice/*Proceeded* to you," where the normal construction "We have proceeded" is interrupted by the clause "with a leavened and preparèd choice." In order to create for yourself sentences that seem more like the English of everyday speech, you may wish to rearrange the words in the way exemplified in this discussion. You will usually find that the sentence will gain in clarity but will lose its rhythm or shift its emphasis.

Locating and rearranging words that "belong together" is especially necessary in passages that separate basic sentence elements by long delaying or expanding interruptions—a structure that is sometimes used in *Measure for Measure.* When Isabella is challenging Angelo's authority for condemning her brother to death, she uses a striking example of such an expanding construction:

> But *man*, proud man,
> Dressed in a little brief authority,
> Most ignorant of what he's most assured,
> His glassy essence, like an angry ape
> *Plays* such fantastic tricks before high heaven
> As makes the angels weep.

Here, after stating the subject of her sentence ("man"), Isabella postpones the verb "plays" until she has fully characterized "man" in a profoundly disturbing way as exercising Godlike authority with no better judgment than "an angry ape."

Often in *Measure for Measure,* rather than separating basic sentence elements, Shakespeare simply holds them back, delaying them until other material to which he wants to give greater emphasis has been presented.

Angelo uses such a construction just as he is about to declare his desire for Isabella to her:

> And from this testimony of your own sex,
> Since I suppose we are made to be no stronger
> Than faults may shake our frames, let me be bold.

The basic sentence elements do not appear until his last four words ("let me be bold"). The emphasis thus falls on the basis for his conviction that Isabella must succumb to his advances, namely, her own testimony that women are "ten times frail" ("this testimony of your own sex"), and his belief that human beings are not strong enough to withstand temptation ("we are made . . . no stronger than faults may shake our frames").

In many of Shakespeare's plays, sentences are sometimes complicated not because of unusual structures or interruptions but because Shakespeare omits words that English sentences normally require. (In conversation, we, too, often omit words. We say "Heard from him yet?" and our hearer supplies the missing "Have you.") Frequent reading of Shakespeare—and of other poets—trains us to supply such missing words. In *Measure for Measure* omissions both maintain the rhythm of the blank verse and contribute to the strong sense of urgency that marks the play. For example, when Angelo is being addressed by his own servant and by the supplicant Isabella, both the servant and Isabella use elliptical constructions as if to signal that Angelo presents himself as so occupied with the administration of justice in Vienna that he will not take the time to hear any more words from others than are absolutely necessary to convey meaning. His servant announces Isabella to him with the words "Here is the sister of the man condemned / Desires access to you" (instead of saying "Here is the condemned man's sister *who* desires access to you"), and Isabella introduces her petition to Angelo saying "I have a brother is condemned to die" instead of "I have a brother *who* is condemned to die." Angelo too addresses himself in soliloquy in language marked by omission, as if the efficient use of language is so habitual to him that it conditions even his innermost thoughts: "God in my mouth, / As if I did but only chew His name, / And in my heart the strong and swelling evil / Of my conception." The more standard construction would be "God [is] in my mouth" and "in my heart [is] the strong and swelling evil."

Shakespearean Wordplay

Shakespeare plays with language so often and so variously that entire books are written on the topic. Here we will discuss in any detail only three kinds of wordplay, puns, similes, and metaphors. A pun is a play on words that sound the same but that have different meanings (or on a single word that has more than one meaning). Much of the humor of *Measure for Measure* depends on puns. One pair of puns early in the play arises in the first speech of the First Gentleman, who is apparently hopeful of bettering himself through service in a military campaign he expects the Duke of Vienna to join in leading against the King of Hungary: "Heaven grant us its peace, but not the King of Hungary's!" The first pun in this speech involves the word *peace*, which has two meanings here. Initially its meaning is "Heaven's peace" or "God's peace," which is asked for in the familiar prayer *Dona nobis pacem*, "grant us thy peace." But this use of the word *peace* becomes a pun when the word acquires the second meaning of "peace treaty" (in "the King of Hungary's" peace). And the First Gentleman's speech also employs the contemporary pun on "Hungary/hungry" and on "Hungarians" as "hungry people." The suggestion is that if peace between warring dukedoms and kingdoms is achieved, he and other soldiers will go hungry.

When these would-be soldiers are approached by the bawd Mistress Overdone, they begin to pun on words about money and syphilis, both associated with prostitution (syphilis being particularly virulent in the period of this play):

LUCIO   Behold, behold, where Madam Mitigation comes! I have purchased as many diseases under her roof as come to—
SECOND GENTLEMAN   To what, I pray?
LUCIO   Judge.
SECOND GENTLEMAN   To three thousand dolors a year.
FIRST GENTLEMAN   Ay, and more.
LUCIO   A French crown more.

In the Second Gentleman's line, "To three thousand dolors a year," the word *dolors* means "pains" or "diseases," including venereal diseases; however, coming after the earlier lines "I have purchased . . . diseases," *dolors* is also a pun on "dollars." And Lucio's use of the term *French crown* is a pun that refers both to a coin and to syphilis, which, in a slur on the French current in England at this time, was known as the "French disease."

Metaphors and similes are plays on words in which one object or idea is expressed as if it were something else, something with which it shares common features. Similes make the verbal act of comparison explicit through the use of "like" or "as"; metaphors simply assert their identification of one thing with another. One particularly vivid simile from early in the play is given to Claudio:

> Our natures do pursue,
> Like rats that raven down their proper bane,
> A thirsty evil, and when we drink, we die.

Here he compares the ravenous appetite exhibited by rats for the poison prepared to destroy them ("their proper bane") with human inclination toward evil and with the deathly consequences, in his case, of having yielded to that inclination.

Vivid though Claudio's figure of speech is, a series of figures employed by the duke in the first scene is perhaps more typical of the play. Like Claudio's simile, the duke's figures are concerned with morality, but, as so often in the language of *Measure for Measure*, they borrow the terms of their comparison from the Bible, specifically from the Christian New Testament. In the following passage the duke begins by alluding to Luke 8.16, which reads: "No man when he lighteth a candle covereth it under a vessel . . . but setteth it on a candlestick that they that enter in may see the light."

> Thyself and thy belongings
> Are not thine own so proper as to waste
> Thyself upon thy virtues, they on thee.
> Heaven doth with us as we with torches do,
> Not light them for themselves; for if our virtues
> Did not go forth of us, 'twere all alike
> As if we had them not. Spirits are not finely touched
> But to fine issues, nor nature never lends
> The smallest scruple of her excellence

But, like a thrifty goddess, she determines
Herself the glory of a creditor,
Both thanks and use.

In the passage in Luke's Gospel, the light of the candle
stands for a gift from God bestowed on an individual, a
gift that, as the passage indicates, carries with it the
obligation that the individual use it for the benefit of
others. Drawing on this passage, the duke constructs a
simile in which Angelo's God-given "virtues" are
"lamps"—torches lit by "Heaven" for the good of
others, not just for himself. As the passage develops,
however, it abandons its biblical allusiveness in favor of
the language of economics, and it takes up a combination of metaphor and simile. "Nature" is first presented
to us, in a metaphor, as a person making a loan: "nature
never lends. . . ." This metaphor is followed by a simile
in which nature is explicitly compared to a "thrifty
goddess, [who] determines herself the glory of a creditor." In her role as "creditor," she seeks to profit from
"use," that is, "interest" on her loan. But "use" is also a
pun, for it means not only "interest" but also the use, for
the benefit of others, to which the creature who
receives nature's excellence is obliged to put it.

   Measure for Measure often contains such series of
figures of speech as we have observed in the duke's
words, series that are complicated because of the suc-
cession and interrelation of the figures. Such weighty
language is perhaps necessary for a play that, though
comic in structure, centers upon issues of lust, prostitution, disease, tyranny, betrayal, and death. The characters, represented as trying to come to terms with inner
and outer pressures, are often given contorted language
to reflect their emotional turmoil and to pull us deeply
into their struggles.

Implied Stage Action

Finally, in reading Shakespeare's plays we should always remember that what we are reading is a performance script. The dialogue is written to be spoken by actors who, at the same time, are moving, gesturing, picking up objects, weeping, shaking their fists. Some stage action is described in what are called "stage directions" (of which there are few in the early printed text of *Measure for Measure*); some is suggested within the dialogue itself. We must learn to be alert to such signals as we stage the play in our imaginations.

Occasionally the dialogue of *Measure for Measure* calls for actors to perform vivid gestures, such as Lucio's struggle with the duke in the last scene, during which the hood of the friar's robe in which the duke is disguised is pulled from his head, revealing his identity. Much of the action demanded by the play's dialogue, however, is more routine. For example, at the beginning of the play, when the duke says to Escalus "There is our commission, / From which we would not have you warp," it is reasonably clear that with these words the duke hands Escalus a document, and we provide a stage direction to this effect. Again, later in the play when a messenger enters and addresses the provost with the words "My lord hath sent you this note," it is fairly certain that this dialogue is accompanied by the transfer of a letter from the messenger to the provost. And so again we provide a stage direction that says as much: *"giving Provost a paper."*

Even such routine action can present problems if the dialogue appears to indicate that while one character is proffering a document to another, the intended recipient is hesitant to take what is offered. Such problems emerge very early in *Measure for Measure* when the duke

says to Angelo "Take thy commission," and Angelo tries
to dissuade the duke from creating him deputy:

> Now, good my lord,
> Let there be some more test made of my mettle
> Before so noble and so great a figure
> Be stamped upon it.

Responding to Angelo, the duke then says in part
"Therefore, take your honors," an order not very different from his earlier command "Take thy commission."
The repetition of the initial command leaves indeterminate the precise location in the dialogue at which
Angelo accepts his commission from the duke. In terms
of the culture of early seventeenth-century Europe, it
seems to us quite unlikely that a subject (Angelo) would
defy the first royal command "Take thy commission"
and leave the duke holding out the document to him
while Angelo tries, in humble words, to persuade the
duke to reconsider the appointment; we have therefore
inserted after this first command the stage direction *"He
hands Angelo a paper."* Some directors choose to have
Angelo wait to accept the commission until the second
command, "Therefore, take your honors," and a good
actor can make Angelo's hesitation an effective moment.

We fully recognize, then, that even though we as
editors have placed stage directions where we feel
reasonably sure our suggestions are valid, readers,
directors, and actors will need to use their own imaginations and their own understandings of the play for their
individual stagings.

It is immensely rewarding to work carefully with
Shakespeare's language so that the words, the sentences, the wordplay, and the implied stage action all
become clear—as readers for the past four centuries
have discovered. It may be more pleasurable to attend a

good performance of a play—though not everyone has thought so. But the joy of being able to stage one of Shakespeare's plays in one's imagination, to return to passages that continue to yield further meanings (or further questions) the more one reads them—these are pleasures that, for many, rival (or at least augment) those of the performed text, and certainly make it worth considerable effort to "break the code" of Elizabethan poetic drama and let free the remarkable language that makes up a Shakespeare text.

Shakespeare's Life

Surviving documents that give us glimpses into the life of William Shakespeare show us a playwright, poet, and actor who grew up in the market town of Stratford-upon-Avon, spent his professional life in London, and returned to Stratford a wealthy landowner. He was born in April 1564, died in April 1616, and is buried inside the chancel of Holy Trinity Church in Stratford.

We wish we could know more about the life of the world's greatest dramatist. His plays and poems are testaments to his wide reading—especially to his knowledge of Virgil, Ovid, Plutarch, Holinshed's *Chronicles*, and the Bible—and to his mastery of the English language, but we can only speculate about his education. We know that the King's New School in Stratford-upon-Avon was considered excellent. The school was one of the English "grammar schools" established to educate young men, primarily in Latin grammar and literature. As in other schools of the time, students began their studies at the age of four or five in the attached "petty school," and there learned to read and

CATECHISMVS

paruus pueris primùm Latinè
qui ediscatur, proponendus
in Scholis.

LONDINI
Apud Iohannem Dayum Typo-
graphum. An. 1573.

Cum Priuilegio Regiæ Maiestatis.

Title page of a 1573 Latin and Greek catechism
for children

write in English, studying primarily the catechism from the Book of Common Prayer. After two years in the petty school, students entered the lower form (grade) of the grammar school, where they began the serious study of Latin grammar and Latin texts that would occupy most of the remainder of their school days. (Several Latin texts that Shakespeare used repeatedly in writing his plays and poems were texts that schoolboys memorized and recited.) Latin comedies were introduced early in the lower form; in the upper form, which the boys entered at age ten or eleven, students wrote their own Latin orations and declamations, studied Latin historians and rhetoricians, and began the study of Greek using the Greek New Testament.

Since the records of the Stratford "grammar school" do not survive, we cannot prove that William Shakespeare attended the school; however, every indication (his father's position as an alderman and bailiff of Stratford, the playwright's own knowledge of the Latin classics, scenes in the plays that recall grammar-school experiences—for example, *The Merry Wives of Windsor*, 4.1) suggests that he did. We also lack generally accepted documentation about Shakespeare's life after his schooling ended and his professional life in London began. His marriage in 1582 (at age eighteen) to Anne Hathaway and the subsequent births of his daughter Susanna (1583) and the twins Judith and Hamnet (1585) are recorded, but how he supported himself and where he lived are not known. Nor do we know when and why he left Stratford for the London theatrical world, nor how he rose to be the important figure in that world that he had become by the early 1590s.

We do know that by 1592 he had achieved some prominence in London as both an actor and a playwright. In that year was published a book by the playwright Robert Greene attacking an actor who had the audacity to write blank-verse drama and who was "in his own conceit [i.e., opinion] the only Shake-scene in a country." Since Greene's attack includes a parody of a line from one of Shakespeare's early plays, there is little doubt that it is Shakespeare to whom he refers, a "Shake-scene" who had aroused Greene's fury by successfully competing with university-educated dramatists like Greene himself. It was also in 1592 that Shakespeare became a published poet. In that year he published his long narrative poem *Venus and Adonis;* in 1593, he followed it with *The Rape of Lucrece.* Both poems were dedicated to the young earl of Southampton (Henry Wriothesley), who may have become Shakespeare's patron.

It seems no coincidence that Shakespeare wrote these narrative poems in years in which the theaters were closed because of the plague, a contagious epidemic disease that devastated the population of London. When the theaters reopened late in 1594, Shakespeare apparently resumed his double career of actor and playwright and began his long (and seemingly profitable) service as an acting-company shareholder. Records from the fall of 1594 show him to be a leading member of the Lord Chamberlain's Men. It was this company of actors, later named the King's Men, for whom he would be a principal actor, dramatist, and shareholder for the rest of his career.

So far as we can tell, that career spanned about twenty years. In the 1590s, he wrote his plays on English history as well as several comedies and at least two tragedies (*Titus Andronicus* and *Romeo and Juliet*). These histories, comedies, and tragedies are the plays credited to him in 1598 in a work, *Palladis Tamia,* that in one chapter compares English writers with "Greek, Latin, and Italian Poets." There the author, Francis

Meres, claims that Shakespeare is comparable to the Latin dramatists Seneca for tragedy and Plautus for comedy, and calls him "the most excellent in both kinds for the stage." He also names him "Mellifluous and honey-tongued Shakespeare": "I say," writes Meres, "that the Muses would speak with Shakespeare's fine filed phrase, if they would speak English." Since Meres also mentions Shakespeare's "sugared sonnets among his private friends," it is assumed that many of Shakespeare's sonnets (not published until 1609) were also written in the 1590s.

In 1599, Shakespeare's company built a theater for themselves across the river from London, naming it the Globe. The plays that are considered by many to be Shakespeare's major tragedies (*Hamlet*, *Othello*, *King Lear*, and *Macbeth*) were written while the company was resident in this theater, as were such comedies as *Twelfth Night* and *Measure for Measure*. Many of Shakespeare's plays were performed at court (both for Queen Elizabeth I and, after her death in 1603, for King James I), some were presented at the Inns of Court (the residences of London's legal societies), and some were doubtless performed in other towns, at the universities, and at great houses when the King's Men went on tour; otherwise, his plays from 1599 to 1608 were, so far as we know, performed only at the Globe. Between 1608 and 1612, Shakespeare wrote several plays—among them *The Winter's Tale* and *The Tempest*—presumably for the company's new indoor Blackfriars theater, though the plays seem to have been performed also at the Globe and at court. Surviving documents describe a performance of *The Winter's Tale* in 1611 at the Globe, for example, and performances of *The Tempest* in 1611 and 1613 at the royal palace of Whitehall.

Shakespeare wrote very little after 1612, the year in

The Globe

A stylized representation of the Globe theater.
From Claes Jansz Visscher, *Londinum florentissima
Britanniae urbs . . .* (c. 1625).

which he probably wrote *King Henry VIII*. (It was at a performance of *Henry VIII* in 1613 that the Globe caught fire and burned to the ground.) Sometime between 1610 and 1613 he seems to have returned to live in Stratford-upon-Avon, where he owned a large house and considerable property, and where his wife and his two daughters and their husbands lived. (His son Hamnet had died in 1596.) During his professional years in London, Shakespeare had presumably derived income from the acting company's profits as well as from his own career as an actor, from the sale of his play manuscripts to the acting company, and, after 1599, from his shares as an owner of the Globe. It was presumably that income, carefully invested in land and other property, which made him the wealthy man that surviving documents show him to have become. It is also assumed that William Shakespeare's growing wealth and reputation played some part in inclining the crown, in 1597, to grant John Shakespeare, William's father, the coat of arms that he had so long sought. William Shakespeare died in Stratford on April 23, 1616 (according to the epitaph carved under his bust in Holy Trinity Church) and was buried on April 25. Seven years after his death, his collected plays were published as *Mr. William Shakespeares Comedies, Histories, & Tragedies* (the work now known as the First Folio).

The years in which Shakespeare wrote were among the most exciting in English history. Intellectually, the discovery, translation, and printing of Greek and Roman classics were making available a set of works and worldviews that interacted complexly with Christian texts and beliefs. The result was a questioning, a vital intellectual ferment, that provided energy for the period's amazing dramatic and literary output and that fed directly into Shakespeare's plays. The Ghost in *Hamlet*,

for example, is wonderfully complicated in part because he is a figure from Roman tragedy—the spirit of
the dead returning to seek revenge—who at the same
time inhabits a Christian hell (or purgatory); Hamlet's
description of humankind reflects at one moment the
Neoplatonic wonderment at mankind ("What a piece of
work is a man!") and, at the next, the Christian dispar-
agement of human sinners ("And yet, to me, what is this
quintessence of dust?").

As intellectual horizons expanded, so also did geo-
graphical and cosmological horizons. New worlds—
both North and South America—were explored, and in
them were found human beings who lived and wor-
shiped in ways radically different from those of Renaissance Europeans and Englishmen. The universe during
these years also seemed to shift and expand. Copernicus
had earlier theorized that the earth was not the center of
the cosmos but revolved as a planet around the sun.
Galileo's telescope, created in 1609, allowed scientists
to see that Copernicus had been correct; the universe
was not organized with the earth at the center, nor was
it so nicely circumscribed as people had, until that time,
thought. In terms of expanding horizons, the impact of
these discoveries on people's beliefs—religious, scien-
tific, and philosophical—cannot be overstated.

London, too, rapidly expanded and changed during the
years (from the early 1590s to around 1610) that Shakespeare lived there. London—the center of England's
government, its economy, its royal court, its overseas
trade—was, during these years, becoming an exciting
metropolis, drawing to it thousands of new citizens every
year. Troubled by overcrowding, by poverty, by recurring
epidemics of the plague, London was also a mecca for
the wealthy and the aristocratic, and for those who
sought advancement at court, or power in government or

finance or trade. One hears in Shakespeare's plays the
voices of London—the struggles for power, the fear of
venereal disease, the language of buying and selling. One
hears as well the voices of Stratford-upon-Avon—
references to the nearby Forest of Arden, to sheep
herding, to small-town gossip, to village fairs and mar-
kets. Part of the richness of Shakespeare's work is the
influence felt there of the various worlds in which he
lived: the world of metropolitan London, the world of
small-town and rural England, the world of the theater,
and the worlds of craftsmen and shepherds.

That Shakespeare inhabited such worlds we know
from surviving London and Stratford documents, as
well as from the evidence of the plays and poems
themselves. From such records we can sketch the dramatist's life. We know from his works that he was a
voracious reader. We know from legal and business
documents that he was a multifaceted theater man who
became a wealthy landowner. We know a bit about his
family life and a fair amount about his legal and
financial dealings. Most scholars today depend upon
such evidence as they draw their picture of the world's
greatest playwright. Such, however, has not always been
the case. Until the late eighteenth century, the William
Shakespeare who lived in most biographies was the
creation of legend and tradition. This was the Shakespeare who was supposedly caught poaching deer at
Charlecote, the estate of Sir Thomas Lucy close by
Stratford; this was the Shakespeare who fled from Sir
Thomas's vengeance and made his way in London by
taking care of horses outside a playhouse; this was the
Shakespeare who reportedly could barely read but
whose natural gifts were extraordinary, whose father
was a butcher who allowed his gifted son sometimes to
help in the butcher shop, where William supposedly

killed calves "in a high style," making a speech for the occasion. It was this legendary William Shakespeare whose Falstaff (in *1* and *2 Henry IV*) so pleased Queen Elizabeth that she demanded a play about Falstaff in love, and demanded that it be written in fourteen days (hence the existence of *The Merry Wives of Windsor*). It was this legendary Shakespeare who reached the top of his acting career in the roles of the Ghost in *Hamlet* and old Adam in *As You Like It*—and who died of a fever contracted by drinking too hard at "a merry meeting" with the poets Michael Drayton and Ben Jonson. This legendary Shakespeare is a rambunctious, undisciplined man, as attractively "wild" as his plays were seen by earlier generations to be. Unfortunately, there is no trace of evidence to support these wonderful stories.

Perhaps in response to the disreputable Shakespeare of legend—or perhaps in response to the fragmentary and, for some, all-too-ordinary Shakespeare documented by surviving records—some people since the mid-nineteenth century have argued that William Shakespeare could not have written the plays that bear his name. These persons have put forward some dozen names as more likely authors, among them Queen Elizabeth, Sir Francis Bacon, Edward de Vere (earl of Oxford), and Christopher Marlowe. Such attempts to find what for these people is a more believable author of the plays is a tribute to the regard in which the plays are held. Unfortunately for their claims, the documents that exist that provide evidence for the facts of Shakespeare's life tie him inextricably to the body of plays and poems that bear his name. Unlikely as it seems to those who want the works to have been written by an aristocrat, a university graduate, or an "important" person, the plays and poems seem clearly to have been produced by a man from Stratford-upon-Avon with a very good "grammar-school" education and a life of experience in London and in the world of the London theater. How this particular man produced the works that dominate the cultures of much of the world almost four hundred years after his death is one of life's mysteries—and one that will continue to tease our imaginations as we continue to delight in his plays and poems.

Shakespeare's Theater

The actors of Shakespeare's time are known to have performed plays in a great variety of locations. They played at court (that is, in the great halls of such royal residences as Whitehall, Hampton Court, and Greenwich); they played in halls at the universities of Oxford and Cambridge, and at the Inns of Court (the residences in London of the legal societies); and they also played in the private houses of great lords and civic officials. Sometimes acting companies went on tour from London into the provinces, often (but not only) when outbreaks of bubonic plague in the capital forced the closing of theaters to reduce the possibility of contagion in crowded audiences. In the provinces the actors usually staged their plays in churches (until around 1600) or in guildhalls. While surviving records show only a handful of occasions when actors played at inns while on tour, London inns were important playing places up until the 1590s.

The building of theaters in London had begun only shortly before Shakespeare wrote his first plays in the 1590s. These theaters were of two kinds: outdoor or public playhouses that could accommodate large numbers of playgoers, and indoor or private theaters for much smaller audiences. What is usually regarded as the first London outdoor public playhouse was called simply the Theatre. James Burbage—the father of Richard Burbage, who was perhaps the most famous actor in Shakespeare's company—built it in 1576 in an area north of the city of London called Shoreditch. Among the more famous of the other public playhouses that capitalized on the new fashion were the Curtain and the Fortune (both also built north of the city), the Rose, the Swan, the Globe, and the Hope (all located on the Bankside, a region just across the Thames south of the city of London). All these playhouses had to be built outside the jurisdiction of the city of London because many civic officials were hostile to the performance of drama and repeatedly petitioned the royal council to abolish it.

The theaters erected on the Bankside (a region under the authority of the Church of England, whose head was the monarch) shared the neighborhood with houses of prostitution and with the Paris Garden, where the blood sports of bearbaiting and bullbaiting were carried on. There may have been no clear distinction between playhouses and buildings for such sports, for we know that the Hope was used for both plays and baiting and that Philip Henslowe, owner of the Rose and, later, partner in the ownership of the Fortune, was also a partner in a monopoly on baiting. All these forms of entertainment were easily accessible to Londoners by boat across the Thames or over London Bridge.

Evidently Shakespeare's company prospered on the Bankside. They moved there in 1599. Threatened by difficulties in renewing the lease on the land where their first theater (the Theatre) had been built, Shakespeare's company took advantage of the Christmas holiday in 1598 to dismantle the Theatre and transport its timbers across the Thames to the Bankside, where, in 1599, these timbers were used in the building of the Globe. The weather in late December 1598 is recorded as having been especially harsh. It was so cold that the Thames was "nigh [nearly] frozen," and there was heavy snow. Perhaps the weather aided Shakespeare's company in eluding their landlord, the snow hiding their activity and the freezing of the Thames allowing them to slide the timbers across to the Bankside without paying tolls for repeated trips over London Bridge. Attractive as this narrative is, it remains just as likely that the heavy snow hampered transport of the timbers in wagons through the London streets to the river. It also must be remembered that the Thames was, according to report, only "nigh frozen" and therefore as impassable as it ever was. Whatever the precise circumstances of this fascinating event in English theater history, Shakespeare's company was able to begin playing at their new Globe theater on the Bankside in 1599. After the first Globe burned down in 1613 during the staging of Shakespeare's *Henry VIII* (its thatch roof was set alight by cannon fire called for by the performance), Shakespeare's company immediately rebuilt on the same location. The second Globe seems to have been a grander structure than its predecessor. It remained in use until the beginning of the English Civil War in 1642, when Parliament officially closed the theaters. Soon thereafter it was pulled down.

The public theaters of Shakespeare's time were very different buildings from our theaters today. First of all, they were open-air playhouses. As recent excavations of the Rose and the Globe confirm, some were polygonal or roughly circular in shape; the Fortune, however, was square. The most recent estimates of their size put the diameter of these buildings at 72 feet (the Rose) to 100 feet (the Globe), but we know that they held vast audiences of two or three thousand, who must have been squeezed together quite tightly. Some of these spectators paid extra to sit or stand in the two or three levels of roofed galleries that extended, on the upper levels, all the way around the theater and surrounded an open space. In this space were the stage and, perhaps, the tiring house (what we would call dressing rooms), as well as the so-called yard. In the yard stood the spectators who chose to pay less, the ones whom Hamlet contemptuously called "groundlings." For a roof they had only the sky, and so they were exposed to all kinds of weather. They stood on a floor that was sometimes made of mortar and sometimes of ash mixed with the shells of hazelnuts. The latter provided a porous and therefore dry footing for the crowd, and the shells may have been more comfortable to stand on because they were not as hard as mortar. Availability of shells may not have been a problem if hazelnuts were a favorite food for Shakespeare's audiences to munch on as they watched his plays. Archaeologists who are today unearthing the remains of theaters from this period have discovered quantities of these nutshells on theater sites.

Unlike the yard, the stage itself was covered by a roof. Its ceiling, called "the heavens," is thought to have been elaborately painted to depict the sun, moon, stars, and planets. Just how big the stage was remains hard to determine. We have a single sketch of part of the interior of the Swan. A Dutchman named Johannes de Witt visited this theater around 1596 and sent a sketch of it back to his friend, Arend van Buchel. Because van Buchel found de Witt's letter and sketch of interest, he copied both into a book. It is van Buchel's copy, adapted, it seems, to the shape and size of the page in his book, that survives. In this sketch, the stage appears to be a large rectangular platform that thrusts far out into the yard, perhaps even as far as the center of the circle formed by the surrounding galleries. This drawing, combined with the specifications for the size of the stage in the building contract for the Fortune, has led scholars to conjecture that the stage on which Shakespeare's plays were performed must have measured approximately 43 feet in width and 27 feet in depth, a vast acting area. But the digging up of a large part of the Rose by archaeologists has provided evidence of a quite different stage design. The Rose stage was a platform tapered at the corners and much shallower than what seems to be depicted in the van Buchel sketch. Indeed, its measurements seem to be about 37.5 feet across at its widest point and only 15.5 feet deep. Because the surviving indications of stage size and design differ from each other so much, it is possible that the stages in other theaters, like the Theatre, the Curtain, and the Globe (the outdoor playhouses where we know that Shakespeare's plays were performed), were different from those at both the Swan and the Rose.

After about 1608 Shakespeare's plays were staged not only at the Globe but also at an indoor or private playhouse in Blackfriars. This theater had been constructed in 1596 by James Burbage in an upper hall of a former Dominican priory or monastic house. Although Henry VIII had dissolved all English monasteries in the 1530s (shortly after he had founded the Church of England), the area remained under church, rather than hostile civic, control. The hall that Burbage had purchased and renovated was a large one in which Parliament had once met. In the private theater that he constructed, the stage, lit by candles, was built across the narrow end of the hall, with boxes flanking it. The rest of the hall offered seating room only. Because there was no provision for standing room, the largest audience it could hold was less than a thousand, or about a quarter of what the Globe could accommodate. Admission to Blackfriars was correspondingly more expensive. Instead of a penny to stand in the yard at the Globe, it cost a minimum of sixpence to get into Blackfriars. The best seats at the Globe (in the Lords' Room in the gallery above and behind the stage) cost sixpence; but the boxes flanking the stage at Blackfriars were half a crown, or five times sixpence. Some spectators who were particularly interested in displaying themselves paid even more to sit on stools on the Blackfriars stage.

Whether in the outdoor or indoor playhouses, the stages of Shakespeare's time were different from ours. They were not separated from the audience by the dropping of a curtain between acts and scenes. Therefore the playwrights of the time had to find other ways of signaling to the audience that one scene (to be imagined as occurring in one location at a given time) had ended and the next (to be imagined at perhaps a different location at a later time) had begun. The customary way used by Shakespeare and many of his contemporaries was to have everyone onstage exit at the end of one scene and have one or more different characters enter to begin the next. In a few cases, where characters remain onstage from one scene to another, the dialogue or stage action makes the change of location clear, and the characters are generally to be imagined as having moved from one place to another. For example, in *Romeo and Juliet*, Romeo and his friends remain onstage in Act 1 from scene 4 to scene 5, but they are represented as having moved between scenes from the street that leads to Capulet's house into Capulet's house itself. The new location is signaled in part by the appearance onstage of Capulet's servingmen carrying napkins, something they would not take into the streets. Playwrights had to be quite resourceful in the use of hand properties, like the napkin, or in the use of dialogue to specify where the action was taking place in their plays because, in contrast to most of today's theaters, the playhouses of Shakespeare's time did not use movable scenery to dress the stage and make the setting precise. As another consequence of this difference, however, the playwrights of Shakespeare's time did not have to specify exactly where the action of their plays was set when they did not choose to do so, and much of the action of their plays is tied to no specific place.

Usually Shakespeare's stage is referred to as a "bare stage," to distinguish it from the stages of the last two or three centuries with their elaborate sets. But the stage in Shakespeare's time was not completely bare. Philip Henslowe, owner of the Rose, lists in his inventory of stage properties a rock, three tombs, and two mossy banks. Stage directions in plays of the time also call for such things as thrones (or "states"), banquets (presumably tables with plaster replicas of food on them), and beds and tombs to be pushed onto the stage. Thus the stage often held more than the actors.

The actors did not limit their performing to the stage alone. Occasionally they went beneath the stage, as the Ghost appears to do in the first act of *Hamlet.* From there they could emerge onto the stage through a trapdoor. They could retire behind the hangings across the back of the stage (or the front of the tiring house), as, for example, the actor playing Polonius does when he hides behind the arras. Sometimes the hangings could be drawn back during a performance to "discover" one or more actors behind them. When performance required that an actor appear "above," as when Juliet is imagined to stand at the window of her chamber in the famous and misnamed "balcony scene," then the actor probably climbed the stairs to the gallery over the back of the stage and temporarily shared it with some of the spectators. The stage was also provided with ropes and winches so that actors could descend from, and reascend to, the "heavens."

Perhaps the greatest difference between dramatic performances in Shakespeare's time and ours was that in Shakespeare's England the roles of women were played by boys. (Some of these boys grew up to take male roles in their maturity.) There were no women in the acting companies, only in the audience. It had not always been so in the history of the English stage. There are records of women on English stages in the thirteenth and fourteenth centuries, two hundred years before Shakespeare's plays were performed. After the accession of James I in 1603, the queen of England and her ladies took part in entertainments at court called masques, and with the reopening of the theaters in 1660 at the restoration of Charles II, women again took their place on the public stage.

The chief competitors for the companies of adult actors such as the one to which Shakespeare belonged and for which he wrote were companies of exclusively boy actors. The competition was most intense in the early 1600s. There were then two principal children's companies: the Children of Paul's (the choirboys from St. Paul's Cathedral, whose private playhouse was near the cathedral); and the Children of the Chapel Royal (the choirboys from the monarch's private chapel, who performed at the Blackfriars theater built by Burbage in 1596, which Shakespeare's company had been stopped from using by local residents who objected to crowds). In *Hamlet* Shakespeare writes of "an aerie [nest] of children, little eyases [hawks], that cry out on the top of question and are most tyrannically clapped for 't. These are now the fashion and . . . berattle the common stages [attack the public theaters]." In the long run, the adult actors prevailed. The Children of Paul's dissolved around 1606. By about 1608 the Children of the Chapel Royal had been forced to stop playing at the Blackfriars theater, which was then taken over by the King's Men, Shakespeare's own troupe.

Acting companies and theaters of Shakespeare's time were organized in different ways. For example, Philip Henslowe owned the Rose and leased it to companies of actors, who paid him from their takings. Henslowe would act as manager of these companies, initially paying playwrights for their plays and buying properties, recovering his outlay from the actors. Shakespeare's company, however, managed itself, with the principal actors, Shakespeare among them, having the status of "sharers" and the right to a share in the takings, as well as the responsibility for a part of the expenses. Five of the sharers themselves, Shakespeare among them, owned the Globe. As actor, as sharer in an acting company and in ownership of theaters, and as playwright, Shakespeare was about as involved in the theatrical industry as one could imagine. Although Shakespeare and his fellows prospered, their status under the law was conditional upon the protection of powerful patrons. "Common players"—those who did not have patrons or masters—were classed in the language of the law with "vagabonds and sturdy beggars." So the actors had to secure for themselves the official rank of servants of patrons. Among the patrons under whose protection Shakespeare's company worked were the lord chamberlain and, after the accession of King James in 1603, the king himself.

We are now perhaps on the verge of learning a great deal more about the theaters in which Shakespeare and his contemporaries performed—or at least of opening up new questions about them. Already about 70 percent of the Rose has been excavated, as has about 10 percent of the second Globe, the one built in 1614. It is to be hoped that soon more will be available for study. These are exciting times for students of Shakespeare's stage.

The Publication of Shakespeare's Plays

Eighteen of Shakespeare's plays found their way into print during the playwright's lifetime, but there is nothing to suggest that he took any interest in their publication. These eighteen appeared separately in editions called quartos. Their pages were not much larger than the one you are now reading, and these little books were sold unbound for a few pence. The earliest of the quartos that still survive were printed in 1594, the year that both *Titus Andronicus* and a version of the play now called *2 King Henry VI* became available. While almost every one of these early quartos displays on its title page the name of the acting company that performed the play, only about half provide the name of the playwright, Shakespeare. The first quarto edition to bear the name Shakespeare on its title page is *Love's Labor's Lost* of 1598. A few of these quartos were popular with the book-buying public of Shakespeare's lifetime; for example, quarto *Richard II* went through five editions between 1597 and 1615. But most of the quartos were far from best-sellers; *Love's Labor's Lost* (1598), for instance, was not reprinted in quarto until 1631. After Shakespeare's death, two more of his plays appeared in quarto format: *Othello* in 1622 and *The Two Noble Kinsmen*, coauthored with John Fletcher, in 1634.

In 1623, seven years after Shakespeare's death, *Mr.*

William Shakespeares Comedies, Histories, & Tragedies
was published. This printing offered readers in a single
book thirty-six of the thirty-eight plays now thought to
have been written by Shakespeare, including eighteen
that had never been printed before. And it offered them
in a style that was then reserved for serious literature
and scholarship. The plays were arranged in double
columns on pages nearly a foot high. This large page size
is called "folio," as opposed to the smaller "quarto,"
and the 1623 volume is usually called the Shakespeare
First Folio. It is reputed to have sold for the lordly price
of a pound. (One copy at the Folger Library is marked
fifteen shillings—that is, three-quarters of a pound.)

In a preface to the First Folio entitled "To the great
Variety of Readers," two of Shakespeare's former fellow
actors in the King's Men, John Heminge and Henry
Condell, wrote that they themselves had collected their
dead companion's plays. They suggested that they had
seen his own papers: "we have scarce received from him
a blot in his papers." The title page of the Folio declared
that the plays within it had been printed "according to
the True Original Copies." Comparing the Folio to the
quartos, Heminge and Condell disparaged the quartos,
advising their readers that "before you were abused
with divers stolen and surreptitious copies, maimed,
and deformed by the frauds and stealths of injurious
impostors." Many Shakespeareans of the eighteenth and
nineteenth centuries believed Heminge and Condell
and regarded the Folio plays as superior to anything in
the quartos.

Once we begin to examine the Folio plays in detail, it
becomes less easy to take at face value the word of
Heminge and Condell about the superiority of the Folio
texts. For example, of the first nine plays in the Folio (one
quarter of the entire collection), four were essentially
reprinted from earlier quarto printings that Heminge

and Condell had disparaged; and four have now been identified as printed from copies written in the hand of a professional scribe of the 1620s named Ralph Crane; the ninth, *The Comedy of Errors*, was apparently also printed from a manuscript, but one whose origin cannot be readily identified. Evidently then, eight of the first nine plays in the First Folio were not printed, in spite of what the Folio title page announces, "according to the True Original Copies," or Shakespeare's own papers, and the source of the ninth is unknown. Since today's editors have been forced to treat Heminge and Condell's pronouncements with skepticism, they must choose whether to base their own editions upon quartos or the Folio on grounds other than Heminge and Condell's story of where the quarto and Folio versions originated.

Editors have often fashioned their own narratives to explain what lies behind the quartos and Folio. They have said that Heminge and Condell meant to criticize only a few of the early quartos, the ones that offer much shorter and sometimes quite different, often garbled, versions of plays. Among the examples of these are the 1600 quarto of *Henry V* (the Folio offers a much fuller version) or the 1603 *Hamlet* quarto (in 1604 a different, much longer form of the play got into print as a quarto). Early in this century editors speculated that these questionable texts were produced when someone in the audience took notes from the plays' dialogue during performances and then employed "hack poets" to fill out the notes. The poor results were then sold to a publisher and presented in print as Shakespeare's plays. More recently this story has given way to another in which the shorter versions are said to be recreations from memory of Shakespeare's plays by actors who wanted to stage them in the provinces but lacked manuscript copies. Most of the quartos offer much better texts than these so-called bad quartos. Indeed, in most of the quartos we find texts that are at least equal to or better than what is printed in the Folio. Many of this century's Shakespeare enthusiasts have persuaded themselves that most of the quartos were set into type directly from Shakespeare's own papers, although there is nothing on which to base this conclusion except the desire for it to be true. Thus speculation continues about how the Shakespeare plays got to be printed. All that we have are the printed texts.

The book collector who was most successful in bringing together copies of the quartos and the First Folio was Henry Clay Folger, founder of the Folger Shakespeare Library in Washington, D.C. While it is estimated that there survive around the world only about 230 copies of the First Folio, Mr. Folger was able to acquire more than seventy-five copies, as well as a large number of fragments, for the library that bears his name. He also amassed a substantial number of quartos. For example, only fourteen copies of the First Quarto of *Love's Labor's Lost* are known to exist, and three are at the Folger Shakespeare Library. As a consequence of Mr. Folger's labors, twentieth-century scholars visiting the Folger Library have been able to learn a great deal about sixteenth- and seventeenth-century printing and, particularly, about the printing of Shakespeare's plays. And Mr. Folger did not stop at the First Folio, but collected many copies of later editions of Shakespeare, beginning with the Second Folio (1632), the Third (1663–64), and the Fourth (1685). Each of these later folios was based on its immediate predecessor and was edited anonymously. The first editor of Shakespeare whose name we know was Nicholas Rowe, whose first edition came out in 1709. Mr. Folger collected this edition and many, many more by Rowe's successors.

An Introduction to This Text

Measure for Measure was first printed in the 1623 collection of Shakespeare's plays now known as the First Folio. The present edition is based directly upon the First Folio version.* For the convenience of the reader, we have modernized the punctuation and the spelling of the Folio. Sometimes we go so far as to modernize certain old forms of words; for example, when *a* means *he,* we change it to *he;* we change *mo* to *more* and *ye* to *you.* But it is not our practice in editing any of the plays to modernize words that sound distinctly different from modern forms. For example, when the early printed texts read *sith* or *apricocks* or *porpentine,* we have not modernized to *since, apricots, porcupine.* When the forms *an, and,* or *and if* appear instead of the modern form *if,* we have reduced *and* to *an* but have not changed any of these forms to their modern equivalent, *if.* We also modernize and, where necessary, correct passages in foreign languages, unless an error in the early printed text can be reasonably explained as a joke.

Whenever we change the wording of the First Folio or add anything to its stage directions, we mark the change by enclosing it in superior half-brackets (⌐ ⌐). We want our readers to be immediately aware when we have intervened. (Only when we correct an obvious typographical error in the First Folio does the change not get marked.) Whenever we change either the First Folio's

---

*We have also consulted the computerized text of the First Folio provided by the Text Archive of the Oxford University Computing Centre, to which we are grateful.

wording or its punctuation so that the meaning changes, we list the change in the textual notes at the back of the book, even if all we have done is fix an obvious error. We regularize a number of the proper names, as is the usual practice in editions of the play. For example, in stage directions the Folio sometimes calls Juliet by the name "Julietta," sometimes names Isabella "Isabell" and sometimes refers to Escalus as "Esculus." We, however, use only the forms Juliet, Isabella, and Escalus in stage directions.

This edition differs from many earlier ones in its efforts to aid the reader in imagining the play as a performance rather than as a series of actual events. Thus stage directions and speech prefixes are written with reference to the stage. For example, when one goes to a production of *Measure for Measure*, one is always aware, after the actor playing the duke has donned his disguise, that he no longer looks the regal figure he appeared to be in the first scene. Instead, the actor playing the duke looks like a friar. In an effort to reproduce in our edition the effect that an audience experiences, we have added to the speech prefix DUKE his disguise name *("as Friar")* whenever he is in dialogue with characters who think they are conversing with a friar. With the addition of this direction to the speech prefix, we hope to give our readers a greater opportunity to stage the play in their own imaginations. For the same reason, whenever it is reasonably certain, in our view, that a speech is accompanied by a particular action, we provide a stage direction describing the action. (Occasional exceptions to this rule occur when the action is so obvious that to add a stage direction would insult the reader.) Stage directions for the entrance of characters in mid-scene are, with rare exceptions, placed so that they immediately precede the characters' participation in the scene, even though these entrances may appear somewhat earlier in the early printed texts. Whenever we move a stage direction, we record this change in the textual notes. Latin stage directions (e.g., *Exeunt*) are translated into English (e.g., *They exit*).

We expand the often severely abbreviated forms of names used as speech headings in early printed texts into the full names of the characters. We also regularize the speakers' names in speech headings, using only a single designation for each character, even though the early printed texts sometimes use a variety of designations. Variations in the speech headings of the early printed texts are recorded in the textual notes.

In the present edition, as well, we mark with a dash any change of address within a speech, unless a stage direction intervenes. When the -ed ending of a word is to be pronounced, we mark it with an accent. Like editors for the past two centuries, we print metrically linked lines in the following way:

LUCIO
  With child, perhaps?
CLAUDIO   Unhappily, even so.

However, when there are a number of short verse lines that can be linked in more than one way, we do not, with rare exceptions, indent any of them.

The Explanatory Notes

The notes that appear on the pages facing the text are designed to provide readers with the help that they may need to enjoy the play. Whenever the meaning of a word in the text is not readily accessible in a good contemporary dictionary, we offer the meaning in a note. Sometimes we provide a note even when the relevant meaning is to be found in the dictionary but the word has acquired since Shakespeare's time other potentially confusing meanings. In our notes, we try to offer modern synonyms for Shakespeare's words. We also try to indicate to the reader the connection between the word in the play and the modern synonym. For example, Shakespeare sometimes uses the word _head_ to mean "source," but, for modern readers, there may be no connection evident between these two words. We provide the connection by explaining Shakespeare's usage as follows: **"head:** fountainhead, source." On some occasions, a whole phrase or clause needs explanation. Then, if space allows, we rephrase in our own words the difficult passage, and add at the end synonyms for individual words in the passage. When scholars have been unable to determine the meaning of a word or phrase, we acknowledge the uncertainty.

MEASURE

FOR

MEASURE

The Scene Vienna.

The names of all the Actors.

Vincentio : *the Duke.*
Angelo, the Deputie.
Escalus, an ancient Lord.
Claudio, a yong Gentleman.
Lucio, a fantastique.
2.Other like Gentlemen.
Prouost.

Thomas.
Peter. } *2. Friers.*
Elbow, a simple Constable.
Froth, a foolish Gentleman.
Clowne.
Abhorson, an Executioner.
Barnardine, a dissolute prisoner.
Isabella, sister to Claudio.
Mariana, betrothed to Angelo.
Iuliet, beloued of Claudio.
Francisca, a Nun.
Mistris Ouer-don, a Bawd.

From the 1623 First Folio.

Characters in the Play

DUKE of Vienna, later called Friar Lodowick
ESCALUS, a judge
PROVOST
ELBOW, a constable
ABHORSON, an executioner
A JUSTICE
VARRIUS, friend to the Duke

ANGELO, deputy to the Duke
MARIANA, betrothed to Angelo
BOY singer
SERVANT to Angelo
MESSENGER from Angelo

ISABELLA, a novice in the Order of Saint Clare
FRANCISCA, a nun

CLAUDIO, brother to Isabella
JULIET, betrothed to Claudio
LUCIO, friend to Claudio
TWO GENTLEMEN, associates of Lucio

FRIAR THOMAS
FRIAR PETER

MISTRESS OVERDONE, a bawd
POMPEY the Clown, her servant
FROTH, Pompey's customer
BARNARDINE, a prisoner

Lords, Officers, Citizens, Servants, and Attendants

MEASURE
FOR
MEASURE

ACT 1

1.1   The Duke of Vienna announces that he has been called away from the city, and that he is leaving Lord Angelo to rule in his place, with full power over life-and-death decisions.

———————

3. **government:** i.e., governing; **properties:** distinctive qualities or traits; **unfold:** explain

4. **t' affect:** to have an affection for

5. **put to know:** obliged to acknowledge; **science:** knowledge

6. **in that:** i.e., in this area; **lists:** limits

8–9. **But that . . . work:** These lines are obscure and metrically faulty. Words or partial lines of text may be missing. **sufficiency:** ability, competence **worth:** high personal merit

10. **institutions:** laws and customs

10–11. **terms / For common justice:** i.e., legal procedures

11. **pregnant:** resourceful, ready

12. **art:** learning

13. **we:** i.e., I (the "royal" plural, which the duke uses often in the remainder of this scene)

14. **warp:** deviate, turn aside

17. **What figure of us think you he will bear?:** i.e., how do you think he will represent me?

18. **with special soul:** i.e., using all of my mental powers

19. **Elected:** chosen; **supply:** make up for

20. **our terror:** i.e., the dread that goes with my office; **dressed him with our love:** perhaps, transferred to him the love that usually comes to me; or, perhaps, gave him my love in giving him the office

ACT 1

Scene 1
Enter Duke, Escalus, Lords, ⌐and Attendants.⌐

DUKE   Escalus.

ESCALUS   My lord.

DUKE

Of government the properties to unfold
Would seem in me t' affect speech and discourse,
Since I am put to know that your own science   5
Exceeds, in that, the lists of all advice
My strength can give you. Then no more remains
But that, to your sufficiency, as your worth is able,
And let them work. The nature of our people,
Our city's institutions, and the terms   10
For common justice, you're as pregnant in
As art and practice hath enrichèd any
That we remember. There is our commission,
                    ⌐*He hands Escalus a paper.*⌐
From which we would not have you warp.—Call
   hither,   15
I say, bid come before us Angelo.
                    ⌐*An Attendant exits.*⌐
What figure of us think you he will bear?
For you must know, we have with special soul
Elected him our absence to supply,
Lent him our terror, dressed him with our love,   20

7

21. **deputation:** appointment as deputy; **organs:** instruments, tools

24. **undergo:** enjoy

30. **character:** i.e., behavior (literally, written sign or symbol) Today's meaning of the word as a combination of characteristics that distinguish the individual is a later development of the word.

32. **unfold:** reveal, disclose; **belongings:** circumstances, relations with others

33. **thine . . . proper:** i.e., so exclusively your own

33–34. **waste / Thyself upon thy virtues:** i.e., use up your powers in making yourself virtuous

34. **they on thee:** i.e., exhaust your virtues on perfecting yourself

35–38. **Heaven . . . them not:** See Luke 8.16: "No man when he lighteth a candle covereth it under a vessel . . . but setteth it on a candlestick that they that enter in may see the light." See also Matthew 5.15–16. **forth of:** i.e., out of   **'twere all alike:** i.e., it would be just the same

38. **touched:** stirred, motivated

39. **issues:** actions, deeds

40. **scruple:** tiny amount (literally, the twenty-fourth part of an ounce)

41. **But . . . determines:** i.e., without . . . demanding

42. **Herself:** i.e., for herself

43. **use:** interest (on the loan); **bend:** direct

44. **advertise:** instruct, inform (accent on second syllable)

45. **Hold:** perhaps, stand firm (But see longer note, page 213.)

(continued)

And given his deputation all the organs
Of our own power. What think you of it?

ESCALUS
  If any in Vienna be of worth
  To undergo such ample grace and honor,
  It is Lord Angelo.   25

            Enter Angelo.

DUKE   Look where he comes.

ANGELO
  Always obedient to your Grace's will,
  I come to know your pleasure.

DUKE   Angelo,
  There is a kind of character in thy life   30
  That to th' observer doth thy history
  Fully unfold. Thyself and thy belongings
  Are not thine own so proper as to waste
  Thyself upon thy virtues, they on thee.
  Heaven doth with us as we with torches do,   35
  Not light them for themselves; for if our virtues
  Did not go forth of us, 'twere all alike
  As if we had them not. Spirits are not finely touched
  But to fine issues, nor nature never lends
  The smallest scruple of her excellence   40
  But, like a thrifty goddess, she determines
  Herself the glory of a creditor,
  Both thanks and use. But I do bend my speech
  To one that can my part in him advertise.
  Hold, therefore, Angelo.   45
  In our remove be thou at full ourself.
  Mortality and mercy in Vienna
  Live in thy tongue and heart. Old Escalus,
  Though first in question, is thy secondary.
  Take thy commission.   ⌜*He hands Angelo a paper.*⌝ 50

ANGELO   Now, good my lord,
  Let there be some more test made of my mettle

46. **remove:** absence; **at full ourself:** i.e., fully myself

47. **Mortality:** (1) death; (2) the power to pass the sentence of death

49. **first in question:** perhaps, the first to be considered for the position; **secondary:** subordinate

51. **good my lord:** i.e., my good lord

52. **mettle:** spirit (A pun on "metal" underlies Angelo's image of himself as a coin that should be subjected to further examination [**some more test**] before the ducal **figure** is **stamped upon it.** See page 206.)

56. **leavened:** i.e., mature, well-considered (The image is of dough through which fermenting yeast has worked.)

58. **of so quick condition:** i.e., in a state requiring such speed

59. **prefers itself:** takes precedence over everything else; **unquestioned:** unexamined, undiscussed

60. **of needful value:** i.e., highly important **needful:** indispensable

61. **concernings:** concerns; **importune:** urge, impel

64–65. **To . . . commissions:** i.e., I leave you to carry out your commissions, no doubt successfully

66. **leave:** permission

67. **bring you something:** i.e., go with you some distance

68. **admit:** i.e., allow

69–70. **have to do / With any scruple:** i.e., have any doubts or hesitations

73–76. **I love the people . . . vehement:** See Historical Background 1, "King James," pages 225–27.

(continued)

Before so noble and so great a figure
Be stamped upon it.
DUKE   No more evasion.   55
We have with a leavened and preparèd choice
Proceeded to you. Therefore, take your honors.
Our haste from hence is of so quick condition
That it prefers itself and leaves unquestioned
Matters of needful value. We shall write to you,   60
As time and our concernings shall importune,
How it goes with us, and do look to know
What doth befall you here. So fare you well.
To th' hopeful execution do I leave you
Of your commissions.   65
ANGELO   Yet give leave, my lord,
That we may bring you something on the way.
DUKE   My haste may not admit it.
Nor need you, on mine honor, have to do
With any scruple. Your scope is as mine own,   70
So to enforce or qualify the laws
As to your soul seems good. Give me your hand.
I'll privily away. I love the people,
But do not like to stage me to their eyes.
Though it do well, I do not relish well   75
Their loud applause and aves vehement,
Nor do I think the man of safe discretion
That does affect it. Once more, fare you well.
ANGELO
The heavens give safety to your purposes.
ESCALUS
Lead forth and bring you back in happiness.   80
DUKE   I thank you. Fare you well.   *He exits.*
ESCALUS, ⌜*to Angelo*⌝
I shall desire you, sir, to give me leave
To have free speech with you; and it concerns me
To look into the bottom of my place.

75. **do well:** i.e., is appropriate
76. **aves:** shouts of welcome
78. **does affect:** is attracted to, likes
84. **look into the bottom:** examine carefully to know the precise nature of; **place:** official position
85. **A power:** i.e., legal or delegated authority
88. **our satisfaction have:** i.e., have our questions fully answered
89. **Touching:** concerning
90. **wait upon:** accompany

1.2 Angelo enforces Vienna's law against fornication, ordering the brothels torn down and having Claudio arrested because his fiancée's pregnancy exposes his guilt in breaking this law. Claudio, sentenced to be executed immediately, sends Lucio to the convent to beg Claudio's sister Isabella, a novice, to intercede with Angelo.

---

2. **composition:** terms, agreement
3. **fall upon:** attack
4–5. **Heaven . . . Hungary's:** See longer note, page 213.
9. **scraped:** erased with a knife; **the table:** i.e., the commandments (English parish churches were required to post "tables of **the ten commandments**" on the wall. At Exodus 24.12 God speaks of writing the commandments on "tables of stone." For the commandments, see Exodus 20.3–17.)
11. **razed:** erased
13–14. **from their functions:** i.e., away from their trade

(continued)

A power I have, but of what strength and nature   85
I am not yet instructed.

ANGELO
'Tis so with me. Let us withdraw together,
And we may soon our satisfaction have
Touching that point.

ESCALUS   I'll wait upon your Honor.   90

They exit.

Scene 2
Enter Lucio and two other Gentlemen.

LUCIO   If the Duke, with the other dukes, come not to
composition with the King of Hungary, why then all
the dukes fall upon the King.

FIRST GENTLEMAN   Heaven grant us its peace, but not
the King of Hungary's!   5

SECOND GENTLEMAN   Amen.

LUCIO   Thou conclud'st like the sanctimonious pirate
that went to sea with the ten commandments but
scraped one out of the table.

SECOND GENTLEMAN   "Thou shalt not steal"?   10

LUCIO   Ay, that he razed.

FIRST GENTLEMAN   Why, 'twas a commandment to command the Captain and all the rest from their functions! They put forth to steal. There's not a soldier of
us all that in the thanksgiving before meat do relish   15
the petition well that prays for peace.

SECOND GENTLEMAN   I never heard any soldier dislike it.

LUCIO   I believe thee, for I think thou never wast where
grace was said.

SECOND GENTLEMAN   No? A dozen times at least.   20

FIRST GENTLEMAN   What? In meter?

LUCIO   In any proportion or in any language.

FIRST GENTLEMAN   I think, or in any religion.

14. **put forth:** embarked, set out (to sea)
15. **meat:** i.e., a meal, food
17. **dislike:** express aversion to
19. **grace:** i.e., the prayer before a meal
21. **In meter:** perhaps a reference to burlesque metrical graces
22. **proportion:** form or shape
24. **Grace is grace:** Through a pun Lucio shifts the meaning of **grace** away from "a prayer before a meal" toward its theological senses of "divine influence" or "God's mercy."; **despite of:** i.e., despite
27–28. **there went . . . us:** i.e., we're made of the same material (proverbial)
29. **lists:** cloth border (See longer note to 1.2.29–30, page 213.)
32. **three-piled piece:** high-quality velvet, whose pile is three times the normal thickness; **warrant:** promise
33. **as lief:** i.e., just as soon; **kersey:** coarse cloth; **piled:** wordplay on "piles" (hemorrhoids) and "pilled" (made bald) Baldness was caused by the mercury treatment for syphilis, "the French disease" (hence the reference to **French velvet**). This is the first of many references to venereal disease. See longer note, pages 213–14.
35. **feelingly:** (1) to the purpose; (2) in a way that can be felt (Lucio responds as if the word carried its meaning of "from actual personal experience.")
38. **begin:** i.e., drink a toast to
39. **after thee:** i.e., from your cup (Montaigne writes in his *Essays* [1603]: "he would not drink after him for fear he should take the pox of him.")
43. **free:** i.e., free from disease

(continued)

14

LUCIO   Ay, why not? Grace is grace, despite of all
    controversy; as, for example, thou thyself art a   25
    wicked villain, despite of all grace.

FIRST GENTLEMAN   Well, there went but a pair of shears
    between us.

LUCIO   I grant, as there may between the lists and the
    velvet. Thou art the list.   30

FIRST GENTLEMAN   And thou the velvet. Thou art good
    velvet; thou'rt a three-piled piece, I warrant thee. I
    had as lief be a list of an English kersey as be piled,
    as thou art piled, for a French velvet. Do I speak
    feelingly now?   35

LUCIO   I think thou dost, and indeed with most painful
    feeling of thy speech. I will, out of thine own
    confession, learn to begin thy health, but, whilst I
    live, forget to drink after thee.

FIRST GENTLEMAN   I think I have done myself wrong,   40
    have I not?

SECOND GENTLEMAN   Yes, that thou hast, whether thou
    art tainted or free.

Enter ⌜*Mistress Overdone, a*⌝ *Bawd.*

LUCIO   Behold, behold, where Madam Mitigation
    comes! I have purchased as many diseases under   45
    her roof as come to—

SECOND GENTLEMAN   To what, I pray?

LUCIO   Judge.

SECOND GENTLEMAN   To three thousand dolors a year.

FIRST GENTLEMAN   Ay, and more.   50

LUCIO   A French crown more.

FIRST GENTLEMAN   Thou art always figuring diseases in
    me, but thou art full of error. I am sound.

LUCIO   Nay, not, as one would say, healthy, but so sound
    as things that are hollow. Thy bones are hollow.   55
    Impiety has made a feast of thee.

44. **Madam Mitigation:** i.e., Mrs. Relief

48. **Judge:** i.e., guess

49. **dolors:** pains, diseases (with a pun on "dollars," the English word for the German *thaler*)

51. **French crown:** (1) a coin; (2) baldness caused by treatment for syphilis

52. **figuring:** imagining

55. **bones are hollow:** Syphilis, in its later stages, attacks the bones.

62. **Marry:** i.e., indeed (originally an oath on the name of the Virgin Mary)

67. **after:** notwithstanding

70. **with child:** i.e., pregnant

74–75. **draws something near:** i.e., approaches **something:** i.e., somewhat

75. **speech:** conversation; **to such a purpose:** i.e., on this subject

79. **sweat:** probably, the sweating treatment given to those suffering from syphilis (as in the illustration on page 212), but possibly also a reference to the plague, a symptom of which was sweating because of high fever

80–81. **am custom-shrunk:** i.e., have fewer customers

81 SD. **Pompey:** In the Folio Pompey is called "Clown," the designation given a servant or lower-class character represented by a comic actor.

83–111. **Yonder . . . Juliet:** See longer note, page 214.

87. **Groping . . . river:** i.e., copulating **Groping:** a method of catching fish by stroking their gills **peculiar:** private

(continued)

FIRST GENTLEMAN, ⌜*to Bawd*⌝ How now, which of your
    hips has the most profound sciatica?

BAWD Well, well. There's one yonder arrested and
    carried to prison was worth five thousand of you all.   60

SECOND GENTLEMAN Who's that, I pray thee?

BAWD Marry, sir, that's Claudio, Signior Claudio.

FIRST GENTLEMAN Claudio to prison? 'Tis not so.

BAWD Nay, but I know 'tis so. I saw him arrested, saw
    him carried away; and, which is more, within these   65
    three days his head to be chopped off.

LUCIO But, after all this fooling, I would not have it so!
    Art thou sure of this?

BAWD I am too sure of it. And it is for getting Madam
    Julietta with child.   70

LUCIO Believe me, this may be. He promised to meet
    me two hours since, and he was ever precise in
    promise-keeping.

SECOND GENTLEMAN Besides, you know, it draws some-
    thing near to the speech we had to such a purpose.   75

FIRST GENTLEMAN But most of all agreeing with the
    proclamation.

LUCIO Away. Let's go learn the truth of it.
                       ⌜*Lucio and Gentlemen*⌝ *exit.*

BAWD Thus, what with the war, what with the sweat,
    what with the gallows, and what with poverty, I am   80
    custom-shrunk.

Enter ⌜*Pompey.*⌝

    How now? What's the news with you?

POMPEY Yonder man is carried to prison.

BAWD Well, what has he done?

POMPEY A woman.   85

BAWD But what's his offense?

POMPEY Groping for trouts in a peculiar river.

BAWD What? Is there a maid with child by him?

88–89. Is . . . by him: Since **maid** meant a virgin (male or female), the pregnant **woman** could not be a **maid,** but the term could be applied to the unborn child.

92. houses: i.e., bawdy houses, brothels (See page 50.); **suburbs:** outskirts (In Shakespeare's London, brothels, theaters, and other buildings of bad repute were usually in the **suburbs.**)

93. plucked down: demolished

95. stand for seed: perhaps, remain standing to provide a future for prostitution, just as unharvested grain provides seed for future plants; **had:** i.e., would have

96. put in for: interceded for; or, offered to buy

102. fear not you: i.e., don't be afraid

107 SD. Provost: an officer charged with arresting and punishing offenders

108. Thomas Tapster: perhaps a nickname for tapsters (See page 46.)

114. in evil disposition: i.e., out of a malicious inclination or nature

115. charge: command

117–19. pay . . . so: See longer note, pages 214–15. **pay down:** pay immediately   **by weight:** i.e., exactly, in full

POMPEY No, but there's a woman with maid by him.
   You have not heard of the proclamation, have you? 90
BAWD What proclamation, man?
POMPEY All houses in the suburbs of Vienna must be
   plucked down.
BAWD And what shall become of those in the city?
POMPEY They shall stand for seed. They had gone down 95
   too, but that a wise burgher put in for them.
BAWD But shall all our houses of resort in the suburbs
   be pulled down?
POMPEY To the ground, mistress.
BAWD Why, here's a change indeed in the common- 100
   wealth! What shall become of me?
POMPEY Come, fear not you. Good counselors lack no
   clients. Though you change your place, you need
   not change your trade. I'll be your tapster still.
   Courage. There will be pity taken on you. You that 105
   have worn your eyes almost out in the service, you
   will be considered.

   Enter Provost, Claudio, Juliet, ⌐and⌐ Officers.

BAWD What's to do here, Thomas Tapster? Let's with-
   draw.
POMPEY Here comes Signior Claudio, led by the Pro- 110
   vost to prison. And there's Madam Juliet.
                          ⌐*Bawd and Pompey*⌐ *exit.*
CLAUDIO, ⌐*to Provost*⌐
   Fellow, why dost thou show me thus to th' world?
   Bear me to prison, where I am committed.
PROVOST
   I do it not in evil disposition,
   But from Lord Angelo by special charge. 115
CLAUDIO
   Thus can the demigod Authority
   Make us pay down for our offense, by weight,

122. **liberty:** (1) licentiousness; (2) freedom

124. **scope:** instance of licentiousness

126. **raven down:** devour; **their proper bane:** i.e., ratsbane, the poison used to kill rats

127. **A thirsty evil:** i.e., an evil that causes thirst

129. **creditors:** an allusion to the practice of creditors arresting those owing them money

130. **foppery:** foolishness, folly

131. **mortality:** deadliness

141. **looked after:** attended to, closely watched

142. **true:** proper

144. **fast:** securely (See below and Historical Background 2, "Betrothal and Marriage," pages 227–32.)

145. **denunciation:** public announcement

146. **order:** administration of a rite or ceremony

A handfasting. (1.2.144)
From George Wither, *A collection of emblemes* . . . (1635).

The words of heaven: on whom it will, it will;
On whom it will not, so; yet still 'tis just.

Enter Lucio and Second Gentleman.

LUCIO
  Why, how now, Claudio? Whence comes this   120
  restraint?
CLAUDIO
  From too much liberty, my Lucio, liberty.
  As surfeit is the father of much fast,
  So every scope by the immoderate use
  Turns to restraint. Our natures do pursue,   125
  Like rats that raven down their proper bane,
  A thirsty evil, and when we drink, we die.
LUCIO If I could speak so wisely under an arrest, I
    would send for certain of my creditors. And yet, to
    say the truth, I had as lief have the foppery of 130
    freedom as the mortality of imprisonment. What's
    thy offense, Claudio?
CLAUDIO
  What but to speak of would offend again.
LUCIO   What, is 't murder?
CLAUDIO   No.   135
LUCIO   Lechery?
CLAUDIO   Call it so.
PROVOST   Away, sir. You must go.
CLAUDIO
  One word, good friend.—Lucio, a word with you.
LUCIO   A hundred, if they'll do you any good. Is lechery 140
    so looked after?
CLAUDIO
  Thus stands it with me: upon a true contract
  I got possession of Julietta's bed.
  You know the lady. She is fast my wife,
  Save that we do the denunciation lack   145
  Of outward order. This we came not to

147. **for propagation of:** perhaps, because of a desire to increase

148. **friends:** i.e., kinsmen

149. **meet:** fitting, proper

150. **for us:** i.e., our allies; **chances:** happens

151. **entertainment:** reception (of each other) **Entertainment** is Claudio's polite way of referring to his sexual relations with Juliet.

152. **character:** handwriting; **gross:** large, evident

156. **glimpse:** perhaps, partial or imperfect vision; **newness:** unfamiliarity

158. **governor:** i.e., ruler (here with the added sense of one who governs—i.e., controls—the horse he rides)

160. **straight:** straightway, immediately

161. **place:** position

163. **stagger in:** i.e., am not sure

164. **Awakes me:** i.e., awakens; **enrollèd:** written

166. **nineteen . . . round:** i.e., nineteen years have passed

167. **for a name:** i.e., in order to establish a reputation

168. **puts:** imposes

170. **tickle:** insecurely, loose

174. **prithee:** i.e., pray thee

175. **should . . . enter:** i.e., is going . . . to enter

176. **receive her approbation:** perhaps, begin her novitiate or probationary period

177. **state:** condition

179. **bid herself assay:** i.e., ask her to approach

Only for propagation of a dower
Remaining in the coffer of her friends,
From whom we thought it meet to hide our love
Till time had made them for us. But it chances   150
The stealth of our most mutual entertainment
With character too gross is writ on Juliet.

LUCIO
With child, perhaps?

CLAUDIO   Unhappily, even so.
And the new deputy now for the Duke—   155
Whether it be the fault and glimpse of newness,
Or whether that the body public be
A horse whereon the governor doth ride,
Who, newly in the seat, that it may know
He can command, lets it straight feel the spur;   160
Whether the tyranny be in his place
Or in his eminence that fills it up,
I stagger in—but this new governor
Awakes me all the enrollèd penalties
Which have, like unscoured armor, hung by th' wall   165
So long that nineteen zodiacs have gone round,
And none of them been worn; and for a name
Now puts the drowsy and neglected act
Freshly on me. 'Tis surely for a name.

LUCIO   I warrant it is. And thy head stands so tickle on 170
    thy shoulders that a milkmaid, if she be in love, may
    sigh it off. Send after the Duke and appeal to him.

CLAUDIO
I have done so, but he's not to be found.
I prithee, Lucio, do me this kind service:
This day my sister should the cloister enter   175
And there receive her approbation.
Acquaint her with the danger of my state;
Implore her, in my voice, that she make friends
To the strict deputy; bid herself assay him.
I have great hope in that, for in her youth   180

181. **prone:** natural
182. **move:** i.e., moves; **art:** skill, learning (here, the art of rhetoric; see page 60)
186. **the like:** perhaps, offenders like Claudio
187. **who:** i.e., which
188–89. **a game of tick-tack:** a mocking reference to sex (literally, a board game in which pegs were placed in holes)

1.3 The duke obtains the clothing of a friar in order to disguise himself and secretly observe the conduct of Angelo and the people of Vienna.

---

2. **dribbling dart:** a scornful allusion to Cupid's arrow, which, by piercing the heart, causes one to fall in love (See page 42.)
3. **complete:** i.e., completely armed, invulnerable (accent on first syllable); **Why:** i.e., the reason why
9. **the life removed:** i.e., a secluded life
10. **held in idle price:** i.e., considered (it) of little worth; **assemblies:** social gatherings
11. **bravery:** ostentation; **keeps:** maintain
13. **stricture:** i.e., strict or rigid behavior
16. **common:** public

There is a prone and speechless dialect
Such as move men. Besides, she hath prosperous art
When she will play with reason and discourse,
And well she can persuade.

LUCIO I pray she may, as well for the encouragement of 185
the like, which else would stand under grievous
imposition, as for the enjoying of thy life, who I
would be sorry should be thus foolishly lost at a
game of tick-tack. I'll to her.

CLAUDIO I thank you, good friend Lucio. 190

LUCIO Within two hours.

CLAUDIO Come, officer, away.

They exit.

⌜Scene 3⌝
Enter Duke and Friar Thomas.

DUKE
No, holy father, throw away that thought.
Believe not that the dribbling dart of love
Can pierce a complete bosom. Why I desire thee
To give me secret harbor hath a purpose
More grave and wrinkled than the aims and ends 5
Of burning youth.

FRIAR THOMAS   May your Grace speak of it?

DUKE
My holy sir, none better knows than you
How I have ever loved the life removed,
And held in idle price to haunt assemblies 10
Where youth and cost witless bravery keeps.
I have delivered to Lord Angelo,
A man of stricture and firm abstinence,
My absolute power and place here in Vienna,
And he supposes me traveled to Poland, 15
For so I have strewed it in the common ear,

21. **weeds:** often emended to "steeds" in order to complete the horseback-riding metaphor begun with **bits** and **curbs** (Such an emendation prevents a mixed metaphor, now regarded as a stylistic fault but not uncommon in Shakespeare's plays.)

22. **let slip:** perhaps, allowed (the **statutes**) to slide; or, perhaps, allowed (the lion's prey) to escape

23–24. **o'ergrown . . . prey:** i.e., a lion too fat or too old to catch its prey

24. **fond:** (1) foolish; (2) doting

25. **twigs of birch:** i.e., the birch rod used for whipping

29. **Dead to infliction:** i.e., never used as punishment

30. **liberty:** i.e., undisciplined freedom, license

33. **It rested in your Grace:** i.e., it remained with you; it was your responsibility

38. **Sith:** since

39. **gall:** harass

40–41. **we bid . . . pass:** i.e., we issue commands to do evil when we fail to punish **evil deeds permissive pass:** i.e., permission to proceed

45. **in th' ambush:** i.e., under the cover; **home:** directly, effectively

46. **nature:** i.e., personal character

47. **To do in slander:** perhaps, to bring discredit on myself (The phrase is obscure.)

49. **prince:** i.e., Angelo (The word **prince** could refer to any person with sovereign authority, regardless of title.)

50. **habit:** clothing (of a friar) See page 196.

51. **formally:** i.e., in proper form; **bear:** i.e., bear myself, behave

And so it is received. Now, pious sir,
You will demand of me why I do this.

FRIAR THOMAS   Gladly, my lord.

DUKE
We have strict statutes and most biting laws, 20
The needful bits and curbs to headstrong weeds,
Which for this fourteen years we have let slip,
Even like an o'ergrown lion in a cave
That goes not out to prey. Now, as fond fathers,
Having bound up the threat'ning twigs of birch 25
Only to stick it in their children's sight
For terror, not to use—in time the rod
More mocked than feared—so our decrees,
Dead to infliction, to themselves are dead,
And liberty plucks justice by the nose, 30
The baby beats the nurse, and quite athwart
Goes all decorum.

FRIAR THOMAS   It rested in your Grace
To unloose this tied-up justice when you pleased,
And it in you more dreadful would have seemed 35
Than in Lord Angelo.

DUKE   I do fear, too dreadful.
Sith 'twas my fault to give the people scope,
'Twould be my tyranny to strike and gall them
For what I bid them do; for we bid this be done 40
When evil deeds have their permissive pass
And not the punishment. Therefore, indeed, my
   father,
I have on Angelo imposed the office,
Who may in th' ambush of my name strike home, 45
And yet my nature never in the fight
To do in slander. And to behold his sway
I will, as 'twere a brother of your order,
Visit both prince and people. Therefore I prithee
Supply me with the habit, and instruct me 50
How I may formally in person bear

53. **more leisure:** i.e., greater leisure

54. **precise:** strict in the observance of rules, fastidious; perhaps, puritanical

55. **at a guard with:** i.e., on his defense against; **envy:** malice, slander

57. **bread than stone:** See Matthew 4.3 (where Jesus, fasting, rejects the devil's temptation to turn stones into bread). See also Matthew 7.9.

58. **If power change purpose:** Proverbial: "Authority shows what a man is."

1.4 Lucio persuades Isabella to intercede with Angelo.

———————

5. **votarists of Saint Clare:** See Historical Background 3, "Isabella and the Order of Poor Clares," pages 232–35, and woodcut, page 34. **votarists:** women under a vow

6 SD. **within:** i.e., from offstage

9. **Turn you the key:** i.e., unlock the door (of the abbey); **know . . . him:** i.e., ask him his **business**

10. **You are yet unsworn:** i.e., you have not yet taken your vows

11–14. **When . . . speak:** See Historical Background 3, "Isabella and the Order of Poor Clares," pages 232–35.

Like a true friar. More reasons for this action
At our more leisure shall I render you.
Only this one: Lord Angelo is precise,
Stands at a guard with envy, scarce confesses   55
That his blood flows or that his appetite
Is more to bread than stone. Hence shall we see,
If power change purpose, what our seemers be.
                                    ⌜*They*⌝ *exit.*

                    ⌜Scene 4⌝
        Enter Isabella and Francisca, a Nun.

ISABELLA
  And have you nuns no farther privileges?
NUN   Are not these large enough?
ISABELLA
  Yes, truly. I speak not as desiring more,
  But rather wishing a more strict restraint
  Upon the sisterhood, the votarists of Saint Clare.   5
LUCIO, *within*
  Ho, peace be in this place!
ISABELLA   Who's that which calls?
NUN
  It is a man's voice. Gentle Isabella,
  Turn you the key and know his business of him.
  You may; I may not. You are yet unsworn.   10
  When you have vowed, you must not speak with men
  But in the presence of the Prioress.
  Then, if you speak, you must not show your face;
  Or if you show your face, you must not speak.
  He calls again. I pray you answer him.   15
ISABELLA
  Peace and prosperity! Who is't that calls?

                    ⌜*Enter Lucio.*⌝

18. **stead:** help

19. **As:** as to

21. **unhappy:** (1) unfortunate; (2) sorrowful

23. **The rather for:** i.e., the more so because

26. **weary:** wearisome, tedious

30. **friend:** i.e., lover

31. **make me not your story:** i.e., do not make a mockery of me

34. **seem the lapwing:** i.e., deceive, play the hypocrite (The **lapwing** deceives predators by calling loudly when far from her nest, thus protecting her fledglings.)

36. **enskied:** i.e., placed in the sky or heaven

37. **renouncement:** i.e., renouncing of the world (by entering the convent)

40. **the good:** perhaps, the real saints to whom Lucio compares Isabella

41. **Fewness and truth:** perhaps, to tell the truth in a few words

44. **seedness:** the state of being strewn with seeds

A lapwing. (1.4.34)
From Konrad Gesner, *Icones animalium* . . . (1560).

LUCIO
  Hail, virgin, if you be, as those cheek-roses
  Proclaim you are no less. Can you so stead me
  As bring me to the sight of Isabella,
  A novice of this place and the fair sister   20
  To her unhappy brother, Claudio?

ISABELLA
  Why "her unhappy brother"? Let me ask,
  The rather for I now must make you know
  I am that Isabella, and his sister.

LUCIO
  Gentle and fair, your brother kindly greets you.   25
  Not to be weary with you, he's in prison.

ISABELLA Woe me, for what?

LUCIO
  For that which, if myself might be his judge,
  He should receive his punishment in thanks:
  He hath got his friend with child.   30

ISABELLA
  Sir, make me not your story.

LUCIO   'Tis true.
  I would not, though 'tis my familiar sin
  With maids to seem the lapwing and to jest,
  Tongue far from heart, play with all virgins so.   35
  I hold you as a thing enskied and sainted,
  By your renouncement an immortal spirit,
  And to be talked with in sincerity
  As with a saint.

ISABELLA
  You do blaspheme the good in mocking me.   40

LUCIO
  Do not believe it. Fewness and truth, 'tis thus:
  Your brother and his lover have embraced;
  As those that feed grow full, as blossoming time
  That from the seedness the bare fallow brings

45. **foison:** abundance

46. **tilth and husbandry:** i.e., tillage of the land (with a pun on "husband")

49. **change:** exchange

50. **vain:** futile or silly; **apt:** appropriate (for **schoolmaids**)

55–56. **Bore . . . hope:** complicated wordplay on "bore in hand," which means "systematically deceived, deluded" (from the French *maintenir*), and "bore in hope," which means "kept in hope"

57. **By those:** i.e., from those

58. **givings-out:** i.e., public assertions

59. **Upon:** i.e., in

60. **line:** extent, scope

62. **very snow-broth:** i.e., nothing but melted snow

63. **motions of the sense:** i.e., sexual impulses

64. **rebate:** make dull; **edge:** desire

65. **With profits of:** i.e., with that which profits

66. **use:** customary behavior, habit; **liberty:** i.e., undisciplined freedom, license

69. **heavy sense:** severe import

73. **grace:** virtue; or, perhaps, good fortune

74. **my pith of business:** i.e., the essence of my business

75. **'Twixt:** i.e., between

76. **he:** i.e., Angelo

To teeming foison, even so her plenteous womb   45
Expresseth his full tilth and husbandry.
ISABELLA
Someone with child by him? My cousin Juliet?
LUCIO   Is she your cousin?
ISABELLA
Adoptedly, as schoolmaids change their names
By vain though apt affection.   50
LUCIO   She it is.
ISABELLA
O, let him marry her!
LUCIO   This is the point.
The Duke is very strangely gone from hence;
Bore many gentlemen, myself being one,   55
In hand, and hope of action; but we do learn,
By those that know the very nerves of state,
His ⌜givings-out⌝ were of an infinite distance
From his true-meant design. Upon his place,
And with full line of his authority,   60
Governs Lord Angelo, a man whose blood
Is very snow-broth; one who never feels
The wanton stings and motions of the sense,
But doth rebate and blunt his natural edge
With profits of the mind: study and fast.   65
He—to give fear to use and liberty,
Which have for long run by the hideous law
As mice by lions—hath picked out an act
Under whose heavy sense your brother's life
Falls into forfeit. He arrests him on it,   70
And follows close the rigor of the statute
To make him an example. All hope is gone
Unless you have the grace by your fair prayer
To soften Angelo. And that's my pith of business
'Twixt you and your poor brother.   75
ISABELLA   Doth he so
Seek his life?

78. **censured:** sentenced

83. **Assay:** try

88. **sue:** petition, entreat

91. **would owe them:** i.e., would wish to have them **owe:** own, possess

94. **will about it:** i.e., will set about doing it

95. **Mother:** head of the religious community

97. **Commend me:** i.e., give my greetings to; **Soon at night:** i.e., early this evening

98. **my success:** the outcome of my efforts

Saint Clare. (1.4.5)
From Petrus de Natalibus, *Catalogus sanctoru[m]* . . . (1519).

LUCIO   Has censured him already,
  And, as I hear, the Provost hath a warrant
  For 's execution.   80
ISABELLA
  Alas, what poor ability's in me
  To do him good?
LUCIO   Assay the power you have.
ISABELLA
  My power? Alas, I doubt—
LUCIO   Our doubts are traitors   85
  And makes us lose the good we oft might win
  By fearing to attempt. Go to Lord Angelo
  And let him learn to know, when maidens sue
  Men give like gods; but when they weep and kneel,
  All their petitions are as freely theirs   90
  As they themselves would owe them.
ISABELLA   I'll see what I can do.
LUCIO   But speedily!
ISABELLA   I will about it straight,
  No longer staying but to give the Mother   95
  Notice of my affair. I humbly thank you.
  Commend me to my brother. Soon at night
  I'll send him certain word of my success.
LUCIO
  I take my leave of you.
ISABELLA   Good sir, adieu.   100

They exit.

MEASURE
FOR
MEASURE

ACT 2

2.1 Escalus tries to persuade Angelo to be less harsh to Claudio. Angelo instead gives orders that Claudio be executed the following morning. Elbow, a constable, brings two prisoners, Pompey and Froth, before Angelo and Escalus. Angelo leaves their trial to Escalus, who tells Froth to stay out of alehouses and tells Pompey that he will be whipped if he is ever brought before Escalus again.

———

2. **fear:** i.e., frighten away
7. **fall:** i.e., let fall
9. **know:** understand
10. **strait:** strict, morally scrupulous
11. **affections:** desires
12. **cohered:** agreed
13. **Or that:** i.e., or if; **blood:** passions, sensual desires
14. **effect:** fulfillment, accomplishment
16. **which:** i.e., for which; **censure:** sentence
19. **not deny:** i.e., do not deny that
20. **passing . . . life:** i.e., giving a verdict in a case where the penalty for the crime is death
22. **open made:** revealed, made obvious

ACT 2

Scene 1
Enter Angelo, Escalus, Servants, ⌜*and a*⌝ *Justice.*

ANGELO
  We must not make a scarecrow of the law,
  Setting it up to fear the birds of prey,
  And let it keep one shape till custom make it
  Their perch and not their terror.
ESCALUS   Ay, but yet   5
  Let us be keen and rather cut a little
  Than fall and bruise to death. Alas, this gentleman
  Whom I would save had a most noble father.
  Let but your Honor know,
  Whom I believe to be most strait in virtue,   10
  That, in the working of your own affections,
  Had time cohered with place, or place with wishing,
  Or that the resolute acting of ⌜your⌝ blood
  Could have attained th' effect of your own purpose,
  Whether you had not sometime in your life   15
  Erred in this point which now you censure him,
  And pulled the law upon you.
ANGELO
  'Tis one thing to be tempted, Escalus,
  Another thing to fall. I not deny
  The jury passing on the prisoner's life   20
  May in the sworn twelve have a thief or two
  Guiltier than him they try. What's open made to
    justice,

24. **laws:** i.e., law
25. **pregnant:** obvious
30. **For:** because, on the grounds that
32. **pattern out:** be the example or precedent for
33. **nothing come in partial:** (1) no argument be heard that is biased in my favor; or, (2) let my judgment be in no way biased
36. **if . . . Honor:** a courteous phrase **like:** please
39. **prepared:** i.e., prepared for death
40. **utmost:** furthest point; **his pilgrimage:** i.e., his life (Proverbial: "Life is a pilgrimage." See below.)
43. **Some run from brakes of ice:** a much-debated figure of speech (See longer note, page 215.)
44. **fault alone:** i.e., mere frailty; or, single frailty
46. **commonweal:** i.e., commonwealth
47. **use:** practice; **common houses:** i.e., brothels
50. **matter:** circumstance, situation

Life as a pilgrimage. (2.1.40)
From Geoffrey Whitney, *A choice of emblemes . . .* (1586).

That justice seizes. What knows the laws
That thieves do pass on thieves? 'Tis very pregnant,   25
The jewel that we find, we stoop and take 't
Because we see it; but what we do not see,
We tread upon and never think of it.
You may not so extenuate his offense
For I have had such faults; but rather tell me,   30
When I that censure him do so offend,
Let mine own judgment pattern out my death,
And nothing come in partial. Sir, he must die.

Enter Provost.

ESCALUS
  Be it as your wisdom will.
ANGELO   Where is the Provost?   35
PROVOST
  Here, if it like your Honor.
ANGELO   See that Claudio
  Be executed by nine tomorrow morning.
  Bring him his confessor, let him be prepared,
  For that's the utmost of his pilgrimage.   40
⌐*Provost exits.*¬

ESCALUS
  Well, heaven forgive him and forgive us all.
  Some rise by sin and some by virtue fall.
  Some run from brakes of ice and answer none,
  And some condemnèd for a fault alone.

Enter Elbow ⌐*and*¬ *Officers,* ⌐*with*¬ *Froth*
⌐*and Pompey.*¬

ELBOW, ⌐*to Officers*¬ Come, bring them away. If these   45
  be good people in a commonweal that do nothing
  but use their abuses in common houses, I know no
  law. Bring them away.
ANGELO How now, sir, what's your name? And what's
  the matter?   50

51–52. poor duke's constable: i.e., duke's poor constable

54. benefactors: i.e., malefactors (This is the first of many comic misuses of words, today called "malapropisms," that characterize Elbow's speech.)

58. precise: probably his error for "precious"—i.e., arrant, egregious

63. Go to: an expression of impatience; **quality:** occupation

66. out at elbow: shabby; impoverished

68. parcel: part; **bawd:** one employed in pandering to sexual debauchery; a procurer

70–71. now . . . hothouse: i.e., now her business is a bathhouse (playing with the word **professes** in its primary sense of taking a religious vow) See page 48.

71. ill: evil

81–82. pity of her life: i.e., a great pity

82. naughty: wicked

85. cardinally: malapropism for "carnally"

Cupid and his arrow. (1.3.2)
From Francesco Petrarca, *Opera* . . . (1508).

ELBOW If it please your Honor, I am the poor duke's
  constable, and my name is Elbow. I do lean upon
  justice, sir, and do bring in here before your good
  Honor two notorious benefactors.

ANGELO Benefactors? Well, what benefactors are they? 55
  Are they not malefactors?

ELBOW If it please your Honor, I know not well what
  they are, but precise villains they are, that I am sure
  of, and void of all profanation in the world that
  good Christians ought to have. 60

ESCALUS, ⌈*to Angelo*⌉ This comes off well. Here's a wise
  officer.

ANGELO, ⌈*to Elbow*⌉ Go to. What quality are they of?
  Elbow is your name? Why dost thou not speak,
  Elbow? 65

POMPEY He cannot, sir. He's out at elbow.

ANGELO What are you, sir?

ELBOW He, sir? A tapster, sir, parcel bawd; one that
  serves a bad woman, whose house, sir, was, as they
  say, plucked down in the suburbs, and now she 70
  professes a hothouse, which I think is a very ill
  house too.

ESCALUS How know you that?

ELBOW My wife, sir, whom I detest before heaven and
  your Honor— 75

ESCALUS How? Thy wife?

ELBOW Ay, sir, whom I thank heaven is an honest
  woman—

ESCALUS Dost thou detest her therefore?

ELBOW I say, sir, I will detest myself also, as well as she, 80
  that this house, if it be not a bawd's house, it is pity
  of her life, for it is a naughty house.

ESCALUS How dost thou know that, constable?

ELBOW Marry, sir, by my wife, who, if she had been a
  woman cardinally given, might have been accused 85

86. **fornication . . . uncleanliness:** Elbow parrots Galatians 5.19: "the works of the flesh are . . . adultery, fornication, uncleanliness."

90. **his, him:** probably referring to Froth, who, at line 151, is the **man** accused by Elbow of propositioning Elbow's wife

95. **misplaces:** i.e., applies the words "varlets" and "honorable" to the wrong people

96. **great with child:** pregnant

97. **saving your Honor's reverence:** i.e., begging your Honor's pardon ("Save your reverence" was a request to be excused for being about to mention something indecent or unsavory.); **stewed prunes:** Stewed prunes were served in houses of prostitution—perhaps in the misplaced belief that they prevented venereal disease.

104. **not of a pin:** i.e., (it) doesn't matter a pin's worth (Proverbial: "not worth a pin")

111–12. **give you . . . again:** i.e., give you . . . back (in change)

114–15. **be remembered:** i.e., remember

119. **wot:** know

120. **diet:** i.e., dietary regimen, prescribed food

in fornication, adultery, and all uncleanliness
there.

ESCALUS By the woman's means?

ELBOW Ay, sir, by Mistress Overdone's means; but as
she spit in his face, so she defied him. 90

POMPEY, ⌜to Escalus⌝ Sir, if it please your Honor, this is
not so.

ELBOW Prove it before these varlets here, thou honorable man, prove it.

ESCALUS, ⌜to Angelo⌝ Do you hear how he misplaces? 95

POMPEY Sir, she came in great with child, and longing,
saving your Honor's reverence, for stewed prunes.
Sir, we had but two in the house, which at that very
distant time stood, as it were, in a fruit dish, a dish
of some three pence; your Honors have seen such 100
dishes; they are not china dishes, but very good
dishes—

ESCALUS Go to, go to. No matter for the dish, sir.

POMPEY No, indeed, sir, not of a pin; you are therein in
the right. But to the point: as I say, this Mistress 105
Elbow, being, as I say, with child, and being great-
bellied, and longing, as I said, for prunes; and
having but two in the dish, as I said, Master Froth
here, this very man, having eaten the rest, as I said,
and, as I say, paying for them very honestly—for, as 110
you know, Master Froth, I could not give you three
pence again—

FROTH No, indeed.

POMPEY Very well. You being then, if you be remembered, cracking the stones of the foresaid prunes— 115

FROTH Ay, so I did indeed.

POMPEY Why, very well. I telling you then, if you be
remembered, that such a one and such a one were
past cure of the thing you wot of, unless they kept
very good diet, as I told you— 120

FROTH All this is true.

125. **Come me:** i.e., come

129. **look into:** i.e., consider; or, look at

130. **of fourscore pound a year:** i.e., with an income (inherited or from property or investments) of eighty pounds a year (Half that amount was considered a good income.)

131. **Hallowmas:** i.e., All Saints' Day (November 1)

133. **All-hallond Eve:** i.e., All Hallows' Eve (October 31)

135. **a lower chair:** possibly an easy chair or couch

136. **Bunch of Grapes:** the name of a room in the house

143. **cause:** case, suit (playing, in line 144, on **cause** as "reason")

151. **this man:** i.e., Froth

A tapster. (1.2.104)
From Guillaume de la Perrière, *La morosophie . . .* (1553).

POMPEY   Why, very well then—

ESCALUS   Come, you are a tedious fool. To the purpose:
what was done to Elbow's wife that he hath cause to
complain of? Come me to what was done to her.   125

POMPEY   Sir, your Honor cannot come to that yet.

ESCALUS   No, sir, nor I mean it not.

POMPEY   Sir, but you shall come to it, by your Honor's
leave. And I beseech you, look into Master Froth
here, sir, a man of fourscore pound a year, whose   130
father died at Hallowmas—was 't not at Hallowmas, Master Froth?

FROTH   All-hallond Eve.

POMPEY   Why, very well. I hope here be truths.—He,
sir, sitting, as I say, in a lower chair, sir—⌈*To Froth.*⌉   135
'Twas in the Bunch of Grapes, where indeed you
have a delight to sit, have you not?

FROTH   I have so, because it is an open room, and good
for winter.

POMPEY   Why, very well then. I hope here be truths.   140

ANGELO, ⌈*to Escalus*⌉
This will last out a night in Russia
When nights are longest there. I'll take my leave,
And leave you to the hearing of the cause,
Hoping you'll find good cause to whip them all.

ESCALUS
I think no less. Good morrow to your Lordship.   145
                              ⌈*Angelo*⌉ *exits.*
Now, sir, come on. What was done to Elbow's wife,
once more?

POMPEY   Once, sir? There was nothing done to her
once.

ELBOW, ⌈*to Escalus*⌉   I beseech you, sir, ask him what   150
this man did to my wife.

POMPEY, ⌈*to Escalus*⌉   I beseech your Honor, ask me.

ESCALUS   Well, sir, what did this gentleman to her?

POMPEY   I beseech you, sir, look in this gentleman's

156. **mark:** observe

163. **supposed:** probably a malapropism for "deposed" or sworn

170. **an it like you:** i.e., if you please; **respected:** probably a malapropism for "suspected"

180. **Justice or Iniquity:** i.e., the constable or the prisoner, here ironically labeled with names of figures from morality plays (or simply personified as abstract qualities)

183. **Hannibal:** the name of a famous Carthaginian general, here perhaps a malapropism for "cannibal" or a confusion of Hannibal with Pompey, a famous Roman general (See page 52.)

187. **have . . . thee:** i.e., sue you for unlawfully beating me

188. **took . . . ear:** i.e., struck you on the head

A hothouse or bathhouse. (2.1.70–72)
From Gregor Reisch, *Margarita philosophica . . .* (1517).

face.—Good Master Froth, look upon his Honor. 155
'Tis for a good purpose.—Doth your Honor mark
his face?

ESCALUS   Ay, sir, very well.

POMPEY   Nay, I beseech you, mark it well.

ESCALUS   Well, I do so. 160

POMPEY   Doth your Honor see any harm in his face?

ESCALUS   Why, no.

POMPEY   I'll be supposed upon a book, his face is the
worst thing about him. Good, then, if his face be the
worst thing about him, how could Master Froth do 165
the Constable's wife any harm? I would know that
of your Honor.

ESCALUS   He's in the right, constable. What say you to
it?

ELBOW   First, an it like you, the house is a respected 170
house; next, this is a respected fellow, and his
mistress is a respected woman.

POMPEY   By this hand, sir, his wife is a more respected
person than any of us all.

ELBOW   Varlet, thou liest; thou liest, wicked varlet! The 175
time is yet to come that she was ever respected with
man, woman, or child.

POMPEY   Sir, she was respected with him before he
married with her.

ESCALUS   Which is the wiser here, Justice or Iniquity? 180
Is this true?

ELBOW, ⌜to Pompey⌝   O thou caitiff! O thou varlet! O
thou wicked Hannibal! I respected with her before I
was married to her?—If ever I was respected with
her, or she with me, let not your Worship think me 185
the poor duke's officer.—Prove this, thou wicked
Hannibal, or I'll have mine action of batt'ry on thee.

ESCALUS   If he took you a box o' th' ear, you might have
your action of slander too.

ELBOW   Marry, I thank your good Worship for it. What 190

194. **discover:** reveal
195. **courses:** conduct
210. **Overdone:** named "Overdone"; worn out
213. **draw:** (1) drain; (2) entice; (3) disembowel (as in "hanging and drawing," an extreme method of execution), with additional wordplay on **Froth,** the foam on beer drawn from a keg
217. **taphouse:** alehouse
218. **drawn in:** enticed in (The phrase could also mean "deluded, tricked.")

A house of prostitution. (1.2.92, 97)
From [Nicholas Goodman,] *Hollands leaguer . . .* (1632).

is 't your Worship's pleasure I shall do with this
wicked caitiff?

ESCALUS   Truly, officer, because he hath some offenses
in him that thou wouldst discover if thou couldst,
let him continue in his courses till thou know'st   195
what they are.

ELBOW   Marry, I thank your Worship for it. ⌈*To Pompey.*⌉ Thou seest, thou wicked varlet, now, what's
come upon thee. Thou art to continue now, thou
varlet, thou art to continue.   200

ESCALUS, ⌈*to Froth*⌉ Where were you born, friend?

FROTH   Here in Vienna, sir.

ESCALUS   Are you of fourscore pounds a year?

FROTH   Yes, an 't please you, sir.

ESCALUS   So. ⌈*To Pompey.*⌉ What trade are you of, sir?   205

POMPEY   A tapster, a poor widow's tapster.

ESCALUS   Your mistress' name?

POMPEY   Mistress Overdone.

ESCALUS   Hath she had any more than one husband?

POMPEY   Nine, sir. Overdone by the last.   210

ESCALUS   Nine?—Come hither to me, Master Froth.
Master Froth, I would not have you acquainted with
tapsters; they will draw you, Master Froth, and you
will hang them. Get you gone, and let me hear no
more of you.   215

FROTH   I thank your Worship. For mine own part, I
never come into any room in a taphouse but I am
drawn in.

ESCALUS   Well, no more of it, Master Froth. Farewell.
⌈*Froth exits.*⌉
Come you hither to me, Master Tapster. What's your   220
name, Master Tapster?

POMPEY   Pompey.

ESCALUS   What else?

POMPEY   Bum, sir.

225. **Troth:** i.e., in troth, indeed

227. **Pompey the Great:** the elder Pompey, a great Roman military leader; **bawd:** See note to 2.1.68.

228. **color:** cloak, disguise

231. **would live:** wants to make a living

238. **splay:** spay, castrate

242. **take order:** make arrangements; **drabs:** prostitutes (also, literally, slovenly women)

244. **is . . . beginning:** i.e., are . . . under way

245. **heading:** i.e., beheading (See page 158.)

247. **together:** without interruption

248. **hold:** stays in force

249. **after:** at the rate of

250. **a bay:** the space lying under one gable

254. **before me:** i.e., brought before me

256–57. **beat . . . Caesar:** When Julius **Caesar** defeated **Pompey** the Great in 48 B.C., Pompey reportedly withdrew to his **tent** when he knew the battle was lost. **shrewd:** harsh, severe

Pompey the Great. (2.1.227)
From [Guillaume Rouillé] . . . *Prima pars promptuarii* . . . (1553).

ESCALUS Troth, and your bum is the greatest thing 225
about you, so that in the beastliest sense you are
Pompey the Great. Pompey, you are partly a bawd,
Pompey, howsoever you color it in being a tapster,
are you not? Come, tell me true. It shall be the
better for you. 230

POMPEY Truly, sir, I am a poor fellow that would live.

ESCALUS How would you live, Pompey? By being a
bawd? What do you think of the trade, Pompey? Is it
a lawful trade?

POMPEY If the law would allow it, sir. 235

ESCALUS But the law will not allow it, Pompey, nor it
shall not be allowed in Vienna.

POMPEY Does your Worship mean to geld and splay all
the youth of the city?

ESCALUS No, Pompey. 240

POMPEY Truly, sir, in my poor opinion, they will to 't
then. If your Worship will take order for the drabs
and the knaves, you need not to fear the bawds.

ESCALUS There is pretty orders beginning, I can tell
you. It is but heading and hanging. 245

POMPEY If you head and hang all that offend that way
but for ten year together, you'll be glad to give out a
commission for more heads. If this law hold in
Vienna ten year, I'll rent the fairest house in it after
three pence a bay. If you live to see this come to 250
pass, say Pompey told you so.

ESCALUS Thank you, good Pompey. And in requital of
your prophecy, hark you: I advise you let me not
find you before me again upon any complaint
whatsoever; no, not for dwelling where you do. If I 255
do, Pompey, I shall beat you to your tent and prove
a shrewd Caesar to you. In plain dealing, Pompey, I
shall have you whipped. So, for this time, Pompey,
fare you well.

POMPEY I thank your Worship for your good counsel. 260

263. **carman:** a driver of a horse and cart; **jade:** a broken-down horse

269. **readiness in the office:** i.e., ease and skill in performing your duties

274. **put . . . upon 't:** i.e., appoint you to the position so often

275. **sufficient:** competent

276. **wit:** intelligence

278. **I do it . . . money:** i.e., they give me money to serve in their place

278–79. **go . . . all:** i.e., perform all the duties

280. **Look you:** i.e., see that you

292. **Mercy . . . so:** proverbial

A bawd or prostitute. (1.2.43 SD)
From *Roxburghe ballads* (printed 1895).

⌜*Aside.*⌝ But I shall follow it as the flesh and fortune
shall better determine.
Whip me? No, no, let carman whip his jade.
The valiant heart's not whipped out of his trade.
                                        He exits.

ESCALUS Come hither to me, Master Elbow. Come 265
hither, Master Constable. How long have you been
in this place of constable?

ELBOW Seven year and a half, sir.

ESCALUS I thought, by the readiness in the office, you
had continued in it some time. You say seven years 270
together?

ELBOW And a half, sir.

ESCALUS Alas, it hath been great pains to you. They do
you wrong to put you so oft upon 't. Are there not
men in your ward sufficient to serve it? 275

ELBOW Faith, sir, few of any wit in such matters. As
they are chosen, they are glad to choose me for
them. I do it for some piece of money and go
through with all.

ESCALUS Look you bring me in the names of some six 280
or seven, the most sufficient of your parish.

ELBOW To your Worship's house, sir?

ESCALUS To my house. Fare you well.
                        ⌜*Elbow and Officers exit.*⌝
⌜*To Justice.*⌝ What's o'clock, think you?

JUSTICE Eleven, sir. 285

ESCALUS I pray you home to dinner with me.

JUSTICE I humbly thank you.

ESCALUS
It grieves me for the death of Claudio,
But there's no remedy.

JUSTICE
Lord Angelo is severe. 290

ESCALUS   It is but needful.
Mercy is not itself that oft looks so.

293. **Pardon . . . woe:** proverbial **still:** always

2.2 Isabella pleads with Angelo for Claudio's life. Angelo refuses to relent but, overcome by desire for Isabella, tells her that he will consider her plea and instructs her to return the following morning.

———————

1. **hearing of:** i.e., hearing; **straight:** i.e., straightway, immediately
5. **His pleasure:** i.e., what Angelo wills or chooses
6. **He:** i.e., Claudio
7. **sects:** classes or ranks (of people)
11. **order:** perhaps a written **order** or warrant
14. **Under . . . correction:** i.e., subject to correction, a formula expressing deference to authority
16. **o'er his doom:** i.e., of its sentence
17. **Go to:** See note to 2.1.63.
19. **well be spared:** i.e., easily be done without

Preparation for a hanging. (2.1.213–14)
From *Warhafftige . . . Verrätherey . . .* (1606).

Pardon is still the nurse of second woe.
But yet, poor Claudio. There is no remedy.
Come, sir.   295

                              They exit.

                        Scene 2
            Enter Provost ⌜and a⌝ Servant.

SERVANT
  He's hearing of a cause. He will come straight.
  I'll tell him of you.
PROVOST   Pray you do.
                              ⌜*Servant exits.*⌝
                         I'll know
  His pleasure. Maybe he will relent. Alas,   5
  He hath but as offended in a dream.
  All sects, all ages smack of this vice, and he
  To die for 't?

                    Enter Angelo.

ANGELO   Now, what's the matter, provost?
PROVOST
  Is it your will Claudio shall die tomorrow?   10
ANGELO
  Did not I tell thee yea? Hadst thou not order?
  Why dost thou ask again?
PROVOST   Lest I might be too rash.
  Under your good correction, I have seen
  When, after execution, judgment hath   15
  Repented o'er his doom.
ANGELO   Go to. Let that be mine.
  Do you your office, or give up your place
  And you shall well be spared.
PROVOST   I crave your Honor's pardon.   20

22. **hour:** i.e., time of delivery
24. **more fitter:** i.e., more appropriate
26. **Desires:** i.e., who desires
32. **fornicatress:** i.e., Juliet
35. **Save:** i.e., God save
38. **suitor:** petitioner
39. **Please . . . hear:** i.e., if you will only hear

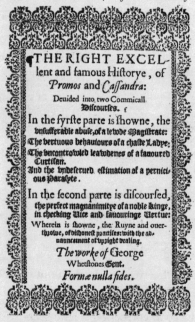

Title page of a primary source of *Measure for Measure*.
From George Whetstone, *The right excellent and famous
Historye, of Promos and Cassandra . . .* [1578].

What shall be done, sir, with the groaning Juliet?
She's very near her hour.
ANGELO   Dispose of her
To some more fitter place, and that with speed.

⌐*Enter Servant.*¬

SERVANT
Here is the sister of the man condemned   25
Desires access to you.
ANGELO   Hath he a sister?
PROVOST
Ay, my good lord, a very virtuous maid,
And to be shortly of a sisterhood,
If not already.   30
ANGELO, ⌐*to Servant*¬ Well, let her be admitted.
                              ⌐*Servant exits.*¬
See you the fornicatress be removed.
Let her have needful but not lavish means.
There shall be order for 't.

Enter Lucio and Isabella.

PROVOST, ⌐*beginning to exit*¬ Save your Honor. 35
ANGELO
Stay a little while. ⌐*To Isabella.*¬ You're welcome.
What's your will?
ISABELLA
I am a woeful suitor to your Honor,
Please but your Honor hear me.
ANGELO   Well, what's your 40
suit?
ISABELLA
There is a vice that most I do abhor,
And most desire should meet the blow of justice,
For which I would not plead, but that I must;

47. **matter:** point in question

48. **is condemned:** i.e., who is condemned

49–50. **let . . . brother:** i.e., condemn his sin rather than condemning him (Proverbial: "Hate not the person but the vice.")

51. **moving:** persuasive, stirring

55. **the very . . . function:** i.e., a completely empty role or office

56. **fine . . . whose fine:** punish . . . whose punishment; **stands in record:** i.e., is set down in legal records **record:** accent second syllable

57. **let . . . actor:** i.e., allow the criminal to go unpunished

60. **Give 't not o'er:** i.e., don't abandon it

62. **cold:** unemotional, aloof, detached

71. **Look what:** whatever

An allegorical figure showing the power of Rhetoric.
(1.2.180–84)
From Sigismondo Fanti, *Triompho di Fortuna* . . . [1526].

For which I must not plead, but that I am   45
At war 'twixt will and will not.

ANGELO   Well, the matter?

ISABELLA
I have a brother is condemned to die.
I do beseech you let it be his fault
And not my brother.   50

PROVOST, ⌜*aside*⌝   Heaven give thee moving
graces.

ANGELO
Condemn the fault, and not the actor of it?
Why, every fault's condemned ere it be done.
Mine were the very cipher of a function   55
To fine the faults whose fine stands in record
And let go by the actor.

ISABELLA   O just but severe law!
I had a brother, then. Heaven keep your Honor.

LUCIO, ⌜*aside to Isabella*⌝
Give 't not o'er so. To him again, entreat him,   60
Kneel down before him, hang upon his gown.
You are too cold. If you should need a pin,
You could not with more tame a tongue desire it.
To him, I say.

ISABELLA, ⌜*to Angelo*⌝
Must he needs die?   65

ANGELO   Maiden, no remedy.

ISABELLA
Yes, I do think that you might pardon him,
And neither heaven nor man grieve at the mercy.

ANGELO
I will not do 't.

ISABELLA   But can you if you would?   70

ANGELO
Look what I will not, that I cannot do.

ISABELLA
But might you do 't and do the world no wrong

73. **If so:** i.e., supposing that; **remorse:** pity

78. **Well believe:** i.e., be assured of

79. **ceremony:** i.e., symbol or attribute of office; **longs:** is appropriate, pertains

80. **deputed:** given to a deputy as a sign of his authority

81. **marshal's truncheon:** baton carried by the chief officer of arms at a royal court

83. **mercy:** Proverbial: "It is in their **mercy** that kings come closest to gods."

84. **as you:** i.e., in your situation

85. **slipped:** sinned, erred; **like you:** i.e., in your position

90. **tell:** make known

92. **touch him:** i.e., challenge him, hit or come near him

93. **vein:** i.e., right way to speak

94. **a forfeit . . . law:** i.e., one who has forfeited his life by breaking the law

97. **forfeit:** lost through error or breach of contract (See longer note to 2.2.97–99, pages 215–16.)

98–99. **And He . . . remedy:** See longer note to 2.2.97–99. **vantage:** advantage, profit **took:** i.e., taken

100. **which:** i.e., who

103. **Like man new-made:** perhaps, like Adam before he sinned; or, perhaps, like a newly redeemed man

If so your heart were touched with that remorse
As mine is to him?
ANGELO   He's sentenced. 'Tis too late.   75
LUCIO, ⌜*aside to Isabella*⌝ You are too cold.
ISABELLA
    Too late? Why, no. I that do speak a word
    May call it ⌜back⌝ again. Well believe this:
    No ceremony that to great ones longs,
    Not the king's crown, nor the deputed sword,   80
    The marshal's truncheon, nor the judge's robe
    Become them with one half so good a grace
    As mercy does.
    If he had been as you, and you as he,
    You would have slipped like him, but he like you   85
    Would not have been so stern.
ANGELO   Pray you begone.
ISABELLA
    I would to heaven I had your potency,
    And you were Isabel. Should it then be thus?
    No. I would tell what 'twere to be a judge   90
    And what a prisoner.
LUCIO, ⌜*aside to Isabella*⌝ Ay, touch him; there's the
       vein.
ANGELO
    Your brother is a forfeit of the law,
    And you but waste your words.   95
ISABELLA   Alas, alas!
    Why all the souls that were were forfeit once,
    And He that might the vantage best have took
    Found out the remedy. How would you be
    If He which is the top of judgment should   100
    But judge you as you are? O, think on that,
    And mercy then will breathe within your lips
    Like man new-made.
ANGELO   Be you content, fair maid.
    It is the law, not I, condemn your brother.   105

110. **of season:** i.e., in its finest condition, in the best state for eating

111. **respect:** care

112–13. **bethink you:** consider, reflect

120. **'tis awake:** i.e., the law is awake

121–22. **prophet . . . glass:** i.e., a soothsayer who uses a magic crystal

123. **now:** i.e., already born; **by remissness:** i.e., because of laxness (of the authorities)

125. **successive degrees:** further stages (of life)

130. **after:** at a later time; **gall:** vex or irritate

131. **do him right that:** i.e., do justice to him who; **answering:** suffering the consequences for

135. **he that suffers:** i.e., Claudio must be the first that undergoes this punishment

Jove throwing a thunderbolt. (2.2.139–40)
From Vincenzo Cartari, *Le vere e noue imagini* . . . (1615).

Were he my kinsman, brother, or my son,
It should be thus with him. He must die tomorrow.

ISABELLA
Tomorrow? O, that's sudden! Spare him, spare him.
He's not prepared for death. Even for our kitchens
We kill the fowl of season. Shall we serve heaven   110
With less respect than we do minister
To our gross selves? Good, good my lord, bethink
     you.
Who is it that hath died for this offense?
There's many have committed it.   115

LUCIO, ⌜*aside to Isabella*⌝   Ay, well said.

ANGELO
The law hath not been dead, though it hath slept.
Those many had not dared to do that evil
If the first that did th' edict infringe
Had answered for his deed. Now 'tis awake,   120
Takes note of what is done, and, like a prophet,
Looks in a glass that shows what future evils—
Either now, or by remissness new-conceived,
And so in progress to be hatched and born—
Are now to have no successive degrees   125
But, ⌜ere⌝ they live, to end.

ISABELLA   Yet show some pity.

ANGELO
I show it most of all when I show justice,
For then I pity those I do not know,
Which a dismissed offense would after gall,   130
And do him right that, answering one foul wrong,
Lives not to act another. Be satisfied;
Your brother dies tomorrow; be content.

ISABELLA
So you must be the first that gives this sentence,
And he that suffers. O, it is excellent   135
To have a giant's strength, but it is tyrannous
To use it like a giant.

139. **great men:** i.e., men in power

139–40. **thunder / As Jove . . . does: Jove,** king of the Greco-Roman gods, was known as the thunder-god or as "thunder-bearer," and was often pictured throwing thunderbolts. (See page 64.)

141. **pelting:** contemptible, paltry

144. **bolt:** i.e., thunderbolt

145. **unwedgeable:** incapable of being split with a wedge

148. **what he's most assured:** i.e., that in which he has most confidence

149. **His glassy essence:** i.e., his being (or existence), which is as frail and brittle as glass

151. **makes:** i.e., make; **spleens:** organs thought to control laughter

152. **themselves laugh mortal:** i.e., laugh themselves to death (Proverbial: "to die laughing")

154. **coming:** i.e., about to yield

156. **We . . . ourself:** i.e., one shouldn't use oneself as a standard by which to judge others

157–58. **Great men . . . profanation:** probably an allusion to the proverb quoted in Shakespeare's source, which says, in Latin, "It is not good to jest with saints." **the less:** i.e., those lower on the social scale

162. **Art advised:** i.e., are you aware, do you know

163. **put . . . upon me:** i.e., apply . . . to me

164–65. **authority . . . itself:** i.e., those in **authority,** even though they sin, find in their positions a kind of healing ointment

LUCIO, ⌈*aside to Isabella*⌉ That's well said.
ISABELLA   Could great men thunder
  As Jove himself does, Jove would never be quiet,   140
  For every pelting, petty officer
  Would use his heaven for thunder,
  Nothing but thunder. Merciful heaven,
  Thou rather with thy sharp and sulphurous bolt
  Splits the unwedgeable and gnarlèd oak,   145
  Than the soft myrtle. But man, proud man,
  Dressed in a little brief authority,
  Most ignorant of what he's most assured,
  His glassy essence, like an angry ape
  Plays such fantastic tricks before high heaven   150
  As makes the angels weep, who with our spleens
  Would all themselves laugh mortal.
LUCIO, ⌈*aside to Isabella*⌉
  O, to him, to him, wench. He will relent.
  He's coming. I perceive 't.
PROVOST, ⌈*aside*⌉   Pray heaven she win him.   155
ISABELLA
  We cannot weigh our brother with ourself.
  Great men may jest with saints; 'tis wit in them,
  But in the less, foul profanation.
LUCIO, ⌈*aside to Isabella*⌉
  Thou'rt i' th' right, girl. More o' that.
ISABELLA
  That in the captain's but a choleric word   160
  Which in the soldier is flat blasphemy.
LUCIO, ⌈*aside to Isabella*⌉
  Art avised o' that? More on 't.
ANGELO
  Why do you put these sayings upon me?
ISABELLA
  Because authority, though it err like others,
  Hath yet a kind of medicine in itself   165

166. **skins . . . top:** i.e., covers over the **vice** without healing it

166–71. **Go . . . life:** See Romans 2.1: "Therefore thou art inexcusable, O man, whosoever thou art that judgest; for wherein thou judgest another, thou condemnest thyself; for thou that judgest doest the same things." See also John 8.3–11 and Galatians 6.1. **natural:** innate

172. **such sense:** i.e., with such meaning (Angelo's **my sense breeds** puns on **sense** as "sensual appetite.")

175. **Gentle my lord:** i.e., my good lord

176. **Come again tomorrow:** See longer note, page 216.

179. **gifts that:** i.e., gifts as

180. **else:** otherwise; i.e., if you had not explained yourself

181. **fond:** foolishly valued; **sicles:** i.e., shekels, coins; **tested:** i.e., refined

182. **stones whose rate are:** i.e., jewels whose worth is (Those who see Isabella as expressing unconscious sexual frustration or awareness note that **stones** could refer to testicles. But see longer note to 2.4.108, pages 218–19.)

185. **preservèd souls:** i.e., spirits protected from the world

193. **Where prayers cross:** perhaps, where your prayer for my honor is at cross-purposes with my desire for you (But see longer note, page 216.)

That skins the vice o' th' top. Go to your bosom,
Knock there, and ask your heart what it doth know
That's like my brother's fault. If it confess
A natural guiltiness such as is his,
Let it not sound a thought upon your tongue   170
Against my brother's life.
ANGELO, ⌜*aside*⌝ She speaks, and 'tis such sense
That my sense breeds with it.   ⌜*He begins to exit.*⌝
       Fare you well.
ISABELLA   Gentle my lord, turn back.   175
ANGELO
I will bethink me. Come again tomorrow.
ISABELLA
Hark how I'll bribe you. Good my lord, turn back.
ANGELO   How? Bribe me?
ISABELLA
Ay, with such gifts that heaven shall share with you.
LUCIO, ⌜*aside to Isabella*⌝ You had marred all else.   180
ISABELLA
Not with fond sicles of the tested gold,
Or stones whose rate are either rich or poor
As fancy values them, but with true prayers
That shall be up at heaven and enter there
Ere sunrise, prayers from preservèd souls,   185
From fasting maids whose minds are dedicate
To nothing temporal.
ANGELO   Well, come to me tomorrow.
LUCIO, ⌜*aside to Isabella*⌝ Go to, 'tis well; away.
ISABELLA
Heaven keep your Honor safe.   190
ANGELO, ⌜*aside*⌝   Amen.
For I am that way going to temptation
Where prayers cross.
ISABELLA   At what hour tomorrow
Shall I attend your Lordship?   195
ANGELO   At any time 'fore noon.

202. **That, lying by the violet:** i.e., that like decaying flesh lying by the violet

203. **Do . . . flower:** Lying **in the sun, carrion** grows more putrid while the **flower** grows more lovely.

204. **Corrupt . . . season:** i.e., in the **season** when the sun gives strength to living things, I, like **carrion**, decay (with wordplay on **virtuous** as "powerful" and "morally good")

205. **betray our sense:** i.e., mislead our desires

206. **lightness:** licentiousness; **waste ground:** i.e., uncultivated and unoccupied land (See longer note to 2.2.206-9, pages 216-17.)

214. **steal themselves:** i.e., themselves are thieves

217-18. **O cunning . . . hook:** Angelo here accuses the devil of using one extremely holy person as a lure to capture the soul of another such person.

219-20. **doth goad . . . virtue:** i.e., uses our love of goodness to draw us into sin

221. **art and nature:** i.e., seductiveness through skill and natural allure

222. **stir my temper:** i.e., shake my composure

224. **fond:** foolishly infatuated

ISABELLA   Save your Honor.
⌜*She exits, with Lucio and Provost.*⌝
ANGELO   From thee, even from thy virtue.
  What's this? What's this? Is this her fault or mine?
  The tempter or the tempted, who sins most, ha?   200
  Not she, nor doth she tempt; but it is I
  That, lying by the violet in the sun,
  Do as the carrion does, not as the flower,
  Corrupt with virtuous season. Can it be
  That modesty may more betray our sense   205
  Than woman's lightness? Having waste ground
    enough,
  Shall we desire to raze the sanctuary
  And pitch our evils there? O fie, fie, fie!
  What dost thou, or what art thou, Angelo?   210
  Dost thou desire her foully for those things
  That make her good? O, let her brother live.
  Thieves for their robbery have authority
  When judges steal themselves. What, do I love her
  That I desire to hear her speak again   215
  And feast upon her eyes? What is 't I dream on?
  O cunning enemy that, to catch a saint,
  With saints dost bait thy hook. Most dangerous
  Is that temptation that doth goad us on
  To sin in loving virtue. Never could the strumpet   220
  With all her double vigor, art and nature,
  Once stir my temper, but this virtuous maid
  Subdues me quite. Ever till now
  When men were fond, I smiled and wondered how.
                                               He exits.

2.3 The duke (in the role of a friar) visits the prison and there meets Juliet, who expresses both her love for Claudio and her repentance for the sinful act that led to her pregnancy. She learns that Claudio must die the following day.

---

1. **so:** i.e., as
5. **Do . . . right:** i.e., grant me the right of every clergyman
10. **of mine:** i.e., in my charge
11. **flaws:** storms, high winds (**Flaws** could also mean "faults" and "passions.")
12. **blistered her report:** i.e., blemished her reputation
13. **got:** i.e., begot, fathered
18. **Stay:** wait
20. **carry:** (1) bear on your conscience; (2) display in your pregnancy
22. **arraign:** examine, interrogate

Scene 3
Enter Duke, ⌜disguised as a Friar,⌝ and Provost.

DUKE, ⌜*as Friar*⌝
  Hail to you, provost, so I think you are.
PROVOST
  I am the Provost. What's your will, good friar?
DUKE, ⌜*as Friar*⌝
  Bound by my charity and my blest order,
  I come to visit the afflicted spirits
  Here in the prison. Do me the common right   5
  To let me see them, and to make me know
  The nature of their crimes, that I may minister
  To them accordingly.
PROVOST
  I would do more than that if more were needful.

Enter Juliet.

  Look, here comes one, a gentlewoman of mine,   10
  Who, falling in the flaws of her own youth,
  Hath blistered her report. She is with child,
  And he that got it, sentenced—a young man,
  More fit to do another such offense
  Than die for this.   15
DUKE, ⌜*as Friar*⌝
  When must he die?
PROVOST   As I do think, tomorrow.
  ⌜*To Juliet.*⌝ I have provided for you. Stay awhile
  And you shall be conducted.
DUKE, ⌜*as Friar, to Juliet*⌝
  Repent you, fair one, of the sin you carry?   20
JULIET
  I do; and bear the shame most patiently.
DUKE, ⌜*as Friar*⌝
  I'll teach you how you shall arraign your conscience,

23. **try:** test

24. **hollowly put on:** i.e., insincerely assumed, hypocritical

27. **the woman . . . him:** i.e., myself

28. **offenseful:** sinful

31. **heavier:** more serious (See longer note, page 217.)

33. **meet so:** i.e., fitting that you should do so

34. **As that:** i.e., because

37. **spare heaven as:** i.e., refrain from offending heaven (through our sins) because

41. **There rest:** i.e., stay at that point (in your thinking)

43. **instruction:** i.e., spiritual lessons

44. **Benedicite:** i.e., Bless you

45–47. **O injurious love . . . horror:** Juliet's pregnancy, the result of the **love** between her and Claudio, has saved her from execution, but the **comfort** of being granted **life** condemns her to the **dying horror** of his death and her continued existence.

48. **pity of:** i.e., a pity about

And try your penitence, if it be sound
Or hollowly put on.
JULIET   I'll gladly learn.   25
DUKE, ⌜*as Friar*⌝ Love you the man that wronged you?
JULIET
Yes, as I love the woman that wronged him.
DUKE, ⌜*as Friar*⌝
So then it seems your most offenseful act
Was mutually committed?
JULIET   Mutually.   30
DUKE, ⌜*as Friar*⌝
Then was your sin of heavier kind than his.
JULIET
I do confess it and repent it, father.
DUKE, ⌜*as Friar*⌝
'Tis meet so, daughter; but lest you do repent
As that the sin hath brought you to this shame,
Which sorrow is always toward ourselves, not   35
  heaven,
Showing we would not spare heaven as we love it,
But as we stand in fear—
JULIET
I do repent me as it is an evil,
And take the shame with joy.   40
DUKE, ⌜*as Friar*⌝   There rest.
Your partner, as I hear, must die tomorrow,
And I am going with instruction to him.
Grace go with you. *Benedicite.*   *He exits.*
JULIET
Must die tomorrow? O injurious love   45
That respites me a life, whose very comfort
Is still a dying horror.
PROVOST   'Tis pity of him.
                                        They exit.

2.4 Angelo tells Isabella that only if she sleeps with him will he set Claudio free; if she refuses, Claudio will be tortured to death. Isabella is certain that Claudio would not want her to commit a mortal sin. She therefore sets off to prepare him for his death.

---

2. **several:** i.e., different, distinct

3. **invention:** i.e., mind

4–7. **God . . . conception:** See longer note, page 217. **chew:** i.e., repeat mindlessly **conception:** thought, idea

7. **state:** i.e., statecraft, political writings

9. **gravity:** importance, dignity

11. **Could I . . . change:** i.e., I could exchange **with boot:** i.e., adding something to make up the difference

12. **for vain:** perhaps, to no purpose, in vain; **place:** high rank or position; **form:** ceremony

13. **case, habit:** clothing

15. **Blood . . . blood:** Angelo may here be acknowledging that he is a mortal, subject to sexual appetite (**blood**), despite his outer trappings that "**awe . . . fools**" and bind "**the wiser souls.**"

16–17. **Let's write . . . crest:** See longer note, page 217.

19. **sister:** i.e., nun (See longer note, pages 217–18.)

20. **Teach:** show

21–24. **Why . . . fitness:** The image is of the **blood** rushing to the **heart** like soldiers assembling in one spot, overcrowding that spot and leaving the remaining territory weakened. **unable:** ineffectual

25. **So play:** thus act

28. **general subject to:** i.e., common subjects of

Scene 4
Enter Angelo.

ANGELO
  When I would pray and think, I think and pray
  To several subjects. Heaven hath my empty words,
  Whilst my invention, hearing not my tongue,
  Anchors on Isabel. ⌜God⌝ in my mouth,
  As if I did but only chew His name,   5
  And in my heart the strong and swelling evil
  Of my conception. The state whereon I studied
  Is, like a good thing being often read,
  Grown ⌜sere⌝ and tedious. Yea, my gravity,
  Wherein—let no man hear me—I take pride,   10
  Could I with boot change for an idle plume
  Which the air beats for vain. O place, O form,
  How often dost thou with thy case, thy habit,
  Wrench awe from fools, and tie the wiser souls
  To thy false seeming! Blood, thou art blood.   15
  Let's write "good angel" on the devil's horn.
  'Tis not the devil's crest. ⌜*Knock within.*⌝ How now,
    who's there?

Enter Servant.

SERVANT
  One Isabel, a sister, desires access to you.
ANGELO
  Teach her the way. ⌜*Servant exits.*⌝ O heavens,   20
  Why does my blood thus muster to my heart,
  Making both it unable for itself
  And dispossessing all my other parts
  Of necessary fitness?
  So play the foolish throngs with one that swoons,   25
  Come all to help him, and so stop the air
  By which he should revive. And even so
  The general subject to a well-wished king

29. **Quit . . . part:** i.e., abandon . . . functions or roles

30. **untaught:** (1) spontaneous; (2) ignorant

34. **know it:** (1) understand that the **pleasure** I seek is carnal; or (2) carnally **know** my **pleasure**

35. **to demand:** i.e., for you to ask

41. **his reprieve:** i.e., the time allowed him

42. **fitted:** prepared

45–46. **that hath . . . made:** i.e., who has killed a man

46–47. **remit . . . that:** i.e., pardon the lustful self-indulgence of those who

47–48. **coin . . . forbid:** i.e., create illegitimate offspring (See longer note, page 218.)

49. **Falsely:** i.e., illegally

50. **put . . . means:** wordplay on **metal**/mettle (gold/spirit) and on **restrainèd** as both "forbidden, illegal" and "illicit" (See longer note to 2.4.47–48.)

51. **false one:** (1) bastard; (2) counterfeit coin

53. **pose:** put a question to

Quit their own part, and in obsequious fondness
Crowd to his presence, where their untaught love   30
Must needs appear offense.

Enter Isabella.

                  How now, fair maid?

ISABELLA   I am come to know your pleasure.

ANGELO
That you might know it would much better please me
Than to demand what 'tis. Your brother cannot live.   35

ISABELLA   Even so. Heaven keep your Honor.

ANGELO
Yet may he live a while. And it may be
As long as you or I. Yet he must die.

ISABELLA   Under your sentence?

ANGELO   Yea.   40

ISABELLA
When, I beseech you? That in his reprieve,
Longer or shorter, he may be so fitted
That his soul sicken not.

ANGELO
Ha! Fie, these filthy vices! It were as good
To pardon him that hath from nature stolen   45
A man already made, as to remit
Their saucy sweetness that do coin ⌈God's⌉ image
In stamps that are forbid. 'Tis all as easy
Falsely to take away a life true made
As to put metal in restrainèd means   50
To make a false one.

ISABELLA
'Tis set down so in heaven, but not in earth.

ANGELO
Say you so? Then I shall pose you quickly:
Which had you rather, that the most just law
Now took your brother's life, ⌈or,⌉ to redeem him,   55

60–61. **Our . . . accompt:** perhaps, sins we are forced to commit may be counted but do not count against us (Proverbial: "Compelled sins are no sins.")

63–64. **Nay . . . say:** perhaps an attempt by Angelo to start over and find a better argument

65. **the recorded law:** i.e., the law as already written

69–71. **Please you . . . charity:** i.e., if you will save Claudio's life, I will put at risk my own soul in order to guarantee that you are not sinning, but showing love

72–73. **Pleased . . . charity:** i.e., if you saved his life at the risk of your soul, sin and charity would weigh equally (**were equal poise**) in your act

75. **You granting of:** i.e., should you grant

78. **nothing of your answer:** i.e., not a sin for which you must answer

80. **Your . . . mine:** i.e., you are not following my meaning

82. **seem so, crafty:** i.e., craftily pretend to be

84. **graciously:** i.e., through divine grace

Give up your body to such sweet uncleanness
As she that he hath stained?
ISABELLA   Sir, believe this:
I had rather give my body than my soul.
ANGELO
I talk not of your soul. Our compelled sins   60
Stand more for number than for accompt.
ISABELLA   How say you?
ANGELO
Nay, I'll not warrant that, for I can speak
Against the thing I say. Answer to this:
I, now the voice of the recorded law,   65
Pronounce a sentence on your brother's life.
Might there not be a charity in sin
To save this brother's life?
ISABELLA   Please you to do 't,
I'll take it as a peril to my soul,   70
It is no sin at all, but charity.
ANGELO
Pleased you to do 't, at peril of your soul,
Were equal poise of sin and charity.
ISABELLA
That I do beg his life, if it be sin
Heaven let me bear it. You granting of my suit,   75
If that be sin, I'll make it my morn prayer
To have it added to the faults of mine
And nothing of your answer.
ANGELO   Nay, but hear me.
Your sense pursues not mine. Either you are   80
    ignorant,
Or seem so, crafty, and that's not good.
ISABELLA
Let ⌜me⌝ be ignorant and in nothing good,
But graciously to know I am no better.
ANGELO
Thus wisdom wishes to appear most bright   85

86. **tax:** accuse; **these black masks:** i.e., dark masks or veils

87. **enshield:** perhaps, concealed, hidden (This word is not recorded elsewhere.)

88. **mark:** i.e., listen to

89. **receivèd plain:** i.e., plainly understood; **gross:** directly

92. **so:** i.e., such; **appears:** is evident

93. **Accountant:** accountable, liable; **upon that pain:** i.e., under that penalty (of death)

95. **Admit:** i.e., grant that there is

96. **As I subscribe . . . other:** i.e., not that I grant assent to this way or any other way of saving his life

97. **in . . . question:** perhaps, now that you have lost the debate (with me)

98. **desired of:** i.e., desired by

99. **or own great place:** i.e., or whose own high position

102. **mean:** course of action

104. **supposed:** i.e., hypothetical person; **let him suffer:** i.e., let your brother die

107. **terms:** i.e., sentence

108. **Th' impression . . . rubies:** See longer note, pages 218–19.

109. **to death . . . bed:** Proverbial: "to go to one's death like a bed"

110. **longing have:** perhaps, **longing** (desire) has; or, perhaps, **longing I have**

113. **the cheaper way:** i.e., the better bargain

114. **at once:** at one stroke

116. **die forever:** i.e., be condemned to eternal damnation (through the sin of fornication)

117. **Were not you:** i.e., would you not be

When it doth tax itself, as these black masks
Proclaim an enshield beauty ten times louder
Than beauty could, displayed. But mark me.
To be receivèd plain, I'll speak more gross:
Your brother is to die.   90

ISABELLA So.

ANGELO
And his offense is so, as it appears,
Accountant to the law upon that pain.

ISABELLA True.

ANGELO
Admit no other way to save his life—   95
As I subscribe not that, nor any other—
But, in the loss of question, that you, his sister,
Finding yourself desired of such a person
Whose credit with the judge, or own great place,
Could fetch your brother from the manacles   100
Of the all-⌜binding⌝ law, and that there were
No earthly mean to save him but that either
You must lay down the treasures of your body
To this supposed, or else to let him suffer.
What would you do?   105

ISABELLA
As much for my poor brother as myself.
That is, were I under the terms of death,
Th' impression of keen whips I'd wear as rubies
And strip myself to death as to a bed
That longing have been sick for, ere I'd yield   110
My body up to shame.

ANGELO Then must your brother die.

ISABELLA And 'twere the cheaper way.
Better it were a brother died at once
Than that a sister, by redeeming him,   115
Should die forever.

ANGELO
Were not you then as cruel as the sentence
That you have slandered so?

119. **Ignomy in ransom:** i.e., an ignominious ransom

120. **of two houses:** i.e., unrelated

122. **of late:** i.e., in our earlier discussion (2.2)

123. **proved:** demonstrated; **sliding of your brother:** i.e., your brother's fall into sin

128. **something:** i.e., somewhat

130. **We are all frail:** Proverbial: "Flesh is frail."

131–33. **Else . . . weakness:** i.e., otherwise, let my brother die only if he alone possesses the frailty you mention (line 130) **fedary:** confederate, accomplice **Owe:** possess, own **succeed:** inherit

135. **glasses:** mirrors (Proverbial: "A woman and a glass are ever in danger.")

136. **easy broke:** i.e., easily broken; **make forms:** i.e., create images (through reflection)

137. **help, heaven:** i.e., heaven help them; **their:** i.e., their own

138. **profiting by:** taking advantage of

139–40. **we . . . prints:** Proverbial: "Soft wax will take any impression." **complexions:** probably, physical constitutions **credulous to false prints:** See longer note, page 219.

142. **of:** (1) about; (2) from

144. **Than:** i.e., than that

145. **that:** that which

146. **If . . . none:** See longer note, page 219.

147. **expressed:** revealed

148. **warrants:** tokens

149. **destined livery:** i.e., clothing for which you are destined (i.e., frailty)

ISABELLA
Ignomy in ransom and free pardon
Are of two houses. Lawful mercy 120
Is nothing kin to foul redemption.

ANGELO
You seemed of late to make the law a tyrant,
And rather proved the sliding of your brother
A merriment than a vice.

ISABELLA
O, pardon me, my lord. It oft falls out, 125
To have what we would have, we speak not what we
mean.
I something do excuse the thing I hate
For his advantage that I dearly love.

ANGELO
We are all frail. 130

ISABELLA   Else let my brother die,
If not a fedary but only he
Owe and succeed thy weakness.

ANGELO Nay, women are frail too.

ISABELLA
Ay, as the glasses where they view themselves, 135
Which are as easy broke as they make forms.
Women—help, heaven—men their creation mar
In profiting by them. Nay, call us ten times frail,
For we are soft as our complexions are,
And credulous to false prints. 140

ANGELO   I think it well.
And from this testimony of your own sex,
Since I suppose we are made to be no stronger
Than faults may shake our frames, let me be bold.
I do arrest your words. Be that you are— 145
That is, a woman. If you be more, you're none.
If you be one, as you are well expressed
By all external warrants, show it now
By putting on the destined livery.

152. **conceive:** understand

156–58. **hath a license . . . others:** i.e., gives you the freedom to pretend to be wicked in order to test others

163. **proclaim:** denounce

164. **a present:** an immediate

167. **What:** i.e., what kind of

170. **vouch:** allegation

176. **Lay by:** put aside; **nicety:** coyness; **prolixious:** i.e., long-drawn-out

177. **sue:** plead

179. **die the death:** a biblical phrase that means "be put to death"

180. **unkindness:** (1) unkind action; (2) unnatural behavior

181. **ling'ring sufferance:** i.e., torture; **Answer:** i.e., say yes to

ISABELLA
  I have no tongue but one. Gentle my lord,   150
  Let me entreat you speak the former language.
ANGELO   Plainly conceive I love you.
ISABELLA   My brother did love Juliet,
  And you tell me that he shall die for 't.
ANGELO
  He shall not, Isabel, if you give me love.   155
ISABELLA
  I know your virtue hath a license in 't
  Which seems a little fouler than it is
  To pluck on others.
ANGELO   Believe me, on mine honor,
  My words express my purpose.   160
ISABELLA
  Ha! Little honor to be much believed,
  And most pernicious purpose. Seeming, seeming!
  I will proclaim thee, Angelo, look for 't.
  Sign me a present pardon for my brother
  Or with an outstretched throat I'll tell the world   165
    aloud
  What man thou art.
ANGELO   Who will believe thee, Isabel?
  My unsoiled name, th' austereness of my life,
  My vouch against you, and my place i' th' state   170
  Will so your accusation overweigh
  That you shall stifle in your own report
  And smell of calumny. I have begun,
  And now I give my sensual race the rein.
  Fit thy consent to my sharp appetite;   175
  Lay by all nicety and prolixious blushes
  That banish what they sue for. Redeem thy brother
  By yielding up thy body to my will,
  Or else he must not only die the death,
  But thy unkindness shall his death draw out   180
  To ling'ring sufferance. Answer me tomorrow,

182. **affection:** desire

185. **Did I tell:** i.e., if I told

188. **Either . . . approof:** i.e., that can either condemn or approve (Proverbial: "Out of one mouth to blow hot and cold.")

192. **by prompture of the blood:** i.e., through passion's (or the body's) instigation

194. **tender down:** lay down in payment

195. **blocks:** i.e., wooden blocks for beheadings (See page 158.)

199. **More . . . chastity:** printed in the Folio with initial quotation marks to signal a moral "sentence" or maxim (In Shakespeare's source, the heroine says "My brother's life is very dear to me, but even dearer to me is my honor.")

201. **fit . . . to:** i.e., prepare . . . for

Or by the affection that now guides me most,
I'll prove a tyrant to him. As for you,
Say what you can, my false o'erweighs your true.

He exits.

ISABELLA
To whom should I complain? Did I tell this,   185
Who would believe me? O, perilous mouths,
That bear in them one and the selfsame tongue,
Either of condemnation or approof,
Bidding the law make curtsy to their will,
Hooking both right and wrong to th' appetite,   190
To follow as it draws. I'll to my brother.
Though he hath fall'n by prompture of the blood,
Yet hath he in him such a mind of honor
That, had he twenty heads to tender down
On twenty bloody blocks, he'd yield them up   195
Before his sister should her body stoop
To such abhorred pollution.
Then, Isabel, live chaste, and, brother, die.
More than our brother is our chastity.
I'll tell him yet of Angelo's request,   200
And fit his mind to death, for his soul's rest.

She exits.

MEASURE
FOR
MEASURE

ACT 3

3.1 The duke, in his guise of "Friar," persuades Claudio that death is preferable to life. When Isabella tells Claudio that he can be freed if she yields her virginity to Angelo, Claudio decides that he wants to live even on these terms. Isabella is horrified. The "Friar," who has been eavesdropping, tells Isabella of a way to save both Claudio and her own honor: they will get Angelo's abandoned fiancée to sleep with Angelo in Isabella's place.

---

1. **of:** i.e., for

7. **If I do lose thee:** This begins a series of statements that Claudio is instructed to say to **life.** (See longer note to 3.1.7–40, pages 219–20.)

9. **Servile . . . influences:** i.e., subject to weather and/or **influences** from stars and planets (See page 188.)

10. **doth:** i.e., do; **this . . . keep'st:** i.e., the body **keep'st:** dwell

11. **fool:** (1) simpleton; (2) buffoon, jester (See page 184.)

13. **still:** always, continually

14. **all . . . bear'st:** i.e., everything you have about you

15. **nursed:** fed, supported; **baseness:** i.e., from base origins

17. **fork:** i.e., forked tongue

18. **worm:** perhaps, snake; or, maggot

19. **provok'st:** invoke; **grossly:** foolishly

ACT 3

Scene 1
Enter Duke ⌐as a Friar,⌐ Claudio, and Provost.

DUKE, ⌐*as Friar*⌐
So then you hope of pardon from Lord Angelo?
CLAUDIO
The miserable have no other medicine
But only hope.
I have hope to live and am prepared to die.
DUKE, ⌐*as Friar*⌐
Be absolute for death. Either death or life   5
Shall thereby be the sweeter. Reason thus with life:
If I do lose thee, I do lose a thing
That none but fools would keep. A breath thou art,
Servile to all the skyey influences
That ⌐doth⌐ this habitation where thou keep'st   10
Hourly afflict. Merely, thou art death's fool,
For him thou labor'st by thy flight to shun,
And yet runn'st toward him still. Thou art not noble,
For all th' accommodations that thou bear'st
Are nursed by baseness. Thou'rt by no means   15
  valiant,
For thou dost fear the soft and tender fork
Of a poor worm. Thy best of rest is sleep,
And that thou oft provok'st, yet grossly fear'st
Thy death, which is no more. Thou art not thyself,   20
For thou exists on many a thousand grains

93

22. **That issue out of dust:** See Genesis 2.7: "And the Lord God formed man of the dust of the ground. . . ."

24. **certain:** constant

25–26. **complexion . . . moon:** i.e., you change as the moon changes **complexion:** temperament, nature **After:** in obedience to

26. **If . . . poor:** See Revelation 3.17: "For thou saist, 'I am rich . . . ' and knowest not how thou art wretched & miserable, and poor."

30–31. **thine own . . . loins:** i.e., your very offspring **bowels:** offspring, children **proper:** own

32. **serpigo:** spreading skin disease, i.e., ringworm; **rheum:** inflammation of nose or throat

33. **nor . . . nor:** i.e., neither . . . nor

36. **Dreaming on both:** i.e., dreaming about both youth and age

37. **as agèd:** i.e., as if old (because youth must **beg** for money)

38. **eld:** old age (See page 102.)

39. **heat:** ardor, passion; **limb:** i.e., use of the body (literally, an organ or body part)

42–43. **death . . . even:** Proverbial: "The end makes all equal."

45. **To sue:** i.e., in petitioning

That issue out of dust. Happy thou art not,
For what thou hast not, still thou striv'st to get,
And what thou hast, forget'st. Thou art not certain,
For thy complexion shifts to strange effects   25
After the moon. If thou art rich, thou'rt poor,
For, like an ass whose back with ingots bows,
Thou bear'st thy heavy riches but a journey,
And death unloads thee. Friend hast thou none,
For thine own bowels which do call thee ⌜sire,⌝   30
The mere effusion of thy proper loins,
Do curse the gout, serpigo, and the rheum
For ending thee no sooner. Thou hast nor youth nor
     age,
But as it were an after-dinner's sleep   35
Dreaming on both, for all thy blessèd youth
Becomes as agèd and doth beg the alms
Of palsied eld; and when thou art old and rich,
Thou hast neither heat, affection, limb, nor beauty
To make thy riches pleasant. What's yet in this   40
That bears the name of life? Yet in this life
Lie hid more thousand deaths; yet death we fear,
That makes these odds all even.
CLAUDIO   I humbly thank you.
To sue to live, I find I seek to die,   45
And seeking death, find life. Let it come on.
ISABELLA, ⌜*within*⌝
What ho! Peace here, grace, and good company.
PROVOST
Who's there? Come in. The wish deserves a welcome.
DUKE, ⌜*as Friar, to Claudio*⌝
Dear sir, ere long I'll visit you again.
CLAUDIO   Most holy sir, I thank you.   50

                    Enter Isabella.

ISABELLA, ⌜*to Provost*⌝
My business is a word or two with Claudio.

57 SD. **exit:** The duke may go behind a curtain or arras, or may leave the stage and be imagined to listen to the conversation from an adjoining room.

61. **affairs to:** i.e., business with

63. **leiger:** An Ambassador Leiger was the permanent representative of his sovereign in a foreign court.

64. **appointment:** i.e., preparation

65. **set on:** go forward

68. **To cleave:** i.e., by cleaving, splitting

74. **Perpetual durance:** Claudio means "life imprisonment," but Isabella gives the words the meaning "in eternal confinement or restraint."

75. **Ay, just:** i.e., yes, exactly

76. **Though . . . had:** i.e., even if you possessed the vastness of the world

77. **determined:** limited, restricted; **scope:** room to move in, space

80. **bark . . . bear:** i.e., strip you of **your honor** (with wordplay on **trunk** as [1] body, [2] tree trunk, and [3] family tree)   **bark:** i.e., strip the bark from

PROVOST
  And very welcome.—Look, signior, here's your
    sister.
DUKE, ⌈*as Friar*⌉ Provost, a word with you.
PROVOST As many as you please.   55
DUKE, ⌈*as Friar, aside to Provost*⌉
  Bring ⌈me⌉ to hear ⌈them⌉ speak, where I may be
    concealed.
                                    ⌈*Duke and Provost exit.*⌉
CLAUDIO Now, sister, what's the comfort?
ISABELLA Why,
  As all comforts are, most good, most good indeed.   60
  Lord Angelo, having affairs to heaven,
  Intends you for his swift ambassador,
  Where you shall be an everlasting leiger;
  Therefore your best appointment make with speed.
  Tomorrow you set on.   65
CLAUDIO   Is there no remedy?
ISABELLA
  None but such remedy as, to save a head,
  To cleave a heart in twain.
CLAUDIO But is there any?
ISABELLA Yes, brother, you may live.   70
  There is a devilish mercy in the judge,
  If you'll implore it, that will free your life
  But fetter you till death.
CLAUDIO   Perpetual durance?
ISABELLA
  Ay, just; perpetual durance, a restraint,   75
  ⌈Though⌉ all the world's vastidity you had,
  To a determined scope.
CLAUDIO   But in what nature?
ISABELLA
  In such a one as, you consenting to 't,
  Would bark your honor from that trunk you bear   80
  And leave you naked.

83. **fear:** distrust, doubt

84. **feverous:** feverish; **entertain:** cherish

85. **more respect:** i.e., hold in higher regard

87. **sense:** feeling or consciousness; **apprehension:** anticipation (The line means, generally, that what is painful about death is its anticipation.)

89. **corporal sufferance:** i.e., bodily suffering

91. **give . . . shame:** i.e., offer me this reproach

92. **a resolution fetch:** i.e., draw resoluteness or firmness of purpose

94. **darkness:** Job 10.21 describes death as "a land . . . dark as darkness itself."

99. **appliances:** subservience; **outward-sainted:** i.e., outwardly holy

100. **settled visage:** sober expression

101. **Nips . . . head:**   overpowers . . . decisively; **enew:** drive (a fowl) into water (The **falcon** attacking the **fowl** [line 102] kills it by "nipping" [striking] at the head; the **falcon** sometimes "enews" the **fowl** as part of the attack.)

103. **cast:** (1) vomited up, as with a falcon being purged; (2) dug up, as with a **pond** (line 104) being cleaned out

105. **prenzie:** This word is unrecorded elsewhere, except where it is used again at 3.1.108. See longer note, page 220.

106–7. **'tis . . . invest:** i.e., this is hell's clever dressing of a damned body   **livery:** action of distributing clothing to servants or retainers   **invest:** clothe

108. **guards:** ornaments, trimmings

113. **So to offend him still:** See longer note, page 220.

CLAUDIO   Let me know the
  point.
ISABELLA
  O, I do fear thee, Claudio, and I quake
  Lest thou a feverous life shouldst entertain,
  And six or seven winters more respect   85
  Than a perpetual honor. Dar'st thou die?
  The sense of death is most in apprehension,
  And the poor beetle that we tread upon
  In corporal sufferance finds a pang as great
  As when a giant dies.   90
CLAUDIO   Why give you me this shame?
  Think you I can a resolution fetch
  From flowery tenderness? If I must die,
  I will encounter darkness as a bride,
  And hug it in mine arms.   95
ISABELLA
  There spake my brother! There my father's grave
  Did utter forth a voice. Yes, thou must die.
  Thou art too noble to conserve a life
  In base appliances. This outward-sainted deputy—
  Whose settled visage and deliberate word   100
  Nips youth i' th' head, and follies doth ⌈enew⌉
  As falcon doth the fowl—is yet a devil.
  His filth within being cast, he would appear
  A pond as deep as hell.
CLAUDIO   The prenzie Angelo?   105
ISABELLA
  O, 'tis the cunning livery of hell
  The damned'st body to invest and cover
  In prenzie guards. Dost thou think, Claudio,
  If I would yield him my virginity
  Thou mightst be freed?   110
CLAUDIO   O heavens, it cannot be!
ISABELLA
  Yes, he would give 't thee; from this rank offense,
  So to offend him still. This night's the time

119. **frankly:** freely

124. **would force:** perhaps, should enforce

125. **deadly seven:** Besides lechery (which Claudio argues is **the least**), the **deadly** sins were pride, envy, sloth, anger, gluttony, and covetousness.

128. **trick:** trifle or illusion

129. **perdurably fined:** eternally punished

134. **in cold obstruction:** i.e., with the vital functions stopped

135. **sensible warm motion:** i.e., living human body **sensible:** capable of sensation, feeling **motion:** capacity to move

136. **delighted spirit:** i.e., the soul, which (in life) is filled with delight

138. **thrilling:** i.e., piercingly cold

139. **viewless:** invisible

141. **pendent world:** i.e., world floating unsupported in space; **worst:** the most unfortunate

142–43. **that lawless . . . howling:** i.e., those **howling** in hell, which uncontrolled **thought** imagines it can hear (See longer note, page 220.)

That I should do what I abhor to name,
Or else thou diest tomorrow.   115
CLAUDIO   Thou shalt not do't.
ISABELLA   O, were it but my life,
  I'd throw it down for your deliverance
  As frankly as a pin.
CLAUDIO   Thanks, dear Isabel.   120
ISABELLA
  Be ready, Claudio, for your death tomorrow.
CLAUDIO   Yes. Has he affections in him
  That thus can make him bite the law by th' nose,
  When he would force it? Sure it is no sin,
  Or of the deadly seven it is the least.   125
ISABELLA   Which is the least?
CLAUDIO
  If it were damnable, he being so wise,
  Why would he for the momentary trick
  Be perdurably fined? O, Isabel—
ISABELLA
  What says my brother?   130
CLAUDIO   Death is a fearful thing.
ISABELLA   And shamèd life a hateful.
CLAUDIO
  Ay, but to die, and go we know not where,
  To lie in cold obstruction and to rot,
  This sensible warm motion to become   135
  A kneaded clod; and the delighted spirit
  To bathe in fiery floods, or to reside
  In thrilling region of thick-ribbèd ice,
  To be imprisoned in the viewless winds
  And blown with restless violence round about   140
  The pendent world; or to be worse than worst
  Of those that lawless and incertain thought
  Imagine howling—'tis too horrible.
  The weariest and most loathèd worldly life
  That age, ache, ⌈penury,⌉ and imprisonment   145

146. **lay on nature:** i.e., impose on human physical powers

151. **Nature:** i.e., natural feeling; **dispenses with:** pardons, excuses

155. **made a man:** i.e., given new life

158. **shield:** i.e., forbid; **played . . . fair:** i.e., was a faithful wife

159. **warpèd:** twisted, perverse; **slip of wilderness:** (1) wild branch (2) licentious descendant

160. **Take my defiance:** i.e., I give you my contempt

167. **accidental:** occasional, casual; **trade:** habit; or, perhaps, occupation

168. **bawd:** procurer, go-between (in serving his wickedness)

173. **dispense with:** do without, forgo

174. **by and by:** immediately

174–75. **The . . . require:** i.e., that which I desire (from our conversation) **require:** entreat, request

"Palsied eld." (3.1.38)
From August Casimir Redel, *Apophtegmata symbolica* . . . [n.d.].

Can lay on nature is a paradise
To what we fear of death.

ISABELLA   Alas, alas!

CLAUDIO   Sweet sister, let me live.
What sin you do to save a brother's life,   150
Nature dispenses with the deed so far
That it becomes a virtue.

ISABELLA   O, you beast!
O faithless coward, O dishonest wretch,
Wilt thou be made a man out of my vice?   155
Is 't not a kind of incest to take life
From thine own sister's shame? What should I think?
Heaven shield my mother played my father fair,
For such a warpèd slip of wilderness
Ne'er issued from his blood. Take my defiance;   160
Die, perish. Might but my bending down
Reprieve thee from thy fate, it should proceed.
I'll pray a thousand prayers for thy death,
No word to save thee.

CLAUDIO   Nay, hear me, Isabel—   165

ISABELLA   O, fie, fie, fie!
Thy sin's not accidental, but a trade.
Mercy to thee would prove itself a bawd.
'Tis best that thou diest quickly.

CLAUDIO   O, hear me, Isabella—   170

⌜*Enter Duke as a Friar.*⌝

DUKE, ⌜*as Friar, to Isabella*⌝
Vouchsafe a word, young sister, but one word.

ISABELLA   What is your will?

DUKE, ⌜*as Friar*⌝   Might you dispense with your leisure, I
would by and by have some speech with you. The
satisfaction I would require is likewise your own   175
benefit.

ISABELLA   I have no superfluous leisure. My stay must

178. **attend you:** wait for you (or, perhaps, listen to you)

183–84. **practice . . . natures:** perhaps, exercise his skills in judging human nature (in order to become more proficient)

186. **gracious:** godly, pious

188. **to death:** i.e., for death (or, to die)

192. **Let . . . pardon:** It is possible in performance that, while the "Friar" talks with the provost at lines 194–201, Claudio speaks to Isabella in pantomime.

193. **sue:** petition

194. **Hold you there:** i.e., stay in that state of mind

199. **promises:** gives assurance; **with my habit:** i.e., along with my (friar's) clothing; **touch:** injure, harm

201. **In good time:** i.e., very well

203–4. **goodness . . . goodness:** an elaboration on the proverbial "beauty and chastity seldom meet" (See longer note, pages 220–21.)

205. **grace:** virtue, piety; **complexion:** disposition, character

206. **fair:** (1) free from moral stain; (2) beautiful; **assault:** (1) temptation to evil; (2) hostile attack

208. **but that:** i.e., except for the fact that; **frailty:** See note to 2.4.130.

209. **falling:** lapse into sin; **wonder:** be struck with astonishment; **How:** i.e., what

210. **substitute:** i.e., deputy

be stolen out of other affairs, but I will attend you
awhile.

DUKE, ⌐*as Friar, taking Claudio aside*⌐ Son, I have over- 180
heard what hath passed between you and your
sister. Angelo had never the purpose to corrupt her;
only he hath made an assay of her virtue, to practice
his judgment with the disposition of natures. She,
having the truth of honor in her, hath made him 185
that gracious denial which he is most glad to
receive. I am confessor to Angelo, and I know this
to be true. Therefore prepare yourself to death. Do
not satisfy your resolution with hopes that are
fallible. Tomorrow you must die. Go to your knees 190
and make ready.

CLAUDIO Let me ask my sister pardon. I am so out of
love with life that I will sue to be rid of it.

DUKE, ⌐*as Friar*⌐ Hold you there. Farewell.—Provost, a
word with you.   195

⌐*Enter Provost.*⌐

PROVOST What's your will, father?

DUKE, ⌐*as Friar*⌐ That now you are come, you will be
gone. Leave me awhile with the maid. My mind
promises with my habit no loss shall touch her by
my company.   200

PROVOST In good time.   *He exits,* ⌐*with Claudio.*⌐

DUKE, ⌐*as Friar, to Isabella*⌐ The hand that hath made
you fair hath made you good. The goodness that is
cheap in beauty makes beauty brief in goodness,
but grace, being the soul of your complexion, shall 205
keep the body of it ever fair. The assault that Angelo
hath made to you, fortune hath conveyed to my
understanding; and but that frailty hath examples
for his falling, I should wonder at Angelo. How will
you do to content this substitute and to save your 210
brother?

212. **resolve him:** i.e., answer Angelo

216–17. **I . . . government:** i.e., if **I open my lips,**
I will expose Angelo's way of behaving (and his way
of governing)   **discover:** reveal, expose

219. **avoid:** make void, refute

220. **he made:** i.e., he will claim that he made

221. **advisings:** counsel

223. **uprighteously:** i.e., in an upright manner

224. **merited:** well-earned

229. **spirit:** courage

231. **spirit:** soul

233. **speak:** talk, discourse

234. **miscarried:** i.e., was lost

238. **should . . . married:** i.e., was to have married (See Historical Background 2, "Betrothal and
Marriage," pages 227–32.)

239. **affianced . . . oath:** a puzzling phrase that
means, perhaps, pledged to her oath, or, perhaps,
betrothed to her promise

239–40. **nuptial appointed:** i.e., day set for the
wedding

241. **limit:** appointed time; **solemnity:** festive celebration

242. **wracked:** shipwrecked

243. **heavily:** dreadfully, painfully

246. **natural:** i.e., brotherly (full of natural feeling); **portion:** inheritance

247. **sinew:** principal support

ISABELLA   I am now going to resolve him. I had rather
   my brother die by the law than my son should be
   unlawfully born. But, O, how much is the good
   duke deceived in Angelo! If ever he return, and I   215
   can speak to him, I will open my lips in vain, or
   discover his government.
DUKE, ⌜*as Friar*⌝   That shall not be much amiss. Yet, as
   the matter now stands, he will avoid your accusation: he made trial of you only. Therefore, fasten   220
   your ear on my advisings. To the love I have in doing
   good, a remedy presents itself. I do make myself
   believe that you may most uprighteously do a poor
   wronged lady a merited benefit, redeem your brother from the angry law, do no stain to your own   225
   gracious person, and much please the absent duke,
   if peradventure he shall ever return to have hearing
   of this business.
ISABELLA   Let me hear you speak farther. I have spirit to
   do anything that appears not foul in the truth of my   230
   spirit.
DUKE, ⌜*as Friar*⌝   Virtue is bold, and goodness never
   fearful. Have you not heard speak of Mariana, the
   sister of Frederick, the great soldier who miscarried
   at sea?   235
ISABELLA   I have heard of the lady, and good words
   went with her name.
DUKE, ⌜*as Friar*⌝   She should this Angelo have married,
   was affianced to her oath, and the nuptial appointed. Between which time of the contract and   240
   limit of the solemnity, her brother Frederick was
   wracked at sea, having in that perished vessel the
   dowry of his sister. But mark how heavily this befell
   to the poor gentlewoman. There she lost a noble
   and renowned brother, in his love toward her ever   245
   most kind and natural; with him, the portion and
   sinew of her fortune, her marriage dowry; with

248. **combinate:** perhaps, contracted, betrothed; **well-seeming:** speciously attractive

253. **pretending . . . dishonor:** i.e., claiming she had been found to be unchaste **pretending:** alleging, putting forth as his reason

253–54. **in few:** briefly, in short

254. **bestowed . . . lamentation:** i.e., gave her to her grief (with wordplay on "bestowed" as "gave in marriage")

255. **wears:** carries about in her heart; **a marble:** i.e., (as if) a figure made of marble

258–59. **What . . . life:** how corrupt is life

260. **avail:** benefit, profit

265. **This . . . maid:** i.e., Mariana (line 233)

265–66. **hath . . . affection:** i.e., is still in love

266. **His:** i.e., Angelo's

270. **requiring:** demand; **plausible:** affable

271. **to the point:** i.e., exactly

272. **refer . . . advantage:** i.e., entrust yourself to this favorable condition **advantage:** something that improves one's position

274–75. **answer to convenience:** i.e., be convenient for you (See longer note, page 221.)

275. **in course:** i.e., as a matter of course

277. **stead up:** i.e., keep, fulfill

278. **encounter:** rendezvous; **acknowledge itself:** i.e., reveal itself

279. **by this:** i.e., through this scheme

282. **scaled:** i.e., weighed (as in a pair of scales); **frame:** prepare; **fit:** ready

283. **attempt:** i.e., assault on her honor; **think well:** i.e., think it a good idea; **carry . . . may:** i.e., carry this out as well as you can

both, her combinate husband, this well-seeming
Angelo.
ISABELLA Can this be so? Did Angelo so leave her? 250
DUKE, ⌜*as Friar*⌝ Left her in her tears and dried not one
of them with his comfort, swallowed his vows
whole, pretending in her discoveries of dishonor; in
few, bestowed her on her own lamentation, which
she yet wears for his sake; and he, a marble to her 255
tears, is washed with them but relents not.
ISABELLA What a merit were it in death to take this
poor maid from the world! What corruption in this
life, that it will let this man live! But how out of this
can she avail? 260
DUKE, ⌜*as Friar*⌝ It is a rupture that you may easily heal,
and the cure of it not only saves your brother, but
keeps you from dishonor in doing it.
ISABELLA Show me how, good father.
DUKE, ⌜*as Friar*⌝ This forenamed maid hath yet in her 265
the continuance of her first affection. His unjust
unkindness, that in all reason should have
quenched her love, hath, like an impediment in the
current, made it more violent and unruly. Go you to
Angelo, answer his requiring with a plausible obedi- 270
ence, agree with his demands to the point. Only
refer yourself to this advantage: first, that your stay
with him may not be long, that the time may have all
shadow and silence in it, and the place answer to
convenience. This being granted in course, and 275
now follows all: we shall advise this wronged maid
to stead up your appointment, go in your place. If
the encounter acknowledge itself hereafter, it may
compel him to her recompense; and here, by this, is
your brother saved, your honor untainted, the poor 280
Mariana advantaged, and the corrupt deputy
scaled. The maid will I frame and make fit for his
attempt. If you think well to carry this as you may,

284. **doubleness of the benefit:** i.e., the **benefit** to both you and Mariana

286. **image:** idea

287. **perfection:** completion, full growth

288. **It lies . . . up:** i.e., it depends primarily on your ability to carry it off **lies . . . in:** consists in, has its ground in

291. **presently:** immediately

291–92. **moated grange:** probably an outlying house belonging to the church and either surrounded by a moat or with a large pond

292. **dejected:** low in fortune and in spirits

293. **dispatch:** make your arrangements speedily

296 SD. **Duke remains:** Though the duke does not exit, the scene seems to change from a secluded to a public space. We have therefore followed the editorial tradition that marks a scene change at this point.

3.2 Pompey is carried off to prison. Lucio refuses to provide bail money for him, and slanders the absent duke to the "Friar," who warns Lucio that he will pay for his slander when the duke "returns." The Bawd, also under arrest, tells Escalus that Lucio fathered an illegitimate child on Kate Keepdown. The "Friar" tells Escalus that Claudio is prepared to die, and has Escalus reassure him about the duke's reputation.

2. **will needs:** i.e., must

3–4. **drink . . . bastard:** To "drink bastard" was to drink sweet wine, but **drink** was also a copulation metaphor.

(continued)

the doubleness of the benefit defends the deceit
from reproof. What think you of it?   285

ISABELLA The image of it gives me content already, and
I trust it will grow to a most prosperous perfection.

DUKE, ⌜*as Friar*⌝ It lies much in your holding up. Haste
you speedily to Angelo. If for this night he entreat
you to his bed, give him promise of satisfaction. I   290
will presently to Saint Luke's. There at the moated
grange resides this dejected Mariana. At that place
call upon me, and dispatch with Angelo that it may
be quickly.

ISABELLA I thank you for this comfort. Fare you well,   295
good father.   *She exits.* ⌜*The Duke remains.*⌝

⌜Scene 2⌝
Enter Elbow, ⌜*Pompey, and*⌝ *Officers.*

ELBOW, ⌜*to Pompey*⌝ Nay, if there be no remedy for it
but that you will needs buy and sell men and
women like beasts, we shall have all the world drink
brown and white bastard.

DUKE, ⌜*as Friar, aside*⌝ O heavens, what stuff is here?   5

POMPEY 'Twas never merry world since, of two usuries,
the merriest was put down, and the worser allowed
by order of law a furred gown to keep him warm,
and furred with fox and lambskins too, to signify
that craft, being richer than innocency, stands for   10
the facing.

ELBOW Come your way, sir.—Bless you, good father
friar.

DUKE, ⌜*as Friar*⌝ And you, good brother father. What
offense hath this man made you, sir?   15

ELBOW Marry, sir, he hath offended the law; and, sir,
we take him to be a thief too, sir, for we have found

6. **two usuries:** i.e., fornication and moneylending

7. **merriest:** i.e., most pleasurable; **put down:** suppressed; **the worser:** i.e., the moneylender

8. **furred gown:** i.e., clothing worn by the wealthy (See *King Lear* 4.6.180–81: "Through tattered clothes small vices do appear. / Robes and furred gowns hide all.")

10. **craft:** craftiness (associated with the **fox**); **richer:** (1) wealthier; (2) costlier

10–11. **stands . . . facing:** i.e., serves as the trim

12. **Come your way:** i.e., come on

14. **brother father:** a joking response to Elbow's clumsy **father friar** (i.e., father brother)

18. **picklock:** The duke's response (lines 20 ff.) suggests that the **picklock** was a sign of the bawd's trade, but there are also general sexual associations with keys and locks.

20. **sirrah:** a term of address to a male social inferior

23. **maw:** belly

27. **living:** livelihood

28. **depending:** (1) sustained, supported; (2) dependent, servile; **mend:** i.e., reform

31. **proofs for:** i.e., arguments in defense of

32. **prove his:** i.e., turn out to be the devil's

33. **Correction:** punishment; **instruction:** spiritual counsel

34. **rude:** uncivilized; **profit:** improve

35. **must:** i.e., must appear; **he has:** i.e., the deputy has

36–37. **whoremaster, whoremonger:** fornicator, one who uses whores

(continued)

upon him, sir, a strange picklock, which we have
sent to the Deputy.

DUKE, ⌜*as Friar, to Pompey*⌝
Fie, sirrah, a bawd, a wicked bawd!   20
The evil that thou causest to be done,
That is thy means to live. Do thou but think
What 'tis to cram a maw or clothe a back
From such a filthy vice; say to thyself,
From their abominable and beastly touches   25
I drink, I eat, ⌜array⌝ myself, and live.
Canst thou believe thy living is a life,
So stinkingly depending? Go mend, go mend.

POMPEY   Indeed, it does stink in some sort, sir. But yet,
sir, I would prove—   30

DUKE, ⌜*as Friar*⌝
Nay, if the devil have given thee proofs for sin,
Thou wilt prove his.—Take him to prison, officer.
Correction and instruction must both work
Ere this rude beast will profit.

ELBOW   He must before the Deputy, sir; he has given   35
him warning. The Deputy cannot abide a whoremaster. If he be a whoremonger and comes before
him, he were as good go a mile on his errand.

DUKE, ⌜*as Friar*⌝
That we were all, as some would seem to be,
From our faults, as faults from seeming, free.   40

ELBOW   His neck will come to your waist—a cord, sir.

Enter Lucio.

POMPEY   I spy comfort, I cry bail. Here's a gentleman
and a friend of mine.

LUCIO   How now, noble Pompey? What, at the wheels of
Caesar? Art thou led in triumph? What, is there   45
none of Pygmalion's images, newly made woman,
to be had now, for putting the hand in the pocket
and extracting ⌜it⌝ clutched? What reply, ha? What

38. **he . . . errand:** perhaps, he would be better off doing anything else (Proverbial: "I will go twenty miles on your errand first.")

39. **That:** i.e., would that (I wish that)

40. **as faults from seeming:** perhaps, as sinners (like Pompey) are **free** from **seeming** (hypocrisy)

41. **will . . . cord:** i.e., will be tied, like the **waist** of a friar's robe, with a **cord** (See page 196.)

42. **cry:** beg for, entreat

44–45. **noble Pompey . . . triumph:** another allusion to Pompey the Great's defeat **at the wheels:** i.e., made to walk as a prisoner behind the chariot **in triumph:** i.e., in Caesar's triumphal procession (See note to 2.1.256–57.)

45–48. **is . . . clutched:** i.e., are there no prostitutes to be bought (See longer note, page 221.)

48–50. **What sayst . . . rain:** perhaps, "How do you like the new regime? Is the old life completely destroyed?" (See the similar questions in lines 51–52.)

50. **trot:** bawd (usually applied to an old woman)

52. **trick:** fashion, custom

55. **Procures she still:** i.e., does she still get women to be prostitutes

56–57. **eaten . . . tub:** wordplay on **beef** (perhaps as male genitals, or perhaps as female prostitutes) and on **the tub,** i.e., the powdering tub, a vessel in which meat was salted and pickled and also the sweating-tub for the treatment of venereal disease (See page 212.)

59. **Ever . . . bawd:** i.e., young prostitutes always become old bawds (**Your** is impersonal, meaning "whores in general" and "bawds in general.") **powdered:** i.e., pickled; also, infected with syphilis

(continued)

sayst thou to this tune, matter, and method? Is 't not
drowned i' th' last rain, ha? What sayst thou, trot? Is 50
the world as it was, man? Which is the way? Is it sad
and few words? Or how? The trick of it?

DUKE, ⌐*as Friar, aside*⌐ Still thus, and thus; still worse.

LUCIO, ⌐*to Pompey*⌐ How doth my dear morsel, thy
mistress? Procures she still, ha? 55

POMPEY Troth, sir, she hath eaten up all her beef, and
she is herself in the tub.

LUCIO Why, 'tis good. It is the right of it. It must be so.
Ever your fresh whore and your powdered bawd, an
unshunned consequence; it must be so. Art going to 60
prison, Pompey?

POMPEY Yes, faith, sir.

LUCIO Why, 'tis not amiss, Pompey. Farewell. Go say I
sent thee thither. For debt, Pompey? Or how?

ELBOW For being a bawd, for being a bawd. 65

LUCIO Well, then, imprison him. If imprisonment be
the due of a bawd, why, 'tis his right. Bawd is he,
doubtless, and of antiquity too. Bawd born.—
Farewell, good Pompey. Commend me to the prison, Pompey. You will turn good husband now, 70
Pompey; you will keep the house.

POMPEY I hope, sir, your good Worship will be my bail.

LUCIO No, indeed, will I not, Pompey; it is not the
wear. I will pray, Pompey, to increase your bondage. If you take it not patiently, why, your mettle is 75
the more. Adieu, trusty Pompey.—Bless you, friar.

DUKE, ⌐*as Friar*⌐ And you.

LUCIO, ⌐*to Pompey*⌐ Does Bridget paint still, Pompey,
ha?

ELBOW, ⌐*to Pompey*⌐ Come your ways, sir, come. 80

POMPEY, ⌐*to Lucio*⌐ You will not bail me, then, sir?

LUCIO Then, Pompey, nor now.—What news abroad,
friar? What news?

ELBOW, ⌐*to Pompey*⌐ Come your ways, sir, come.

60. **unshunned:** unavoidable

68. **of antiquity:** longstanding; **Bawd born:** i.e., born a bawd

70–71. **husband ... house:** wordplay on **husband** as (1) male head of the house and (2) frugal manager, and on **keep the house** as (1) stay indoors and (2) take care of the home

72. **be my bail:** i.e., provide the money for my bail

74. **wear:** fashion

75. **mettle:** (1) spirit; (2) metal (of his chains)

78. **paint:** i.e., use cosmetics

82. **Then:** i.e., neither then; **abroad:** current in the outside world

89. **other some:** i.e., certain others (say)

93. **fantastical:** whimsical, capricious; **steal:** i.e., steal away

94. **usurp the beggary:** wrongfully take on a beggarly status (Lucio, complaining that the duke has abandoned his high status, describes unawares the duke's actual disguise as a poor friar.)

96. **puts ... to 't:** i.e., drives ... to extremities

99. **Something too crabbed:** somewhat too harsh

100. **It:** i.e., lechery; **general:** prevalent

102. **in good sooth:** indeed; **a great kindred:** a large family

103. **is well allied:** i.e., has strong allies; **extirp:** eradicate

104. **put down:** suppressed

105–6. **after ... way:** i.e., in accordance with the straightforward way

109. **sea-maid:** i.e., mermaid (See page 178.)

110. **stockfishes:** dried codfish

(continued)

LUCIO Go to kennel, Pompey, go.   85
                    ⌜*Elbow, Pompey, and Officers exit.*⌝
        What news, friar, of the Duke?
DUKE, ⌜*as Friar*⌝ I know none. Can you tell me of any?
LUCIO Some say he is with the Emperor of Russia;
        other some, he is in Rome. But where is he, think
        you?   90
DUKE, ⌜*as Friar*⌝ I know not where, but wheresoever, I
        wish him well.
LUCIO It was a mad fantastical trick of him to steal
        from the state and usurp the beggary he was never
        born to. Lord Angelo dukes it well in his absence.   95
        He puts transgression to 't.
DUKE, ⌜*as Friar*⌝ He does well in 't.
LUCIO A little more lenity to lechery would do no harm
        in him. Something too crabbed that way, friar.
DUKE, ⌜*as Friar*⌝ It is too general a vice, and severity 100
        must cure it.
LUCIO Yes, in good sooth, the vice is of a great kindred;
        it is well allied, but it is impossible to extirp it quite,
        friar, till eating and drinking be put down. They say
        this Angelo was not made by man and woman after 105
        this downright way of creation. Is it true, think
        you?
DUKE, ⌜*as Friar*⌝ How should he be made, then?
LUCIO Some report a sea-maid spawned him; some,
        that he was begot between two stockfishes. But it is 110
        certain that when he makes water, his urine is
        congealed ice; that I know to be true. And he is a
        motion generative, that's infallible.
DUKE, ⌜*as Friar*⌝ You are pleasant, sir, and speak apace.
LUCIO Why, what a ruthless thing is this in him, for the 115
        rebellion of a codpiece to take away the life of a
        man! Would the duke that is absent have done this?
        Ere he would have hanged a man for the getting
        a hundred bastards, he would have paid for the

113. **motion:** puppet; **generative:** perhaps a reference to his male gender (often emended to "ungenerative," incapable of procreation)

114. **pleasant:** merry

116. **rebellion of a codpiece:** i.e., illicit sex **codpiece:** the showy appendage to the front of a man's breeches, here meaning the genitals themselves

118. **getting:** begetting

120–21. **the sport, the service:** sexual action, intercourse

124. **detected for women:** i.e., accused of womanizing

127. **your beggar of fifty:** i.e., fifty-year-old beggars (**Your** is impersonal, meaning "beggars in general.")

128. **use:** custom; **ducat:** gold coin; **clack-dish:** beggar's bowl (Lucio here implies that the beggar to whom the duke gave money was actually his whore.)

129. **crotchets:** strange whims

132. **inward:** familiar acquaintance; **shy:** cautious

133–34. **withdrawing:** departure

138. **the . . . subject:** i.e., the majority of subjects

141. **unweighing:** thoughtless

142. **envy:** malice

144. **helmed:** steered

144–45. **upon . . . need:** i.e., should there be a genuine **need** for the duke to defend himself **warranted:** justified

145. **proclamation:** i.e., public description

146. **testimonied:** tested by evidence; **bringings-forth:** achievements

147. **envious:** malicious

148. **unskillfully:** foolishly, ignorantly

149. **darkened:** clouded

nursing a thousand. He had some feeling of the   120
sport, he knew the service, and that instructed him
to mercy.

DUKE, ⌜*as Friar*⌝ I never heard the absent duke much
detected for women. He was not inclined that way.

LUCIO O, sir, you are deceived.   125

DUKE, ⌜*as Friar*⌝ 'Tis not possible.

LUCIO Who, not the Duke? Yes, your beggar of fifty;
and his use was to put a ducat in her clack-dish. The
Duke had crotchets in him. He would be drunk too,
that let me inform you.   130

DUKE, ⌜*as Friar*⌝ You do him wrong, surely.

LUCIO Sir, I was an inward of his. A shy fellow was the
Duke, and I believe I know the cause of his withdrawing.

DUKE, ⌜*as Friar*⌝ What, I prithee, might be the cause?   135

LUCIO No, pardon. 'Tis a secret must be locked within
the teeth and the lips. But this I can let you
understand: the greater file of the subject held the
Duke to be wise.

DUKE, ⌜*as Friar*⌝ Wise? Why, no question but he was.   140

LUCIO A very superficial, ignorant, unweighing fellow.

DUKE, ⌜*as Friar*⌝ Either this is envy in you, folly, or
mistaking. The very stream of his life and the
business he hath helmed must, upon a warranted
need, give him a better proclamation. Let him be   145
but testimonied in his own bringings-forth, and he
shall appear to the envious a scholar, a statesman,
and a soldier. Therefore you speak unskillfully. Or,
if your knowledge be more, it is much darkened in
your malice.   150

LUCIO Sir, I know him, and I love him.

DUKE, ⌜*as Friar*⌝ Love talks with better knowledge, and
knowledge with ⌜dearer⌝ love.

LUCIO Come, sir, I know what I know.

DUKE, ⌜*as Friar*⌝ I can hardly believe that, since you   155

163. **report:** describe, give an account of

166. **unhurtful:** harmless

166–67. **opposite:** adversary

168. **forswear:** repudiate; **again:** another time

173. **tundish:** funnel (Both **bottle** and **tundish** could allude to sexual organs.); **would:** wish

174. **were returned again:** i.e., were back

175. **ungenitured:** sexless, without genitals; **agent:** deputy

178. **darkly:** secretly

179. **Would:** I wish

180. **untrussing:** i.e., undressing (literally, untying the laces that hold up a man's breeches)

182–83. **eat . . . Fridays:** wordplay on eating meat **on Fridays** (forbidden by the church) and on eating **mutton** (i.e., visiting prostitutes)

184. **mouth with:** i.e., kiss; **smelt:** i.e., smelled of

185. **brown bread:** i.e., coarse rye bread of the poor (The wealthy ate white bread.)

186. **mortality:** human life

187. **censure scape:** i.e., escape hostile criticism

187–88. **Back-wounding . . . strikes:** Proverbial: "Calumny shoots at the fairest mark." **Back-wounding:** i.e., backbiting, slandering behind a person's back

know not what you speak. But if ever the Duke
return, as our prayers are he may, let me desire you
to make your answer before him. If it be honest you
have spoke, you have courage to maintain it. I am
bound to call upon you, and, I pray you, your name? 160

LUCIO Sir, my name is Lucio, well known to the Duke.

DUKE, ⌈*as Friar*⌉ He shall know you better, sir, if I may
live to report you.

LUCIO I fear you not.

DUKE, ⌈*as Friar*⌉ O, you hope the Duke will return no 165
more, or you imagine me too unhurtful an opposite. But indeed I can do you little harm; you'll
forswear this again.

LUCIO I'll be hanged first. Thou art deceived in me,
friar. But no more of this. Canst thou tell if Claudio 170
die tomorrow or no?

DUKE, ⌈*as Friar*⌉ Why should he die, sir?

LUCIO Why? For filling a bottle with a tundish. I would
the Duke we talk of were returned again. This
ungenitured agent will unpeople the province with 175
continency. Sparrows must not build in his house
eaves, because they are lecherous. The Duke yet
would have dark deeds darkly answered. He would
never bring them to light. Would he were returned.
Marry, this Claudio is condemned for untrussing. 180
Farewell, good friar. I prithee pray for me. The
Duke, I say to thee again, would eat mutton on
Fridays. He's now past it, yet—and I say to thee—
he would mouth with a beggar though she smelt
brown bread and garlic. Say that I said so. Farewell. 185
He exits.

DUKE
No might nor greatness in mortality
Can censure scape. Back-wounding calumny
The whitest virtue strikes. What king so strong

189. **gall:** bitterness

194. **Double . . . admonition:** i.e., warned two and three times

194–95. **forfeit . . . kind:** i.e., liable to punishment for the same offense

195–96. **mercy swear:** Proverbial: "Enough to make a saint swear."

199–200. **information:** accusation

201. **he promised:** i.e., Lucio promised

203. **come . . . Jacob:** i.e., next May 1, the feast of Saints Philip and James (See longer note, pages 221–22.)

204. **goes . . . me:** i.e., tries to slander me

205. **license:** disregard of the law

207. **Go to:** an expression of impatience

208. **brother:** fellow justice, colleague

210. **divines:** clergymen (See page 154.)

211. **wrought . . . pity:** i.e., acted in line with the pity that I feel

212. **him:** i.e., Claudio

214. **entertainment:** acceptance

218. **chance:** fortune, lot

219. **use it:** dwell in it

Can tie the gall up in the slanderous tongue?
But who comes here?   190

Enter Escalus, Provost, ⌜*Officers,*⌝ *and* ⌜*Mistress*
Overdone, a⌝ *Bawd.*

ESCALUS, ⌜*to Officers*⌝ Go, away with her to prison.
BAWD Good my lord, be good to me. Your Honor is
accounted a merciful man, good my lord.
ESCALUS Double and treble admonition, and still forfeit in the same kind? This would make mercy 195
swear and play the tyrant.
PROVOST A bawd of eleven years' continuance, may it
please your Honor.
BAWD, ⌜*to Escalus*⌝ My lord, this is one Lucio's information against me. Mistress Kate Keepdown was 200
with child by him in the Duke's time; he promised
her marriage. His child is a year and a quarter old
come Philip and Jacob. I have kept it myself, and see
how he goes about to abuse me.
ESCALUS That fellow is a fellow of much license. Let 205
him be called before us. Away with her to prison.—
Go to, no more words.   ⌜*Officers exit with Bawd.*⌝
Provost, my brother Angelo will not be altered.
Claudio must die tomorrow. Let him be furnished
with divines and have all charitable preparation. If 210
my brother wrought by my pity, it should not be so
with him.
PROVOST So please you, this friar hath been with him,
and advised him for th' entertainment of death.
ESCALUS Good even, good father.   215
DUKE, ⌜*as Friar*⌝ Bliss and goodness on you.
ESCALUS Of whence are you?
DUKE, ⌜*as Friar*⌝
Not of this country, though my chance is now
To use it for my time. I am a brother

220. **gracious:** holy, pious; **the See: i.e.,** the Holy See (the papal court in Rome)

223–31. **None . . . news:** See longer note, page 222.

223–24. **there . . . cure it:** i.e., **goodness** is so sick that (only) death can cure the disease

225. **Novelty . . . request:** i.e., only "the latest thing" is in demand

226. **aged:** persistent

228. **societies:** partnerships; associations; **security:** excessive self-confidence

229. **fellowships:** associations; guilds, companies (nearly synonymous with **societies** in line 228); **upon:** according to

233. **strifes:** endeavors, efforts; **contended:** strove earnestly

235. **given to:** inclined

239. **his events:** i.e., the outcome of his affairs

242. **lent him visitation:** i.e., visited him

244. **sinister measure:** unfair treatment

245. **determination:** decision; **Yet:** nonetheless

246. **framed to:** i.e., devised for

246–47. **by . . . frailty:** i.e., prompted by his human weakness

247–48. **by my good leisure:** i.e., by degrees, slowly

250–51. **paid . . . calling:** i.e., fulfilled your duties as a friar both to God and to the prisoner **function:** role

252–53. **extremest . . . modesty:** i.e., as far as I could without giving offense **modesty:** freedom from presumption or impudence

253. **brother justice:** i.e., fellow judge

Of gracious order, late come from the See   220
In special business from his Holiness.

ESCALUS What news abroad i' th' world?

DUKE, ⌜*as Friar*⌝ None but that there is so great a fever
on goodness that the dissolution of it must cure it.
Novelty is only in request, and it is as dangerous to   225
be aged in any kind of course as it is virtuous to be
constant in any undertaking. There is scarce truth
enough alive to make societies secure, but security
enough to make fellowships accursed. Much upon
this riddle runs the wisdom of the world. This news   230
is old enough, yet it is every day's news. I pray you,
sir, of what disposition was the Duke?

ESCALUS One that, above all other strifes, contended
especially to know himself.

DUKE, ⌜*as Friar*⌝ What pleasure was he given to?   235

ESCALUS Rather rejoicing to see another merry than
merry at anything which professed to make him
rejoice—a gentleman of all temperance. But leave
we him to his events, with a prayer they may prove
prosperous, and let me desire to know how you find   240
Claudio prepared. I am made to understand that
you have lent him visitation.

DUKE, ⌜*as Friar*⌝ He professes to have received no
sinister measure from his judge but most willingly
humbles himself to the determination of justice. Yet   245
had he framed to himself, by the instruction of his
frailty, many deceiving promises of life, which I, by
my good leisure, have discredited to him, and now
is he resolved to die.

ESCALUS You have paid the heavens your function and   250
the prisoner the very debt of your calling. I have
labored for the poor gentleman to the extremest
shore of my modesty, but my brother justice have I
found so severe that he hath forced me to tell him
he is indeed Justice.   255

256. **answer the straitness:** i.e., match the strictness

261–82. **He who . . . contracting:** See longer note, page 222.

263. **Pattern . . . know:** perhaps, find the **pattern** of proper conduct in himself

264. **Grace . . . go:** i.e., find in himself the grace to be upright and the strength to go forward

265–66. **More . . . weighing:** i.e., not punishing others more or less severely than his own conscience dictates, after he has reflected on his own failings **self-offenses:** his own offenses

270. **my vice:** i.e., the **vice** I allowed (through not enforcing the law)

273–76. **How . . . things:** Editors suggest that a couplet has dropped out after line 274. The lines as they now stand make little sense.

277. **Craft:** (1) deceit; (2) ingenuity

279. **despisèd:** scorned

280. **th' disguisèd:** i.e., Mariana

281. **Pay:** render in retribution; **falsehood:** deception; **false exacting:** treacherous exaction, extortion

282. **perform:** fulfill; **contracting:** contract, betrothal

DUKE, ⌜*as Friar*⌝ If his own life answer the straitness of
  his proceeding, it shall become him well; wherein if
  he chance to fail, he hath sentenced himself.
ESCALUS I am going to visit the prisoner. Fare you well.
DUKE, ⌜*as Friar*⌝ Peace be with you.   260
                              ⌜*Escalus and Provost exit.*⌝
⌜DUKE⌝
  He who the sword of heaven will bear
  Should be as holy as severe,
  Pattern in himself to know,
  Grace to stand, and virtue go;
  More nor less to others paying   265
  Than by self-offenses weighing.
  Shame to him whose cruel striking
  Kills for faults of his own liking.
  Twice treble shame on Angelo,
  To weed my vice, and let his grow.   270
  O, what may man within him hide,
  Though angel on the outward side!
  How may likeness made in crimes,
  Making practice on the times,
  To draw with idle spiders' strings   275
  Most ponderous and substantial things.
  Craft against vice I must apply.
  With Angelo tonight shall lie
  His old betrothèd but despisèd.
  So disguise shall, by th' disguisèd,   280
  Pay with falsehood false exacting
  And perform an old contracting.
                                              He exits.

MEASURE
FOR
MEASURE

ACT 4

4.1 Isabella reports to the "Friar" about the arrangements made with Angelo for that night's assignation; Mariana agrees to sleep with Angelo in Isabella's place.

———————

2. **were forsworn:** i.e., falsely promised (to be faithful)

5. **bring again:** i.e., bring back, return

9. **brawling:** clamorous

10. **cry you mercy:** i.e., beg your pardon

12. **excuse me:** i.e., excuse myself; **believe me so:** i.e., believe what I'm about to say

14. **charm:** power of enchanting or bewitching the mind

15. **bad good:** i.e., the bad seem good

A garden with "a planchèd gate." (4.1.28–30)
From [Thomas Hill,] *The gardeners labyrinth* . . . (1577).

ACT 4

Scene 1
Enter Mariana, and Boy singing.

Song.

> *Take, O take those lips away,*
> > *That so sweetly were forsworn,*
> *And those eyes, the break of day,*
> > *Lights that do mislead the morn.*
> *But my kisses bring again, bring again,*   5
> *Seals of love, but sealed in vain, sealed in vain.*

Enter Duke ⌜as a Friar.⌝

MARIANA, ⌜to Boy⌝
Break off thy song and haste thee quick away.
Here comes a man of comfort, whose advice
Hath often stilled my brawling discontent.
                              ⌜*Boy exits.*⌝
I cry you mercy, sir, and well could wish   10
You had not found me here so musical.
Let me excuse me, and believe me so,
My mirth it much displeased, but pleased my woe.
DUKE, ⌜as Friar⌝
'Tis good, though music oft hath such a charm
To make bad good and good provoke to harm.   15
  I pray you tell me, hath anybody inquired for me

131

17. **Much upon:** i.e., at; or, just about

18. **meet:** keep an appointment

21. **constantly:** confidently

22–23. **crave . . . little:** i.e., ask you to leave for a while

23. **anon:** soon

28. **circummured:** walled around

30. **to that vineyard:** i.e., (opening) into that vineyard; **planchèd gate:** i.e., a gate made of planks or boards (See page 130.)

31. **makes his opening:** i.e., is opened   **his:** its

32. **other:** i.e., other key

34. **upon:** during

35. **Heavy:** (1) sleepy; (2) gloomy

36. **shall . . . knowledge:** perhaps, will you know how to

39–40. **In action . . . o'er:** See longer note, pages 222–23.

42. **'greed:** i.e., agreed upon; **her observance:** i.e., what she must do

43. **repair:** i.e., visit

44. **possessed:** informed; **most:** i.e., longest

here today? Much upon this time have I promised
here to meet.

MARIANA You have not been inquired after. I have sat
here all day.   20

Enter Isabella.

DUKE, ⌜*as Friar*⌝ I do constantly believe you. The time is
come even now. I shall crave your forbearance a
little. Maybe I will call upon you anon for some
advantage to yourself.

MARIANA I am always bound to you.   *She exits.* 25

DUKE, ⌜*as Friar*⌝ Very well met, and welcome.
  What is the news from this good deputy?

ISABELLA
  He hath a garden circummured with brick,
  Whose western side is with a vineyard backed;
  And to that vineyard is a planchèd gate   30
  That makes his opening with this bigger key.
  This other doth command a little door
  Which from the vineyard to the garden leads.
  There have I made my promise, upon the
  Heavy middle of the night, to call upon him. 35

DUKE, ⌜*as Friar*⌝
  But shall you on your knowledge find this way?

ISABELLA
  I have ta'en a due and wary note upon 't.
  With whispering and most guilty diligence,
  In action all of precept, he did show me
  The way twice o'er.   40

DUKE, ⌜*as Friar*⌝   Are there no other tokens
  Between you 'greed concerning her observance?

ISABELLA
  No, none, but only a repair i' th' dark,
  And that I have possessed him my most stay
  Can be but brief, for I have made him know 45
  I have a servant comes with me along

47. **stays upon:** waits for; **persuasion:** belief

49. **borne up:** kept up, supported, maintained

56. **respect:** esteem, have a high regard for

57. **found it:** i.e., found it to be true

60. **attend your leisure:** i.e., await you

63. **false:** treacherous

64. **stuck:** fixed; **volumes of report:** i.e., a mass of rumors

65–66. **Run . . . doings:** a hunting metaphor, in which hostile (**contrarious**) hounds (i.e., the **volumes of report**) accompany the treacherous **eyes** (the **false**) and **quest upon** (i.e., bark at the sight of) the quarry (i.e., the ruler's **doings**)

66. **escapes:** flights, sallies

67. **father . . . dream:** i.e., source of their imaginings

68. **rack:** torture, tear apart (See below.)

Victims on a rack. (4.1.68, 5.1.349)
From Girolamo Maggi, *De tintinnabulis liber . . .* (1689).

That stays upon me, whose persuasion is
I come about my brother.
DUKE, ⌜*as Friar*⌝   'Tis well borne up.
I have not yet made known to Mariana   50
A word of this.—What ho, within; come forth.

Enter Mariana.

⌜*To Mariana.*⌝ I pray you be acquainted with this
  maid.
She comes to do you good.
ISABELLA   I do desire the like.   55
DUKE, ⌜*as Friar, to Mariana*⌝
Do you persuade yourself that I respect you?
MARIANA
Good friar, I know you do, and have found it.
DUKE, ⌜*as Friar*⌝
Take then this your companion by the hand,
Who hath a story ready for your ear.
I shall attend your leisure. But make haste.   60
The vaporous night approaches.
MARIANA, ⌜*to Isabella*⌝   Will 't please you walk aside?
                         ⌜*Isabella and Mariana*⌝ *exit.*

DUKE
O place and greatness, millions of false eyes
Are stuck upon thee; volumes of report
Run with these false, and, most contrarious, quest   65
Upon thy doings; thousand escapes of wit
Make thee the father of their idle dream
And rack thee in their fancies.

Enter Mariana and Isabella.

⌜DUKE, *as Friar*⌝   Welcome. How agreed?
ISABELLA
She'll take the enterprise upon her, father,   70
If you advise it.

72. **not my consent:** i.e., not only my consent

77. **Fear me not:** i.e., don't distrust or doubt me

78. **fear you not:** i.e., don't be afraid

81. **Sith that:** i.e., since

82. **flourish:** embellish

83. **Our . . . sow:** i.e., we can't yet **reap** our harvest since we have yet to **sow** our grain   **corn:** i.e., wheat   **to reap:** i.e., still to be reaped   **tithe:** perhaps, seed that will yield the tithe-corn (the tenth of the harvest due the church)   **to sow:** i.e., to be sown

4.2 At the prison, Pompey agrees to serve as the assistant to Abhorson, the public executioner. The duke, in his role of Friar, impatiently awaits Angelo's pardon for Claudio. But Angelo instead sends an order that Claudio be put to death immediately and that his head be brought to Angelo. The "Friar" persuades the Provost to delay the beheading of Claudio and to send Angelo the disguised head of Barnardine, a prisoner who is also scheduled for execution.

———————

4. **his wife's head:** See Ephesians 5.23: "For the husband is the head of the wife, even as Christ is the head of the church." See also 1 Corinthians 11.3.

6. **leave . . . snatches:** i.e., leave your quibbles

9. **common:** public; **office:** function (as executioner)

11. **gyves:** shackles (See page 142.)

DUKE, ⌜*as Friar*⌝   It is not my consent
　But my entreaty too.
ISABELLA, ⌜*to Mariana*⌝ Little have you to say
　When you depart from him, but, soft and low,   75
　"Remember now my brother."
MARIANA   Fear me not.
DUKE, ⌜*as Friar*⌝
　Nor, gentle daughter, fear you not at all.
　He is your husband on a precontract.
　To bring you thus together 'tis no sin,   80
　Sith that the justice of your title to him
　Doth flourish the deceit. Come, let us go.
　Our corn's to reap, for yet our tithe's to sow.
                                        They exit.

Scene 2
Enter Provost, ⌜Pompey, and Officer.⌝

PROVOST   Come hither, sirrah. Can you cut off a man's
　head?
POMPEY   If the man be a bachelor, sir, I can; but if he be
　a married man, he's his wife's head, and I can never
　cut off a woman's head.   5
PROVOST   Come, sir, leave me your snatches, and yield
　me a direct answer. Tomorrow morning are to die
　Claudio and Barnardine. Here is in our prison a
　common executioner, who in his office lacks a
　helper. If you will take it on you to assist him, it   10
　shall redeem you from your gyves; if not, you shall
　have your full time of imprisonment and your
　deliverance with an unpitied whipping, for you have
　been a notorious bawd.
POMPEY   Sir, I have been an unlawful bawd time out of   15
　mind, but yet I will be content to be a lawful

19. **Abhorson:** a name that combines "abhor" and "whoreson" (i.e., bastard)

23. **meet:** fitting, proper

23–24. **compound:** make arrangements, contract

26. **estimation:** reputation

29. **mystery:** profession, calling, art

32. **by . . . favor:** a courteous phrase, "if you please," but with a punning reference (line 33) to Abhorson's **favor,** or face

33–34. **a hanging look:** (1) gloomy expression; (2) look of a hangman; (3) look of one born to be hanged

36. **Painting:** i.e., the profession of the artist (but, in line 38, meaning "using cosmetics")

37. **your whores:** i.e., whores (impersonal **your**)

43–47. **Every . . . thief:** Abhorson's **proof** involves (1) the relationship between the **true man** (i.e., honest man) and the **thief,** and (2) wordplay on **big** (large, valuable) and **little** (small, insignificant). Attempts to explain how his proof demonstrates that **hanging** is a **mystery** are generally unpersuasive.

hangman. I would be glad to receive some instruction from my fellow partner.

PROVOST What ho, Abhorson!—Where's Abhorson
there?   20

Enter Abhorson.

ABHORSON Do you call, sir?

PROVOST Sirrah, here's a fellow will help you tomorrow in your execution. If you think it meet, compound with him by the year and let him abide here
with you; if not, use him for the present and dismiss   25
him. He cannot plead his estimation with you; he
hath been a bawd.

ABHORSON A bawd, sir? Fie upon him! He will discredit
our mystery.

PROVOST Go to, sir; you weigh equally. A feather will   30
turn the scale.   *He exits.*

POMPEY Pray, sir, by your good favor—for surely, sir, a
good favor you have, but that you have a hanging
look—do you call, sir, your occupation a mystery?

ABHORSON Ay, sir, a mystery.   35

POMPEY Painting, sir, I have heard say, is a mystery;
and your whores, sir, being members of my occupation, using painting, do prove my occupation a
mystery; but what mystery there should be in hanging, if I should be hanged, I cannot imagine.   40

ABHORSON Sir, it is a mystery.

POMPEY Proof?

ABHORSON Every true man's apparel fits your thief. If it
be too little for your thief, your true man thinks it
big enough; if it be too big for your thief, your thief   45
thinks it little enough. So every true man's apparel
fits your thief.

Enter Provost.

PROVOST Are you agreed?

51. **ask forgiveness:** "The common executioner . . . / Falls not the axe upon the humbled neck / But first begs pardon" (*As You Like It* 3.5.3–7).

52. **block:** See note to 2.4.195, and page 158.

57. **for your own turn:** i.e., when you are executed

58. **yare:** ready, prepared

59. **a good turn:** (1) a kind service; (2) an expert hanging (playing on the phrase "to turn someone off," which meant "to hang someone")

66. **sleep . . . labor:** See Ecclesiastes 5.12: "The sleep of a laboring man is sweet."

67. **starkly:** stiffly; **traveler's:** perhaps, laborer's ("Travel" and "travail" [meaning "labor"] were interchangeable spellings.)

69. **do good on:** benefit

75. **gentle:** i.e., good (a complimentary epithet)

POMPEY   Sir, I will serve him, for I do find your hangman is a more penitent trade than your bawd. He 50
  doth oftener ask forgiveness.
PROVOST, ⌜to Abhorson⌝   You, sirrah, provide your block
  and your axe tomorrow, four o' clock.
ABHORSON, ⌜to Pompey⌝   Come on, bawd. I will instruct
  thee in my trade. Follow. 55
POMPEY   I do desire to learn, sir; and I hope, if you have
  occasion to use me for your own turn, you shall find
  me ⌜yare.⌝ For truly, sir, for your kindness, I owe
  you a good turn.   ⌜Pompey and Abhorson⌝ exit.
PROVOST, ⌜to Officer⌝
  Call hither Barnardine and Claudio. 60

           ⌜Officer exits.⌝

  Th' one has my pity; not a jot the other,
  Being a murderer, though he were my brother.

    Enter Claudio, ⌜*with Officer.*⌝

  Look, here's the warrant, Claudio, for thy death.
  'Tis now dead midnight, and by eight tomorrow
  Thou must be made immortal. Where's Barnardine? 65
CLAUDIO
  As fast locked up in sleep as guiltless labor
  When it lies starkly in the traveler's bones.
  He will not wake.
PROVOST   Who can do good on him?
  Well, go, prepare yourself. ⌜Knock within.⌝ But hark, 70
  what noise?—
  Heaven give your spirits comfort. ⌜Claudio exits,
  with Officer. Knock within.⌝ By and by!—
  I hope it is some pardon or reprieve
  For the most gentle Claudio. 75

    Enter Duke, ⌜*as a Friar.*⌝

      Welcome, father.

79. **curfew:** the ringing of a bell at a fixed hour (8 or 9 o'clock) in the evening

85. **bitter:** cruel, severe

86. **is paralleled:** i.e., conforms

87. **stroke and line:** i.e., straight course

90. **qualify:** temper, moderate; **mealed:** spotted, stained

92. **this being so:** i.e., his life being so virtuous

94. **gentle:** kind; **Seldom when:** i.e., it is seldom that

95. **steelèd:** hardened

98. **unsisting:** perhaps, unresisting (often emended to "unshifting"); **postern:** small rear or side gate (providing a private entrance)

99. **There . . . stay:** i.e., the person knocking must stay at the gate

100. **called up:** i.e., summoned to get up

A man in gyves. (4.2.11)
From Cesare Vecellio, *Degli habiti antichi et moderni . . .* (1590).

DUKE, ⌜*as Friar*⌝
  The best and wholesom'st spirits of the night
  Envelop you, good provost. Who called here of late?
PROVOST
  None since the curfew rung.
DUKE, ⌜*as Friar*⌝   Not Isabel?   80
PROVOST   No.
DUKE, ⌜*as Friar*⌝   They will, then, ere 't be long.
PROVOST   What comfort is for Claudio?
DUKE, ⌜*as Friar*⌝
  There's some in hope.
PROVOST   It is a bitter deputy.   85
DUKE, ⌜*as Friar*⌝
  Not so, not so. His life is paralleled
  Even with the stroke and line of his great justice.
  He doth with holy abstinence subdue
  That in himself which he spurs on his power
  To qualify in others. Were he mealed with that   90
  Which he corrects, then were he tyrannous,
  But this being so, he's just. ⌜*Knock within.*⌝ Now are
    they come.   ⌜*Provost exits.*⌝
  This is a gentle provost. Seldom when
  The steelèd jailer is the friend of men.   95

        ⌜*Enter Provost. Knocking continues.*⌝

  How now, what noise? That spirit's possessed with
    haste
  That wounds th' unsisting postern with these strokes.
PROVOST
  There he must stay until the officer
  Arise to let him in. He is called up.   100
DUKE, ⌜*as Friar*⌝
  Have you no countermand for Claudio yet,
  But he must die tomorrow?
PROVOST   None, sir, none.

106. **Happily:** i.e., haply, perhaps
109. **siege:** seat
112. **his Lordship's man:** i.e., Angelo's servant
115. **charge:** order
118. **morrow:** i.e., morning
122–23. **Hence ... authority:** perhaps, **an offense** of which the ruler is guilty is quickly pardoned
his: its
125. **the fault's love:** i.e., love of the fault;
friended: i.e., befriended
127. **belike:** perhaps
128. **awakens me:** stirs me to action
129. **putting-on:** incitement
130. **used it:** i.e., done such a thing

DUKE, ⌜*as Friar*⌝
　As near the dawning, provost, as it is,
　You shall hear more ere morning.   105
PROVOST   Happily
　You something know, yet I believe there comes
　No countermand. No such example have we.
　Besides, upon the very siege of justice
　Lord Angelo hath to the public ear   110
　Professed the contrary.

                    Enter a Messenger.

                           This is his ⌜Lordship's⌝ man.
⌜DUKE, *as Friar*⌝　And here comes Claudio's pardon.
MESSENGER, ⌜*giving Provost a paper*⌝　My lord hath sent
　you this note, and by me this further charge: that   115
　you swerve not from the smallest article of it,
　neither in time, matter, or other circumstance.
　Good morrow, for, as I take it, it is almost day.
PROVOST　I shall obey him.   ⌜*Provost reads message.*
                              Messenger exits.⌝
DUKE, ⌜*aside*⌝
　This is his pardon, purchased by such sin   120
　For which the pardoner himself is in.
　Hence hath offense his quick celerity
　When it is borne in high authority.
　When vice makes mercy, mercy's so extended
　That for the fault's love is th' offender friended.   125
　⌜*As Friar.*⌝ Now, sir, what news?
PROVOST　I told you: Lord Angelo, belike thinking me
　remiss in mine office, awakens me with this un-
　wonted putting-on, methinks strangely; for he hath
　not used it before.   130
DUKE, ⌜*as Friar*⌝　Pray you let's hear.
⌜PROVOST, *reads*⌝ *the letter.*
　　Whatsoever you may hear to the contrary, let Claudio
　　be executed by four of the clock, and in the afternoon

137. **deliver:** communicate

137–38. **Thus . . . peril:** a standard legal statement in orders to jailers

143. **bred:** educated, brought up; **is . . . old:** i.e., has been a prisoner for nine years

147. **His:** i.e., Barnardine's; **still wrought:** continually brought about

148. **fact:** crime, deed; **government:** term of office

149. **undoubtful:** certain

150. **apparent:** plainly seen

152. **borne:** conducted

153. **touched:** affected

154–55. **no more . . . as:** i.e., as no more dreadful than

156–57. **insensible of mortality:** i.e., indifferent to death

158. **wants advice:** needs spiritual counsel

159–60. **the liberty of:** unrestricted use of; permission to go anywhere within

168. **beguiles:** deceives

168–69. **in . . . cunning:** i.e., confident of my skill

169. **lay . . . hazard:** i.e., put myself in jeopardy

Barnardine. For my better satisfaction, let me have
Claudio's head sent me by five. Let this be duly 135
performed with a thought that more depends on it
than we must yet deliver. Thus fail not to do your
office, as you will answer it at your peril.
What say you to this, sir?

DUKE, ⌜*as Friar*⌝ What is that Barnardine who is to be 140
  executed in th' afternoon?

PROVOST A Bohemian born, but here nursed up and
  bred; one that is a prisoner nine years old.

DUKE, ⌜*as Friar*⌝ How came it that the absent duke had
  not either delivered him to his liberty, or executed 145
  him? I have heard it was ever his manner to do so.

PROVOST His friends still wrought reprieves for him;
  and indeed his fact, till now in the government of
  Lord Angelo, came not to an undoubtful proof.

DUKE, ⌜*as Friar*⌝ It is now apparent? 150

PROVOST Most manifest, and not denied by himself.

DUKE, ⌜*as Friar*⌝ Hath he borne himself penitently in
  prison? How seems he to be touched?

PROVOST A man that apprehends death no more dreadfully but as a drunken sleep; careless, reckless, and 155
  fearless of what's past, present, or to come; insensible of mortality and desperately mortal.

DUKE, ⌜*as Friar*⌝ He wants advice.

PROVOST He will hear none. He hath evermore had the
  liberty of the prison; give him leave to escape 160
  hence, he would not. Drunk many times a day, if not
  many days entirely drunk. We have very oft awaked
  him, as if to carry him to execution, and showed
  him a seeming warrant for it. It hath not moved him
  at all. 165

DUKE, ⌜*as Friar*⌝ More of him anon. There is written in
  your brow, provost, honesty and constancy; if I read
  it not truly, my ancient skill beguiles me. But in the
  boldness of my cunning, I will lay myself in hazard.

171. **no . . . law:** i.e., no more liable to the law, no guiltier

173. **manifested effect:** clear demonstration

174. **present:** immediate

179. **limited:** fixed, appointed

181. **make . . . Claudio's:** i.e., put myself in the same plight as Claudio; **to cross:** i.e., if I oppose

182. **smallest:** i.e., least

183–84. **warrant you:** guarantee your safety

187. **discover:** distinguish, discern

188. **favor:** appearance, features

190. **tie the beard:** See longer note, page 223.

192. **course:** practice

193. **fall to you upon:** i.e., befall you because of

194. **by . . . profess:** i.e., to whose order I have made my vow

196. **Pardon me:** i.e., I'm sorry

197. **Were you sworn:** i.e., did you take your **oath**

199. **him:** i.e., the duke

201. **avouch:** answer for

204. **Not a resemblance:** i.e., not only a likelihood

205. **coat:** religious habit (See page 196.)

Claudio, whom here you have warrant to execute, is 170
no greater forfeit to the law than Angelo, who hath
sentenced him. To make you understand this in a
manifested effect, I crave but four days' respite, for
the which you are to do me both a present and a
dangerous courtesy. 175

PROVOST Pray, sir, in what?

DUKE, ⌐*as Friar*⌐ In the delaying death.

PROVOST Alack, how may I do it, having the hour
limited, and an express command, under penalty,
to deliver his head in the view of Angelo? I may 180
make my case as Claudio's, to cross this in the
smallest.

DUKE, ⌐*as Friar*⌐ By the vow of mine order I warrant
you, if my instructions may be your guide. Let this
Barnardine be this morning executed and his head 185
borne to Angelo.

PROVOST Angelo hath seen them both and will discover
the favor.

DUKE, ⌐*as Friar*⌐ O, death's a great disguiser, and you
may add to it. Shave the head and tie the beard, and 190
say it was the desire of the penitent to be so bared
before his death. You know the course is common.
If anything fall to you upon this, more than thanks
and good fortune, by the saint whom I profess, I
will plead against it with my life. 195

PROVOST Pardon me, good father, it is against my oath.

DUKE, ⌐*as Friar*⌐ Were you sworn to the Duke or to the
Deputy?

PROVOST To him and to his substitutes.

DUKE, ⌐*as Friar*⌐ You will think you have made no 200
offense if the Duke avouch the justice of your
dealing?

PROVOST But what likelihood is in that?

DUKE, ⌐*as Friar*⌐ Not a resemblance, but a certainty; yet
since I see you fearful, that neither my coat, integri- 205

206. **attempt you:** try to win you over, tempt you

208. **hand:** handwriting

210. **character:** style of writing; **strange:** unfamiliar

214. **overread:** read through

217. **tenor:** substance, drift

218. **entering:** i.e., of his entering

219. **by chance:** i.e., as it falls out, incidentally (wordplay on **perchance** [i.e., perhaps], line 218)

220–21. **th' unfolding . . . shepherd:** i.e., the morning star signals the **shepherd** to release his sheep from the fold

222–23. **All . . . known:** Proverbial: "Everything is easy after it has been done."

224–25. **a present shrift:** i.e., immediate confession and absolution (See page 154.)

225. **a better place:** i.e., heaven; **Yet:** still

226. **amazed:** astounded, stunned; **resolve you:** i.e., answer your doubts

4.3 Barnardine declares himself not ready to die. The provost and the "Friar" agree to spare him temporarily and to send Angelo instead the head of a dead prisoner, Ragozine. Claudio will be safely hidden in a secret prison cell. When Isabella comes to ask about Claudio, the "Friar" tells her that Claudio has been executed, but that the duke is returning and that she will soon be able to get revenge on Angelo.

1. **well:** i.e., widely

2. **house of profession:** See longer note, page 223.

(continued)

ty, nor persuasion can with ease attempt you, I will
go further than I meant, to pluck all fears out of
you. Look you, sir, here is the hand and seal of the
Duke. ⌜*He shows the Provost a paper.*⌝ You know the
character, I doubt not, and the signet is not strange 210
to you.

PROVOST I know them both.

DUKE, ⌜*as Friar*⌝ The contents of this is the return of the
Duke; you shall anon overread it at your pleasure,
where you shall find within these two days he will 215
be here. This is a thing that Angelo knows not, for
he this very day receives letters of strange tenor,
perchance of the Duke's death, perchance entering
into some monastery, but by chance nothing of
what is writ. Look, th' unfolding star calls up the 220
shepherd. Put not yourself into amazement how
these things should be. All difficulties are but easy
when they are known. Call your executioner, and
off with Barnardine's head. I will give him a present
shrift, and advise him for a better place. Yet you are 225
amazed, but this shall absolutely resolve you.
⌜*He gives the Provost the paper.*⌝
Come away; it is almost clear dawn.
⌜*They*⌝ *exit.*

Scene 3
Enter ⌜*Pompey.*⌝

POMPEY I am as well acquainted here as I was in our
house of profession. One would think it were Mistress Overdone's own house, for here be many of
her old customers. First, here's young Master Rash.
He's in for a commodity of brown paper and old 5
ginger, ninescore and seventeen pounds, of which
he made five marks ready money. Marry, then

4. **Rash:** impetuous (Each of the prisoners listed in this speech is given a name that characterizes him. Many, like **Rash**, are imprisoned for debt.)

5–7. **commodity . . . money:** See longer note, page 223.

8. **old women:** Shakespeare's *The Merchant of Venice* (3.1.9–10) also links old women with a love of **ginger.**

9. **Caper:** i.e., a frisky movement, a frolicsome leap

10. **at the suit of:** i.e., having been sued by (with a pun on **suits** in line 11); **Three-pile:** See note to 1.2.32; **mercer:** a dealer in textiles

12. **peaches him:** indicts him as (with a pun on **peach-colored**)

14. **Copper-spur:** See longer note, page 224.; **Starve-lackey:** i.e., a gallant too needy or too miserly to feed his menial servants

14–15. **rapier-and-dagger man:** i.e., quarreler, dueler

15–16. **Drop-heir . . . Pudding:** See longer note, page 224.

16. **Forth-light:** perhaps in error for "forthright," a jousting term; **tilter:** jouster

17. **brave:** gorgeously dressed; **Shoe-tie:** Fancy bows on shoes were associated with travelers' affectations.

18. **Half-can, Pots:** Both are names of drinking tankards.

19. **doers in our trade:** i.e., frequenters of prostitutes

19–20. **for . . . sake:** the cry of poor prisoners begging for food through the prison windows

ginger was not much in request, for the old women
were all dead. Then is there here one Master Caper,
at the suit of Master Three-pile the mercer, for some   10
four suits of peach-colored satin, which now
peaches him a beggar. Then have we here young
Dizzy and young Master Deep-vow, and Master
Copper-spur and Master Starve-lackey the rapier-
and-dagger man, and young Drop-heir that killed   15
lusty Pudding, and Master Forth-light the tilter, and
brave Master Shoe-tie the great traveler, and wild
Half-can that stabbed Pots, and I think forty more,
all great doers in our trade, and are now "for the
Lord's sake."   20

Enter Abhorson.

ABHORSON   Sirrah, bring Barnardine hither.
POMPEY, ⌜*calling*⌝   Master Barnardine, you must rise
and be hanged, Master Barnardine.
ABHORSON, ⌜*calling*⌝   What ho, Barnardine!
BARNARDINE, *within*   A pox o' your throats! Who makes   25
that noise there? What are you?
POMPEY, ⌜*calling to Barnardine offstage*⌝   Your friends,
sir, the hangman. You must be so good, sir, to rise
and be put to death.
BARNARDINE, ⌜*within*⌝   Away, you rogue, away! I am   30
sleepy.
ABHORSON, ⌜*to Pompey*⌝   Tell him he must awake, and
that quickly too.
POMPEY, ⌜*calling*⌝   Pray, Master Barnardine, awake till
you are executed, and sleep afterwards.   35
ABHORSON   Go in to him, and fetch him out.
POMPEY   He is coming, sir, he is coming. I hear his
straw rustle.
ABHORSON   Is the axe upon the block, sirrah?
POMPEY   Very ready, sir.   40

Enter Barnardine.

43–44. **clap . . . prayers:** i.e., start praying right away

48. **betimes:** early

51. **ghostly father:** i.e., father confessor

57. **will . . . me:** i.e., must have more time to prepare myself

58. **shall beat:** i.e., will have to beat; **billets:** sticks of wood

61–62. **shall go:** i.e., are to go

67. **my ward:** i.e., the part of the prison where I stay

68. **gravel heart:** i.e., heart of flint

Condemned prisoners making their last confessions. (3.2.209–10)
From Joost Damhouder, *Praxis rerum criminalium . . .* (1570).

BARNARDINE How now, Abhorson? What's the news
    with you?

ABHORSON Truly, sir, I would desire you to clap into
    your prayers, for, look you, the warrant's come.

BARNARDINE You rogue, I have been drinking all night. 45
    I am not fitted for 't.

POMPEY O, the better, sir, for he that drinks all night
    and is hanged betimes in the morning may sleep the
    sounder all the next day.

Enter Duke, ⌈as a Friar.⌉

ABHORSON, ⌈*to Barnardine*⌉ Look you, sir, here comes 50
    your ghostly father. Do we jest now, think you?

DUKE, ⌈*as Friar, to Barnardine*⌉ Sir, induced by my
    charity, and hearing how hastily you are to depart, I
    am come to advise you, comfort you, and pray with
    you.   55

BARNARDINE Friar, not I. I have been drinking hard all
    night, and I will have more time to prepare me, or
    they shall beat out my brains with billets. I will not
    consent to die this day, that's certain.

DUKE, ⌈*as Friar*⌉ O, sir, you must. And therefore I 60
    beseech you look forward on the journey you shall
    go.

BARNARDINE I swear I will not die today for any man's
    persuasion.

DUKE, ⌈*as Friar*⌉ But hear you—   65

BARNARDINE Not a word. If you have anything to say to
    me, come to my ward, for thence will not I today.
                            He exits.

DUKE, ⌈*as Friar*⌉
  Unfit to live or die. O gravel heart!
  After him, fellows; bring him to the block.
              ⌈*Abhorson and Pompey exit.*⌉

Enter Provost.

71. **unprepared:** i.e., spiritually unprepared; **unmeet:** unfit

72. **transport him:** i.e., send him from this world to the next

78–79. **omit / This reprobate:** i.e., forget about Barnardine **omit:** leave disregarded

84. **Prefixed:** appointed

89. **continue:** preserve, retain

93. **holds:** cells

95. **journal:** daily

96. **yonder generation:** perhaps, those outside the prison **generation:** those alive at this moment

98. **free dependent:** i.e., willing servant

A man being led to prison. (1.2.110–13, 3.2.66)
From Joost Damhouder, *Praxis rerum criminalium* . . . (1570).

PROVOST
　Now, sir, how do you find the prisoner?　　　　　　　70
DUKE, ⌈*as Friar*⌉
　A creature unprepared, unmeet for death,
　And to transport him in the mind he is
　Were damnable.
PROVOST　　　　　　　Here in the prison, father,
　There died this morning of a cruel fever　　　　　　75
　One Ragozine, a most notorious pirate,
　A man of Claudio's years, his beard and head
　Just of his color. What if we do omit
　This reprobate till he were well inclined,
　And satisfy the Deputy with the visage　　　　　　80
　Of Ragozine, more like to Claudio?
DUKE, ⌈*as Friar*⌉
　O, 'tis an accident that heaven provides!
　Dispatch it presently. The hour draws on
　Prefixed by Angelo. See this be done
　And sent according to command, whiles I　　　　　85
　Persuade this rude wretch willingly to die.
PROVOST
　This shall be done, good father, presently.
　But Barnardine must die this afternoon,
　And how shall we continue Claudio,
　To save me from the danger that might come　　　90
　If he were known alive?
DUKE, ⌈*as Friar*⌉　　　　　Let this be done:
　Put them in secret holds, both Barnardine and
　　Claudio.
　Ere twice the sun hath made his journal greeting　95
　To ⌈yonder⌉ generation, you shall find
　Your safety manifested.
PROVOST　I am your free dependent.
DUKE, ⌈*as Friar*⌉
　Quick, dispatch, and send the head to Angelo.
　　　　　　　　　　　　　　　　⌈*Provost*⌉ *exits.*

102. **near at:** i.e., nearly at; or, near

106. **A league:** i.e., three miles

107. **gradation:** step by step advancing; **form:** legal procedure

110. **Convenient:** proper, suitable

111. **commune:** talk (accent on first syllable)

118. **make . . . despair:** i.e., turn her despair into heavenly comfort

Beheading and hanging. (2.1.245)
From [Richard Verstegen,] *Theatre des cruautez . . . de nostre temps . . .* (1607).

⌈DUKE⌉
  Now will I write letters to Angelo—   100
  The Provost he shall bear them—whose contents
  Shall witness to him I am near at home
  And that by great injunctions I am bound
  To enter publicly. Him I'll desire
  To meet me at the consecrated fount   105
  A league below the city; and from thence,
  By cold gradation and well-balanced form,
  We shall proceed with Angelo.

Enter Provost, ⌈*carrying a head.*⌉

PROVOST
  Here is the head. I'll carry it myself.
DUKE, ⌈*as Friar*⌉
  Convenient is it. Make a swift return,   110
  For I would commune with you of such things
  That want no ear but yours.
PROVOST   I'll make all speed.
                              He exits.

ISABELLA, *within*   Peace, ho, be here.
DUKE
  The tongue of Isabel. She's come to know   115
  If yet her brother's pardon be come hither.
  But I will keep her ignorant of her good
  To make her heavenly comforts of despair
  When it is least expected.

Enter Isabella.

ISABELLA   Ho, by your leave.   120
DUKE, ⌈*as Friar*⌉
  Good morning to you, fair and gracious daughter.
ISABELLA
  The better, given me by so holy a man.
  Hath yet the Deputy sent my brother's pardon?

128. **close patience:** i.e., quiet or rigorous self-control

133. **nor hurts:** i.e., neither hurts

135. **Mark:** pay attention to

136. **a faithful verity:** i.e., truth you can rely on

139. **convent:** religious order

140. **instance:** proof; **he:** i.e., the duke

143–44. **pace your wisdom:** i.e., teach your wisdom to walk

146. **your bosom on:** i.e., your desire (inflicted) on

147. **Grace of the Duke:** i.e., the duke's favor; **to your heart:** i.e., in accordance with your heart's desire

Lucio's image of the duke as a "fantastical duke of dark corners." (4.3.170)
From *Le centre de l'amour . . .* [1650?]

DUKE, ⌈*as Friar*⌉
  He hath released him, Isabel, from the world.
  His head is off, and sent to Angelo. 125
ISABELLA
  Nay, but it is not so.
DUKE, ⌈*as Friar*⌉   It is no other.
  Show your wisdom, daughter, in your close patience.
ISABELLA
  O, I will to him and pluck out his eyes!
DUKE, ⌈*as Friar*⌉
  You shall not be admitted to his sight. 130
ISABELLA
  Unhappy Claudio, wretched Isabel,
  Injurious world, most damnèd Angelo!
DUKE, ⌈*as Friar*⌉
  This nor hurts him nor profits you a jot.
  Forbear it, therefore; give your cause to heaven.
  Mark what I say, which you shall find 135
  By every syllable a faithful verity.
  The Duke comes home tomorrow—nay, dry your
    eyes.
  One of our convent, and his confessor,
  Gives me this instance. Already he hath carried 140
  Notice to Escalus and Angelo,
  Who do prepare to meet him at the gates,
  There to give up their power. If you can, pace your
    wisdom
  In that good path that I would wish it go, 145
  And you shall have your bosom on this wretch,
  Grace of the Duke, revenges to your heart,
  And general honor.
ISABELLA   I am directed by you.
DUKE, ⌈*as Friar, showing her a paper*⌉
  This letter, then, to Friar Peter give. 150
  'Tis that he sent me of the Duke's return.
  Say, by this token, I desire his company

154. **perfect him withal:** inform him about completely (**Perfect** is accented on the first syllable.)

155. **to . . . Angelo:** i.e., to Angelo's face

157. **combinèd:** perhaps, bound

158. **Wend you:** i.e., go

159. **fretting:** (1) fretful; (2) corroding, wasting

161. **pervert your course:** i.e., lead you in a wrong direction

165. **patient:** calm; **fain:** compelled

166–67. **for my head:** i.e., for fear of being beheaded

167. **fruitful:** abundant

167–68. **set me to 't:** perhaps, make me lustful (and therefore in danger of the law)

170. **fantastical:** whimsical, capricious (See page 160.)

171. **he had lived:** i.e., Claudio would have lived

172–73. **beholding:** indebted

173–74. **lives . . . them:** (1) i.e., is not represented accurately by them; (2) i.e., is not dependent on them for his reputation

176. **woodman:** womanizer

177. **answer:** pay the penalty for

184. **before him:** i.e., a defendant before his court

At Mariana's house tonight. Her cause and yours
I'll perfect him withal, and he shall bring you
Before the Duke, and to the head of Angelo   155
Accuse him home and home. For my poor self,
I am combinèd by a sacred vow
And shall be absent. Wend you with this letter.
⌈*He hands her the paper.*⌉
Command these fretting waters from your eyes
With a light heart. Trust not my holy order   160
If I pervert your course.—Who's here?

Enter Lucio.

LUCIO Good even, friar, where's the Provost?
DUKE, ⌈*as Friar*⌉ Not within, sir.
LUCIO O, pretty Isabella, I am pale at mine heart to see
thine eyes so red. Thou must be patient. I am fain to 165
dine and sup with water and bran. I dare not for my
head fill my belly. One fruitful meal would set me to
't. But they say the Duke will be here tomorrow. By
my troth, Isabel, I loved thy brother. If the old
fantastical duke of dark corners had been at home, 170
he had lived.   ⌈*Isabella exits.*⌉
DUKE, ⌈*as Friar*⌉ Sir, the Duke is marvelous little beholding to your reports, but the best is, he lives not
in them.
LUCIO Friar, thou knowest not the Duke so well as I do. 175
He's a better woodman than thou tak'st him for.
DUKE, ⌈*as Friar*⌉ Well, you'll answer this one day. Fare
you well.
LUCIO Nay, tarry, I'll go along with thee. I can tell thee
pretty tales of the Duke.   180
DUKE, ⌈*as Friar*⌉ You have told me too many of him
already, sir, if they be true; if not true, none were
enough.
LUCIO I was once before him for getting a wench with
child.   185

187. **forswear it:** deny it under oath

188-89. **rotten medlar:** A **medlar** was a small apple with a cup-shaped eye; it was called in slang an "open-arse." (See page 186.) The word was often associated with prostitutes.

190. **fairer:** perhaps a reference to Lucio's fancy clothes (In the Folio cast-of-characters list, Lucio is called "a fantastique." See page 2.)

194. **burr:** Proverbial: "To stick like burrs."

4.4 Angelo learns of the duke's return. Alone, he expresses his anguish that he has raped Isabella and had Claudio killed.

---

1. **disvouched:** contradicted

2. **other:** each preceding one

3. **uneven:** irregular

4-5. **his . . . tainted:** i.e., he is not suffering from a mental illness

7. **I guess not:** i.e., I cannot guess

8. **in an hour:** i.e., an hour

10. **exhibit:** officially present

12-13. **dispatch:** prompt settlement

13. **deliver:** save; **devices:** contrived complaints

14-15. **stand against:** oppose

17. **Betimes:** early; **call:** call upon

18. **sort and suit:** rank and following

DUKE, ⌜*as Friar*⌝ Did you such a thing?

LUCIO   Yes, marry, did I, but I was fain to forswear it.
They would else have married me to the rotten
medlar.

DUKE, ⌜*as Friar*⌝ Sir, your company is fairer than hon-   190
est. Rest you well.

LUCIO   By my troth, I'll go with thee to the lane's end. If
bawdy talk offend you, we'll have very little of it.
Nay, friar, I am a kind of burr. I shall stick.

They exit.

Scene 4
Enter Angelo and Escalus.

ESCALUS   Every letter he hath writ hath disvouched
other.

ANGELO   In most uneven and distracted manner. His
actions show much like to madness. Pray heaven his
wisdom be not tainted. And why meet him at the   5
gates and ⌜deliver⌝ our authorities there?

ESCALUS   I guess not.

ANGELO   And why should we proclaim it in an hour
before his entering, that if any crave redress of
injustice, they should exhibit their petitions in the   10
street?

ESCALUS   He shows his reason for that: to have a dispatch of complaints, and to deliver us from devices
hereafter, which shall then have no power to stand
against us.   15

ANGELO   Well, I beseech you let it be proclaimed.
Betimes i' th' morn, I'll call you at your house. Give
notice to such men of sort and suit as are to meet
him.

ESCALUS   I shall, sir. Fare you well.   20

22. **unshapes:** i.e., destroys; **unpregnant:** unready, unresourceful

24. **body:** i.e., person

26. **proclaim . . . loss:** i.e., announce her loss of virginity

27. **tongue:** reproach; **dares her no:** i.e., forbids her

28. **bears . . . bulk:** i.e., carries such credibility

30. **confounds:** ruins; **breather:** i.e., speaker (of the **scandal**)

30–31. **He . . . that:** i.e., I would have let Claudio live, except that

31. **riotous youth:** i.e., youthful lack of restraint; **sense:** passion

33. **By:** i.e., because of

34. **With . . . shame:** i.e., through paying such a shameful price; **Would yet:** i.e., I wish even so

35. **grace:** virtue

36. **We . . . not:** See Romans 7.15: "what I would, that do I not; but what I hate, that do I."

4.5 The duke makes plans with Friar Peter, whom he sends away on errands, and then greets Varrius.

1. **deliver me:** i.e., deliver for me
3. **keep:** remember
4. **drift:** aim, scheme
5. **blench:** swerve, deviate
6. **As . . . minister:** i.e., as the affair prompts you
7. **like:** i.e., same
9. **trumpets:** i.e., trumpeters

(continued)

ANGELO   Good night.   ⌜*Escalus*⌝ *exits.*
    This deed unshapes me quite, makes me unpregnant
    And dull to all proceedings. A deflowered maid,
    And by an eminent body that enforced
    The law against it. But that her tender shame   25
    Will not proclaim against her maiden loss,
    How might she tongue me! Yet reason dares her no,
    For my authority bears of a credent bulk
    That no particular scandal once can touch
    But it confounds the breather. He should have lived,   30
    Save that his riotous youth with dangerous sense
    Might in the times to come have ta'en revenge
    By so receiving a dishonored life
    With ransom of such shame. Would yet he had lived.
    Alack, when once our grace we have forgot,   35
    Nothing goes right. We would, and we would not.
                                        He exits.

                        Scene 5
                Enter Duke and Friar Peter.

DUKE, ⌜*giving the Friar papers.*⌝
    These letters at fit time deliver me.
    The Provost knows our purpose and our plot.
    The matter being afoot, keep your instruction
    And hold you ever to our special drift,
    Though sometimes you do blench from this to that   5
    As cause doth minister. Go call at ⌜Flavius'⌝ house
    And tell him where I stay. Give the like notice
    To Valencius, Rowland, and to Crassus,
    And bid them bring the trumpets to the gate.
    But send me Flavius first.   10
FRIAR PETER   It shall be speeded well.   ⌜*He exits.*⌝

                Enter Varrius.

11. **speeded:** concluded (with possible wordplay on "hastened")

14. **gentle:** i.e., good

4.6 Isabella and Mariana discuss the roles they are to play when they meet the duke, who is about to enter the city gates.

------

1. **indirectly:** dishonestly
2. **accuse him so:** i.e., utter charges against Angelo
3. **part:** role; **do it:** i.e., to **speak . . . indirectly**
4. **He:** i.e., Friar Peter (See longer note, page 224.)
8–9. **'tis . . . end:** Proverbial: "Men take bitter potions for sweet health." **physic:** medicine
12. **stand:** place to stand (literally, a place for shooting at game)
13. **have such vantage on:** i.e., have such a superior position in relation to
16. **generous:** i.e., highest born
17. **hent:** arrived at; **near upon:** i.e., soon

DUKE
  I thank thee, Varrius. Thou hast made good haste.
  Come, we will walk. There's other of our friends
  Will greet us here anon. My gentle Varrius.

                                        They exit.

                        Scene 6
              Enter Isabella and Mariana.

ISABELLA
  To speak so indirectly I am loath.
  I would say the truth, but to accuse him so
  That is your part; yet I am advised to do it,
  He says, to veil full purpose.
MARIANA   Be ruled by him.   5
ISABELLA
  Besides, he tells me that, if peradventure
  He speak against me on the adverse side,
  I should not think it strange, for 'tis a physic
  That's bitter to sweet end.
MARIANA   I would Friar Peter—   10

                  Enter ⌈Friar⌉ Peter.

ISABELLA   O peace, the Friar is come.
FRIAR PETER
  Come, I have found you out a stand most fit,
  Where you may have such vantage on the Duke
  He shall not pass you. Twice have the trumpets
     sounded.   15
  The generous and gravest citizens
  Have hent the gates, and very near upon
  The Duke is entering. Therefore hence, away.

                                        They exit.

MEASURE
FOR
MEASURE

ACT 5

5.1 The duke, on his entry, is met by Isabella, who accuses Angelo of violating her chastity. She is arrested for slander. Mariana claims Angelo as her husband. Angelo protests his innocence until the duke, who re-enters disguised as the friar, is stripped of his friar's hood by Lucio. Angelo then confesses his crimes, and is sentenced first to marry Mariana and then to be executed for Claudio's death. (Scene heading continues on page 202.)

---

0 SD. **several:** separate

1. **cousin:** a term used by a sovereign in addressing a noble; **fairly met:** an expression of welcome

2. **Our, we:** the royal plural, used by the duke through much of the scene

5. **thankings:** thanks

8. **Cannot . . . to:** i.e., must give you

9. **more requital:** i.e., greater reward

12. **wards . . . bosom:** i.e., my heart's secret places

13. **characters of brass:** i.e., bronze letters

14. **forted:** fortified; **tooth of time:** Proverbial: "Time devours all things."

15. **razure of oblivion:** i.e., obliteration through being completely forgotten

16. **the subject:** i.e., my subjects

17. **fain:** happily

18. **keep within:** i.e., reside in the heart

ACT 5

Scene 1
Enter Duke, Varrius, Lords, Angelo, Escalus, Lucio,
⌜*Provost, Officers, and*⌝ *Citizens at several doors.*

DUKE, ⌜*to Angelo*⌝
  My very worthy cousin, fairly met.
  ⌜*To Escalus.*⌝ Our old and faithful friend, we are
    glad to see you.
ANGELO, ESCALUS
  Happy return be to your royal Grace.
DUKE
  Many and hearty thankings to you both.   5
  We have made inquiry of you, and we hear
  Such goodness of your justice that our soul
  Cannot but yield you forth to public thanks,
  Forerunning more requital.
ANGELO You make my bonds still greater.   10
DUKE
  O, your desert speaks loud, and I should wrong it
  To lock it in the wards of covert bosom
  When it deserves with characters of brass
  A forted residence 'gainst the tooth of time
  And razure of oblivion. Give ⌜me⌝ your hand   15
  And let the subject see, to make them know
  That outward courtesies would fain proclaim
  Favors that keep within.—Come, Escalus,

173

20. **supporters:** attendants as in a processional (with wordplay on "helpers, assistants," and "heraldic figures that appear to hold up a shield")

22. **Vail your regard:** i.e., look down

30. **Reveal yourself:** i.e., make your complaint known

39. **Cut off:** i.e., executed; **by course of:** i.e., in accordance with the procedures of

43. **Angelo's forsworn:** i.e., Angelo has perjured himself (or, has broken his oath)

45. **adulterous thief:** This charge points to Angelo's betrothal to Mariana, supposedly violated in the **adulterous** meeting with Isabella, and to the theft of Isabella's virginity.

Justice. (1.3.30; 2.2.128; 5.1.27, 39, 266)
From Thomas Peyton, *The glasse of time . . .* (1620).

You must walk by us on our other hand.
And good supporters are you.   20

Enter ⌈Friar⌉ Peter and Isabella.

FRIAR PETER, ⌈*to Isabella*⌉
　Now is your time. Speak loud, and kneel before him.
ISABELLA, ⌈*kneeling*⌉
　Justice, O royal duke. Vail your regard
　Upon a wronged—I would fain have said, a maid.
　O worthy prince, dishonor not your eye
　By throwing it on any other object   25
　Till you have heard me in my true complaint
　And given me justice, justice, justice, justice.
DUKE
　Relate your wrongs. In what, by whom? Be brief.
　Here is Lord Angelo shall give you justice.
　Reveal yourself to him.   30
ISABELLA　　　　　　　　　　O worthy duke,
　You bid me seek redemption of the devil.
　Hear me yourself, for that which I must speak
　Must either punish me, not being believed,
　Or wring redress from you. Hear me, O hear me,   35
　　here.
ANGELO
　My lord, her wits, I fear me, are not firm.
　She hath been a suitor to me for her brother
　Cut off by course of justice.
ISABELLA, ⌈*standing*⌉　　　　By course of justice!   40
ANGELO
　And she will speak most bitterly and strange.
ISABELLA
　Most strange, but yet most truly will I speak.
　That Angelo's forsworn, is it not strange?
　That Angelo's a murderer, is 't not strange?
　That Angelo is an adulterous thief,   45

50. **Than this:** i.e., than that this; **is all as true:** i.e., is just as true

51. **truth is truth:** proverbial

54. **in . . . sense:** i.e., from a diseased mind

55. **conjure:** implore

57. **with that opinion:** i.e., because you believe

58. **Make not:** i.e., do not regard as

60. **but seems unlike:** i.e., merely seems unlikely

61. **But one:** i.e., but that one who is; **caitiff:** villain; **on the ground:** i.e., living

62. **shy:** i.e., reserved; **absolute:** perfect

64. **dressings:** robes of office; **caracts:** badges of rank; **forms:** ceremonies

70. **oddest . . . sense:** i.e., most remarkable rational structure

71. **a dependency . . . thing:** i.e., a coherent logical sequence

74. **on that:** i.e., on my (presumed) madness

74–75. **banish . . . inequality:** perhaps, dismiss rational statements because of a disparity (between them and what people think)

77. **And hide:** i.e., and let **truth hide** (the **false**); **seems:** i.e., that seems

An hypocrite, a virgin-violator,
Is it not strange, and strange?
DUKE   Nay, it is ten times strange.
ISABELLA
It is not truer he is Angelo
Than this is all as true as it is strange.   50
Nay, it is ten times true, for truth is truth
To th' end of reck'ning.
DUKE   Away with her. Poor soul,
She speaks this in th' infirmity of sense.
ISABELLA
O prince, I conjure thee, as thou believest   55
There is another comfort than this world,
That thou neglect me not with that opinion
That I am touched with madness. Make not
     impossible
That which but seems unlike. 'Tis not impossible   60
But one, the wicked'st caitiff on the ground,
May seem as shy, as grave, as just, as absolute
As Angelo. Even so may Angelo,
In all his dressings, caracts, titles, forms,
Be an archvillain. Believe it, royal prince,   65
If he be less, he's nothing, but he's more,
Had I more name for badness.
DUKE   By mine honesty,
If she be mad—as I believe no other—
Her madness hath the oddest frame of sense,   70
Such a dependency of thing on thing,
As e'er I heard in madness.
ISABELLA   O gracious duke,
Harp not on that; nor do not banish reason
For inequality, but let your reason serve   75
To make the truth appear where it seems hid,
And hide the false seems true.
DUKE   Many that are not mad
Have, sure, more lack of reason. What would you
     say?   80

84. **in probation of a sisterhood:** See note to 1.2.176.

86. **As then:** i.e., being at that time

87. **an 't like:** i.e., if it please

88. **desired:** requested

94. **Nor wished:** i.e., nor was I commanded; **hold my peace:** i.e., stay silent

97. **business:** difficulty; **for yourself:** i.e., that involves you

98. **perfect:** i.e., letter-perfect

99. **warrant:** assure (The duke's response plays on **warrant** as a judicial writ for an arrest.)

101. **somewhat:** something

109. **to the matter:** to the point, relevant

A sea-maid or mermaid. (3.2.109)
From August Casimir Redel, *Apophtegmata symbolica* . . . [n.d.]

ISABELLA
  I am the sister of one Claudio,
  Condemned upon the act of fornication
  To lose his head, condemned by Angelo.
  I, in probation of a sisterhood,
  Was sent to by my brother; one Lucio   85
  As then the messenger—
LUCIO, ⌈*to Duke*⌉ That's I, an 't like your Grace.
  I came to her from Claudio and desired her
  To try her gracious fortune with Lord Angelo
  For her poor brother's pardon.   90
ISABELLA, ⌈*to Duke*⌉   That's he indeed.
DUKE, ⌈*to Lucio*⌉
  You were not bid to speak.
LUCIO   No, my good lord,
  Nor wished to hold my peace.
DUKE   I wish you now, then. 95
  Pray you take note of it, and when you have
  A business for yourself, pray heaven you then
  Be perfect.
LUCIO   I warrant your Honor.
DUKE
  The warrant's for yourself. Take heed to 't.   100
ISABELLA
  This gentleman told somewhat of my tale.
LUCIO   Right.
DUKE
  It may be right, but you are i' the wrong
  To speak before your time.—Proceed.
ISABELLA   I went 105
  To this pernicious caitiff deputy—
DUKE
  That's somewhat madly spoken.
ISABELLA   Pardon it;
  The phrase is to the matter.

110. **Mended again:** i.e., once again set right

111. **set . . . by:** i.e., to put aside the narrative, which is here unnecessary

113. **refelled:** refuted; rejected; repelled

117. **concupiscible:** vehemently desirous

118. **debatement:** argument, debate

119. **remorse:** pity; **confutes:** overcomes, silences

120. **betimes:** early

121. **surfeiting:** grown sick through overindulgence

124. **like:** probable

125. **fond:** foolish

128. **practice:** deception, stratagem

129. **it imports no reason:** i.e., it is not rational

130. **pursue:** i.e., persecute

131. **proper:** i.e., belonging

132. **weighed:** i.e., judged

133. **set you on:** incited you

137. **ministers above:** i.e., angels

139. **Unfold:** bring to light

140. **In countenance:** (1) by patronage or authority; (2) through outward show, or facial expression, or self-confidence

DUKE
　Mended again. The matter; proceed.　　　　　　　110
ISABELLA
　In brief, to set the needless process by:
　How I persuaded, how I prayed and kneeled,
　How he refelled me, and how I replied—
　For this was of much length—the vile conclusion
　I now begin with grief and shame to utter.　　　115
　He would not, but by gift of my chaste body
　To his concupiscible intemperate lust,
　Release my brother; and after much debatement,
　My sisterly remorse confutes mine honor,
　And I did yield to him. But the next morn betimes,　120
　His purpose surfeiting, he sends a warrant
　For my poor brother's head.
DUKE　　　　　　　　　　This is most likely!
ISABELLA
　O, that it were as like as it is true!
DUKE
　By heaven, fond wretch, thou know'st not what　125
　　thou speak'st,
　Or else thou art suborned against his honor
　In hateful practice. First, his integrity
　Stands without blemish; next, it imports no reason
　That with such vehemency he should pursue　　130
　Faults proper to himself. If he had so offended,
　He would have weighed thy brother by himself
　And not have cut him off. Someone hath set you on.
　Confess the truth, and say by whose advice
　Thou cam'st here to complain.　　　　　　　135
ISABELLA　　　　　　　　　And is this all?
　Then, O you blessèd ministers above,
　Keep me in patience, and with ripened time
　Unfold the evil which is here wrapped up
　In countenance. Heaven shield your Grace from　140
　　woe,

143. **fain:** gladly

145. **blasting:** blighting, withering

146. **needs:** necessarily, inevitably; **practice:** plot, trick

148. **would:** wish; **Lodowick:** the name used by the duke in his disguise as a friar

149. **ghostly:** spiritual (with perhaps a pun on "shadowy, insubstantial"); **belike:** in all likelihood

151. **lay:** i.e., secular, a layman

153. **In your retirement:** i.e., when you were away

154. **This':** i.e., this is

158. **saucy:** insolent

162. **abused:** deceived, imposed upon

164. **touch or soil:** i.e., sexual contact or moral stain

165. **ungot:** i.e., unborn (literally, unbegotten, never conceived)

As I, thus wrongèd, hence unbelievèd go.
DUKE
I know you'd fain be gone.—An officer!
⌐*An Officer comes forward.*⌐
To prison with her. Shall we thus permit
A blasting and a scandalous breath to fall   145
On him so near us? This needs must be a practice.—
Who knew of your intent and coming hither?
ISABELLA
One that I would were here, Friar Lodowick.
⌐*Officer exits with Isabella.*⌐
DUKE
A ghostly father, belike. Who knows that Lodowick?
LUCIO
My lord, I know him. 'Tis a meddling friar.   150
I do not like the man. Had he been lay, my lord,
For certain words he spake against your Grace
In your retirement, I had swinged him soundly.
DUKE
Words against me? This' a good friar, belike.
And to set on this wretched woman here   155
Against our substitute! Let this friar be found.
LUCIO
But yesternight, my lord, she and that friar,
I saw them at the prison. A saucy friar,
A very scurvy fellow.
FRIAR PETER, ⌐*to Duke*⌐ Blessed be your royal Grace.   160
I have stood by, my lord, and I have heard
Your royal ear abused. First hath this woman
Most wrongfully accused your substitute,
Who is as free from touch or soil with her
As she from one ungot.   165
DUKE   We did believe no less.
Know you that Friar Lodowick that she speaks of?
FRIAR PETER
I know him for a man divine and holy,

169. **temporary meddler:** i.e., meddler in temporal affairs

176. **his mere request:** i.e., a request from him alone

179. **his mouth:** i.e., the mouth of Friar Lodowick

181. **probation:** proof; **make up full clear:** i.e., supply as fully evident

182. **convented:** summoned

183. **justify:** vindicate

184. **vulgarly:** publicly

185. **to her eyes:** i.e., to her face

194. **after:** afterward

Death with a Fool. (3.1.11)
From *Todten-Tantz* . . . (1696).

Not scurvy, nor a temporary meddler,
As he's reported by this gentleman;   170
And on my trust, a man that never yet
Did, as he vouches, misreport your Grace.

LUCIO
My lord, most villainously, believe it.

FRIAR PETER
Well, he in time may come to clear himself;
But at this instant he is sick, my lord,   175
Of a strange fever. Upon his mere request,
Being come to knowledge that there was complaint
Intended 'gainst Lord Angelo, came I hither
To speak as from his mouth, what he doth know
Is true and false, and what he with his oath   180
And all probation will make up full clear
Whensoever he's convented. First, for this woman,
To justify this worthy nobleman,
So vulgarly and personally accused,
Her shall you hear disprovèd to her eyes   185
Till she herself confess it.

DUKE   Good friar, let's hear it.—
Do you not smile at this, Lord Angelo?
O heaven, the vanity of wretched fools!—
Give us some seats.—Come, cousin Angelo,   190
In this I'll be impartial. Be you judge
Of your own cause.   ⌜*Duke and Angelo are seated.*⌝

Enter Mariana, ⌜*veiled.*⌝

                     Is this the witness, friar?
First, let her show ⌜her⌝ face, and after speak.

MARIANA
Pardon, my lord, I will not show my face   195
Until my husband bid me.

DUKE   What, are you married?

MARIANA   No, my lord.

DUKE   Are you a maid?

203–4. **neither . . . wife:** Proverbial: "She is neither maid, wife, nor widow" (often used as the definition of a whore).

205. **punk:** prostitute

212, 213. **known, knew:** had sexual relations with

218. **witness for:** evidence on behalf of

222. **with such a time:** i.e., at the very time

224. **effect:** outward manifestation

228. **just:** i.e., exactly

231. **abuse:** (1) deception; (2) delusion; (3) injury, wrongdoing

Medlars. (4.3.189)
From *The grete herball* [1529].

MARIANA   No, my lord.   200
DUKE   A widow, then?
MARIANA   Neither, my lord.
DUKE   Why you are nothing, then, neither maid, widow,
   nor wife?
LUCIO   My lord, she may be a punk, for many of them   205
   are neither maid, widow, nor wife.
DUKE   Silence that fellow. I would he had some cause
   to prattle for himself.
LUCIO   Well, my lord.
MARIANA
   My lord, I do confess I ne'er was married,   210
   And I confess besides I am no maid.
   I have known my husband, yet my husband
   Knows not that ever he knew me.
LUCIO   He was drunk, then, my lord; it can be no better.
DUKE   For the benefit of silence, would thou wert so   215
   too.
LUCIO   Well, my lord.
DUKE
   This is no witness for Lord Angelo.
MARIANA   Now I come to 't, my lord.
   She that accuses him of fornication   220
   In selfsame manner doth accuse my husband,
   And charges him, my lord, with such a time
   When, I'll depose, I had him in mine arms
   With all th' effect of love.
ANGELO   Charges she more than me?   225
MARIANA   Not that I know.
DUKE   No? You say your husband.
MARIANA
   Why, just, my lord, and that is Angelo,
   Who thinks he knows that he ne'er knew my body,
   But knows, he thinks, that he knows Isabel's.   230
ANGELO
   This is a strange abuse. Let's see thy face.

237. **match:** appointment (with perhaps some wordplay on "the action of marrying")

238. **supply:** satisfy

245. **since:** ago

248. **for that:** i.e., because; **proportions:** i.e., marriage portion

249. **composition:** i.e., (our) agreement; **in chief:** i.e., chiefly

250. **disvalued:** diminished in value

251. **In levity:** i.e., because of unbecoming conduct; **Since . . . years:** i.e., from five years ago until now

260. **But . . . gone:** i.e., only this past Tuesday night

263. **confixèd:** fixed firmly

Astrologers assessing "skyey influences." (3.1.9)
From Jakob Rüff, *De conceptu et generatione hominis . . .* (1580).

MARIANA
    My husband bids me. Now I will unmask.
                        ⌜*She removes her veil.*⌝
    This is that face, thou cruel Angelo,
    Which once thou swor'st was worth the looking on.
    This is the hand which, with a vowed contract,   235
    Was fast belocked in thine. This is the body
    That took away the match from Isabel
    And did supply thee at thy garden house
    In her imagined person.
DUKE, ⌜*to Angelo*⌝ Know you this woman?   240
LUCIO   Carnally, she says.
DUKE   Sirrah, no more.
LUCIO   Enough, my lord.
ANGELO
    My lord, I must confess I know this woman,
    And five years since there was some speech of   245
        marriage
    Betwixt myself and her, which was broke off,
    Partly for that her promisèd proportions
    Came short of composition, but in chief
    For that her reputation was disvalued   250
    In levity. Since which time of five years
    I never spake with her, saw her, nor heard from her,
    Upon my faith and honor.
MARIANA, ⌜*kneeling, to Duke*⌝ Noble prince,
    As there comes light from heaven and words from   255
        breath,
    As there is sense in truth and truth in virtue,
    I am affianced this man's wife as strongly
    As words could make up vows. And, my good lord,
    But Tuesday night last gone in 's garden house   260
    He knew me as a wife. As this is true,
    Let me in safety raise me from my knees,
    Or else forever be confixèd here
    A marble monument.

266. **scope of:** i.e., freedom (to employ)

268. **informal:** perhaps, mentally disturbed

269. **more mightier member:** i.e., more powerful person

271. **practice:** plot, trick

275. **Compact:** in league

280. **That's sealed in approbation:** i.e., who has been ratified (as if through the affixing of a seal) in my public statement of approval

281. **cousin:** i.e., Angelo (See note to 5.1.1.); **kind pains:** i.e., best efforts

282. **abuse:** deception

290. **well-warranted:** i.e., approved by good authority

292. **forth:** through to the end

293–94. **Do . . . chastisement:** i.e., deal with the offenses against you through imposing whatever punishment seems best to you   **seems you:** i.e., seems to you

296. **Well determined upon:** i.e., made a careful decision about

297. **throughly:** thoroughly, completely

ANGELO   I did but smile till now.   265
  Now, good my lord, give me the scope of justice.
  My patience here is touched. I do perceive
  These poor informal women are no more
  But instruments of some more mightier member
  That sets them on. Let me have way, my lord,   270
  To find this practice out.
DUKE   Ay, with my heart,
  And punish them to your height of pleasure.—
  Thou foolish friar, and thou pernicious woman,
  Compact with her that's gone, think'st thou thy   275
    oaths,
  Though they would swear down each particular
    saint,
  Were testimonies against his worth and credit
  That's sealed in approbation?—You, Lord Escalus,   280
  Sit with my cousin; lend him your kind pains
  To find out this abuse, whence 'tis derived.
                ⌜*The Duke rises. Escalus is seated.*⌝
  There is another friar that set them on.
  Let him be sent for.
FRIAR PETER
  Would he were here, my lord, for he indeed   285
  Hath set the women on to this complaint;
  Your provost knows the place where he abides,
  And he may fetch him.
DUKE, ⌜*to Provost*⌝   Go, do it instantly.
                                     ⌜*Provost exits.*⌝
  ⌜*To Angelo.*⌝ And you, my noble and well-warranted   290
    cousin,
  Whom it concerns to hear this matter forth,
  Do with your injuries as seems you best
  In any chastisement. I for a while
  Will leave you; but stir not you till you have   295
  Well determined upon these slanderers.
ESCALUS   My lord, we'll do it throughly.   ⌜*Duke*⌝ *exits.*

300. **Cucullus . . . monachum:** Proverbial: "A cowl does not make a monk."

301. **clothes:** i.e., friar's habit

304. **enforce:** urge

305. **notable:** notorious

313. **handled:** i.e., stroked, fondled

316. **darkly:** i.e., cryptically, mysteriously (Lucio responds as if the word were intended to mean "privately" or "in the dark.")

317. **light:** wanton (The sentence was a common saying.)

319. **denies:** i.e., who denies

322. **In . . . time:** i.e., at exactly the right moment

324. **Mum:** Proverbial: "I will say nought but mum."

329. **How?:** an interjection meaning "What?" or "What!"

"Pressing to death." (5.1.596)
From *The life and death of Griffin Flood informer . . .* (1623).

Signior Lucio, did not you say you knew that Friar
Lodowick to be a dishonest person?

LUCIO *Cucullus non facit monachum*, honest in nothing 300
but in his clothes, and one that hath spoke most
villainous speeches of the Duke.

ESCALUS We shall entreat you to abide here till he
come, and enforce them against him. We shall find
this friar a notable fellow. 305

LUCIO As any in Vienna, on my word.

ESCALUS Call that same Isabel here once again. I would
speak with her. ⌜*An Attendant exits.*⌝
⌜*To Angelo.*⌝ Pray you, my lord, give me leave to
question. You shall see how I'll handle her. 310

LUCIO Not better than he, by her own report.

ESCALUS Say you?

LUCIO Marry, sir, I think, if you handled her privately,
she would sooner confess; perchance publicly she'll
be ashamed. 315

ESCALUS I will go darkly to work with her.

LUCIO That's the way, for women are light at midnight.

Enter Duke ⌜*as a Friar,*⌝ *Provost,* ⌜*and*⌝ *Isabella,*
⌜*with Officers.*⌝

ESCALUS, ⌜*to Isabella*⌝ Come on, mistress. Here's a gentlewoman denies all that you have said.

LUCIO My lord, here comes the rascal I spoke of, here 320
with the Provost.

ESCALUS In very good time. Speak not you to him till
we call upon you.

LUCIO Mum.

ESCALUS, ⌜*to disguised Duke*⌝ Come, sir, did you set 325
these women on to slander Lord Angelo? They have
confessed you did.

DUKE, ⌜*as Friar*⌝
'Tis false.

ESCALUS How? Know you where you are?

334. **Look you:** i.e., see that you

336. **seek . . . fox:** Proverbial: "Do not let the wolf guard the sheep." (Shakespeare standardly changes "wolf" to "fox" in his use of this proverb.)

337. **Good . . . redress:** i.e., farewell to any hope of help for you

339. **retort:** i.e., turn back (to Angelo); **manifest:** clear, open; **appeal:** accusation, charge

341. **Which:** i.e., whom

343. **unreverend:** irreverent; **unhallowed:** impious, wicked

345. **mouth:** i.e., language

346. **in the witness . . . ear:** i.e., with his own **ear** as **witness**

347. **glance:** i.e., move obliquely, shift the attack

348. **tax him with:** i.e., accuse him of

349. **rack:** an instrument of torture on which a victim's limbs were torn apart (See page 134.)

349–50. **touse him:** i.e., pull him apart

356. **Nor here provincial:** i.e., not a member of this ecclesiastical province

359. **it o'errun the stew:** i.e., the caldron boils over (with possible wordplay on **stew** as "brothel")

360. **countenanced:** encouraged, favored

DUKE, ⌜*as Friar*⌝
  Respect to your great place, and let the devil   330
  Be sometime honored for his burning throne.
  Where is the Duke? 'Tis he should hear me speak.
ESCALUS
  The Duke's in us, and we will hear you speak.
  Look you speak justly.
DUKE, ⌜*as Friar*⌝
  Boldly, at least.—But, O, poor souls,   335
  Come you to seek the lamb here of the fox?
  Good night to your redress. Is the Duke gone?
  Then is your cause gone too. The Duke's unjust
  Thus to retort your manifest appeal,
  And put your trial in the villain's mouth   340
  Which here you come to accuse.
LUCIO
  This is the rascal; this is he I spoke of.
ESCALUS, ⌜*to disguised Duke*⌝
  Why, thou unreverend and unhallowed friar,
  Is 't not enough thou hast suborned these women
  To accuse this worthy man, but, in foul mouth   345
  And in the witness of his proper ear,
  To call him villain? And then to glance from him
  To th' Duke himself, to tax him with injustice?—
  Take him hence. To th' rack with him. We'll touse
    ⌜him⌝   350
  Joint by joint, but we will know his purpose.
  What? "Unjust"?
DUKE, ⌜*as Friar*⌝   Be not so hot. The Duke
  Dare no more stretch this finger of mine than he
  Dare rack his own. His subject am I not,   355
  Nor here provincial. My business in this state
  Made me a looker-on here in Vienna,
  Where I have seen corruption boil and bubble
  Till it o'errun the stew. Laws for all faults,
  But faults so countenanced that the strong statutes   360

361. **forfeits . . . shop:** i.e., penalties for misbehavior (listed but with no means for enforcement)

362. **As . . . mark:** i.e., as much mocked as heeded

367. **Goodman:** indicates a social rank below that of a gentleman; **Baldpate:** A friar would normally have the crown of his head shaved. (The duke's head is covered by his friar's cowl.)

374. **notedly:** especially, particularly

375. **fleshmonger:** fornicator

385. **close:** (1) conclude; or (2) come to terms

387. **withal:** i.e., with

389. **bolts:** leg-irons

391. **giglets:** lewd women

391–92. **confederate companion:** i.e., fellow in league with them (i.e., Friar Peter)

393. **Stay:** wait

394. **he:** i.e., "Friar Lodowick"; **him:** i.e., the provost

A Franciscan friar. (1.3.50)
From Niccolo Catalano, *Fiume del terrestre paradiso . . .* (1652).

Stand like the forfeits in a barber's shop,
As much in mock as mark.
ESCALUS   Slander to th' state!
Away with him to prison.
ANGELO, ⌜to Lucio⌝
What can you vouch against him, Signior Lucio?   365
Is this the man that you did tell us of?
LUCIO 'Tis he, my lord.—Come hither, Goodman Bald-
pate. Do you know me?
DUKE, ⌜as Friar⌝ I remember you, sir, by the sound of
your voice. I met you at the prison in the absence of   370
the Duke.
LUCIO O, did you so? And do you remember what you
said of the Duke?
DUKE, ⌜as Friar⌝ Most notedly, sir.
LUCIO Do you so, sir? And was the Duke a fleshmonger,   375
a fool, and a coward, as you then reported him to
be?
DUKE, ⌜as Friar⌝ You must, sir, change persons with me
ere you make that my report. You indeed spoke so
of him, and much more, much worse.   380
LUCIO O, thou damnable fellow! Did not I pluck thee by
the nose for thy speeches?
DUKE, ⌜as Friar⌝ I protest I love the Duke as I love
myself.
ANGELO Hark how the villain would close now, after   385
his treasonable abuses!
ESCALUS Such a fellow is not to be talked withal. Away
with him to prison. Where is the Provost? ⌜Provost
comes forward.⌝ Away with him to prison. Lay bolts
enough upon him. Let him speak no more. Away   390
with those giglets too, and with the other confederate companion.
                    ⌜Provost seizes the disguised Duke.⌝
DUKE, ⌜as Friar⌝ Stay, sir, stay awhile.
ANGELO What, resists he?—Help him, Lucio.
LUCIO, ⌜to the disguised Duke⌝ Come, sir, come, sir,   395

397. **hooded:** covered with a hood

398. **sheep-biting:** (1) thieving; (2) whoremongering

399. **be hanged an hour:** i.e., be hanged; **Will 't not off:** i.e., won't the hood come off

400. **mad'st:** created

401. **these gentle three:** Isabella, Mariana, and Friar Peter

407. **of him:** i.e., from Angelo

409. **or word:** i.e., either word

410. **office:** service

415. **undiscernible:** i.e., beyond being discerned or perceived

417. **my passes:** i.e., what I have done (perhaps with a suggestion of the word "trespasses")

418. **session:** i.e., trial, judicial sitting

420. **sequent death:** i.e., death following as a consequence

come, sir. Foh, sir! Why you bald-pated, lying rascal,
you must be hooded, must you? Show your knave's
visage, with a pox to you! Show your sheep-biting
face, and be hanged an hour! Will 't not off?
⌈*He pulls off the friar's hood, and reveals the Duke.
Angelo and Escalus stand.*⌉

DUKE
Thou art the first knave that e'er mad'st a duke.— 400
First, provost, let me bail these gentle three.
⌈*To Lucio.*⌉ Sneak not away, sir, for the friar and
    you
Must have a word anon.—Lay hold on him.

LUCIO   This may prove worse than hanging. 405

DUKE, ⌈*to Escalus*⌉
What you have spoke I pardon. Sit you down.
We'll borrow place of him. ⌈*To Angelo.*⌉ Sir, by your
    leave.
Hast thou or word, or wit, or impudence
That yet can do thee office? If thou hast, 410
Rely upon it till my tale be heard,
And hold no longer out.

ANGELO   O my dread lord,
I should be guiltier than my guiltiness
To think I can be undiscernible, 415
When I perceive your Grace, like power divine,
Hath looked upon my passes. Then, good prince,
No longer session hold upon my shame,
But let my trial be mine own confession.
Immediate sentence then and sequent death 420
Is all the grace I beg.

DUKE   Come hither, Mariana.
                ⌈*Mariana stands and comes forward.*⌉
⌈*To Angelo.*⌉ Say, wast thou e'er contracted to this
    woman?

ANGELO   I was, my lord. 425

DUKE
Go take her hence and marry her instantly.

428. **consummate:** completed

431. **strangeness of it:** i.e., strange form it took

434. **Advertising:** attentive

435. **habit:** clothing

436. **Attorneyed at:** i.e., serving as an agent in

438. **pained:** i.e., troubled

439. **unknown:** undisclosed

442. **free:** generous

443. **sits at:** i.e., weighs on

446. **remonstrance:** demonstration

450. **brained:** i.e., destroyed (as in killing by knocking out the brains)

453. **So . . . brother:** i.e., that your brother has that happiness (of not fearing death)

456. **salt:** lecherous; **yet:** notwithstanding (i.e., despite the fact that he did wrong only in **imagination**)

⌐*To Friar Peter.*⌐ Do you the office, friar, which
    consummate,
Return him here again.—Go with him, provost.
        ⌐*Angelo, Mariana, Friar Peter, and Provost*⌐ *exit.*

ESCALUS
    My lord, I am more amazed at his dishonor   430
    Than at the strangeness of it.
DUKE   Come hither, Isabel.
    Your friar is now your prince. As I was then
    Advertising and holy to your business,
    Not changing heart with habit, I am still   435
    Attorneyed at your service.
ISABELLA   O, give me pardon
    That I, your vassal, have employed and pained
    Your unknown sovereignty.
DUKE   You are pardoned,   440
    Isabel.
    And now, dear maid, be you as free to us.
    Your brother's death, I know, sits at your heart,
    And you may marvel why I obscured myself,
    Laboring to save his life, and would not rather   445
    Make rash remonstrance of my hidden power
    Than let him so be lost. O most kind maid,
    It was the swift celerity of his death,
    Which I did think with slower foot came on,
    That brained my purpose. But peace be with him.   450
    That life is better life past fearing death
    Than that which lives to fear. Make it your comfort,
    So happy is your brother.
ISABELLA   I do, my lord.

Enter Angelo, ⌐*Mariana,*⌐ ⌐*Friar*⌐ *Peter,* ⌐*and*⌐ *Provost.*

DUKE
    For this new-married man approaching here,   455
    Whose salt imagination yet hath wronged
    Your well-defended honor, you must pardon

458. **adjudged:** condemned

460. **criminal . . . violation:** i.e., doubly criminal in violation

461. **promise-breach:** See longer note to 5.1.460–62, page 224.

463. **mercy of the law:** See lines 2.2.127–28: "Yet show some pity." "I show it most of all when I show justice."

464. **his proper:** i.e., its own

465. **death for death:** a proverbial way of stating the doctrine of retribution, "an eye for an eye" (Deuteronomy 19.21)

466. **still pays:** i.e., always repays; **leisure:** i.e., deliberation

467. **Like . . . like:** Proverbial: "Like will to like." **quit:** reward

467–68. **measure . . . measure:** See Historical Background 4, "Measure for Measure," pages 235–38.

471. **vantage:** benefit

473. **like:** equal

5.1 (continued) Mariana begs for Angelo's life and persuades Isabella to join in the plea, despite Claudio's death. Isabella begs the duke to spare Angelo. The duke refuses and has Barnardine and another prisoner brought in. When this second prisoner is unmuffled, he is revealed to be Claudio. Angelo's death sentence is revoked, Lucio is sentenced to marry Kate Keepdown, and Claudio is instructed to marry Juliet. The duke offers his hand in marriage to Isabella.

(continued)

For Mariana's sake. But as he adjudged your
  brother—
Being criminal in double violation   460
Of sacred chastity and of promise-breach
Thereon dependent for your brother's life—
The very mercy of the law cries out
Most audible, even from his proper tongue,
"An Angelo for Claudio, death for death."   465
Haste still pays haste, and leisure answers leisure;
Like doth quit like, and measure still for
  measure.—
Then, Angelo, thy fault's thus manifested,
Which, though thou wouldst deny, denies thee   470
  vantage.
We do condemn thee to the very block
Where Claudio stooped to death, and with like
  haste.—
Away with him.   475

MARIANA   O my most gracious lord,
  I hope you will not mock me with a husband.

DUKE
  It is your husband mocked you with a husband.
  Consenting to the safeguard of your honor,
  I thought your marriage fit. Else imputation,   480
  For that he knew you, might reproach your life
  And choke your good to come. For his possessions,
  Although by ⌜confiscation⌝ they are ours,
  We do instate and widow you with all
  To buy you a better husband.   485

MARIANA   O my dear lord,
  I crave no other nor no better man.

DUKE
  Never crave him. We are definitive.

MARIANA, ⌜kneeling⌝
  Gentle my liege—

DUKE   You do but lose your labor.—   490

477. **mock:** delude, tantalize

478. **husband mocked:** i.e., husband who mocked

479. **Consenting:** i.e., in accord with; **safeguard:** protection

480–81. **Else . . . knew you:** otherwise the accusation that he had had intercourse with you

482. **choke:** obstruct, prevent; **For:** i.e., as for

484. **instate:** endow; **widow:** provide a widow's right; **with all:** i.e., with his **possessions**

488. **We are definitive:** i.e., my decision is final

489. **Gentle my liege:** i.e., my gracious sovereign

494. **Lend me your knees:** i.e., kneel with me

496. **importune:** implore, beg (accent on second syllable)

497. **in mercy of this fact:** i.e., to plead for mercy for this crime

498. **his pavèd bed:** i.e., the stone slab over his burial place

501. **yet:** nevertheless; **but:** only

504. **the most:** i.e., the most part

515. **For:** i.e., as for

516. **o'ertake:** (1) overtake along **the way** (line 518); (2) accomplish

518. **Thoughts . . . subjects:** i.e., thoughts (1) have no real independent existence, (2) are not subject to our control (Proverbial: "Thought is free.")

522. **bethought me:** remembered

Away with him to death. ⌜*To Lucio.*⌝ Now, sir, to
   you.

MARIANA
   O, my good lord.—Sweet Isabel, take my part.
   Lend me your knees, and all my life to come
   I'll lend you all my life to do you service.   495

DUKE
   Against all sense you do importune her.
   Should she kneel down in mercy of this fact,
   Her brother's ghost his pavèd bed would break
   And take her hence in horror.

MARIANA   Isabel,   500
   Sweet Isabel, do yet but kneel by me,
   Hold up your hands, say nothing. I'll speak all.
   They say best men are molded out of faults,
   And, for the most, become much more the better
   For being a little bad. So may my husband.   505
   O Isabel, will you not lend a knee?

DUKE
   He dies for Claudio's death.

ISABELLA, ⌜*kneeling*⌝   Most bounteous sir,
   Look, if it please you, on this man condemned
   As if my brother lived. I partly think   510
   A due sincerity governed his deeds
   Till he did look on me. Since it is so,
   Let him not die. My brother had but justice,
   In that he did the thing for which he died.
   For Angelo,   515
   His act did not o'ertake his bad intent,
   And must be buried but as an intent
   That perished by the way. Thoughts are no subjects,
   Intents but merely thoughts.

MARIANA   Merely, my lord.   520

DUKE
   Your suit's unprofitable. Stand up, I say.
                                          ⌜*They stand.*⌝
   I have bethought me of another fault.—

531. **knew it not:** i.e., was not certain of it

532. **repent me:** change my mind; **advice:** deliberation; consultation

533. **For testimony whereof:** i.e., as evidence of which (i.e., of the fact that I changed my mind about beheading on the authority of a **private message** alone) **testimony:** evidence

538. **by:** in the case of

539. **him:** i.e., Barnardine

541. **still:** always

542. **slip:** sin, err; **blood:** sexual appetite

543. **tempered:** temperate

Metal being tested on a touchstone. (1.1.52)
From George Wither, *A collection of emblemes* . . . (1635).

Provost, how came it Claudio was beheaded
At an unusual hour?
PROVOST   It was commanded so.   525
DUKE
  Had you a special warrant for the deed?
PROVOST
  No, my good lord, it was by private message.
DUKE
  For which I do discharge you of your office.
  Give up your keys.
PROVOST   Pardon me, noble lord.   530
  I thought it was a fault, but knew it not,
  Yet did repent me after more advice,
  For testimony whereof, one in the prison
  That should by private order else have died,
  I have reserved alive.   535
DUKE   What's he?
PROVOST   His name is Barnardine.
DUKE
  I would thou hadst done so by Claudio.
  Go fetch him hither. Let me look upon him.
                                        ⌜*Provost exits.*⌝
ESCALUS, ⌜*to Angelo*⌝
  I am sorry one so learnèd and so wise   540
  As you, Lord Angelo, have still appeared,
  Should slip so grossly, both in the heat of blood
  And lack of tempered judgment afterward.
ANGELO
  I am sorry that such sorrow I procure;
  And so deep sticks it in my penitent heart   545
  That I crave death more willingly than mercy.
  'Tis my deserving, and I do entreat it.

  Enter Barnardine and Provost, Claudio, ⌜*muffled,
                  and*⌝ *Juliet.*

DUKE, ⌜*to Provost*⌝
  Which is that Barnardine?

550. **told:** i.e., who told

553. **squar'st:** frame; **according:** i.e., accordingly

554. **for:** as regards; **quit:** remit, forgive

555. **mercy:** act of mercy

556. **advise:** counsel spiritually

564. **Give me:** i.e., if you will give me

566. **By this:** i.e., by this time

567. **Methinks:** i.e., it seems to me; **quick'ning:** The verb "to quicken" means to receive or recover life.

568. **quits:** repays, rewards

569. **Look that:** i.e., see to it that

569–70. **her worth worth yours:** her worth is the equal of yours (i.e., she is worthy to be your wife)

571. **apt remission:** appropriate inclination toward pardon

572. **in place:** present

575. **luxury:** lechery

578–79. **I spoke . . . trick:** i.e., (1) it was only a joke; (2) it was a foolish and thoughtless act; (3) it was just my way of talking

PROVOST   This, my
   lord.

DUKE
  There was a friar told me of this man.—   550
  Sirrah, thou art said to have a stubborn soul
  That apprehends no further than this world,
  And squar'st thy life according. Thou'rt condemned.
  But, for those earthly faults, I quit them all,
  And pray thee take this mercy to provide   555
  For better times to come.—Friar, advise him.
  I leave him to your hand.—What muffled fellow's
    that?

PROVOST
  This is another prisoner that I saved
  Who should have died when Claudio lost his head,   560
  As like almost to Claudio as himself.
                ⌜*He unmuffles Claudio.*⌝

DUKE, ⌜*to Isabella*⌝
  If he be like your brother, for his sake
  Is he pardoned; and for your lovely sake,
  Give me your hand and say you will be mine,
  He is my brother too. But fitter time for that.   565
  By this Lord Angelo perceives he's safe;
  Methinks I see a quick'ning in his eye.—
  Well, Angelo, your evil quits you well.
  Look that you love your wife, her worth worth
    yours.   570
  I find an apt remission in myself.
  And yet here's one in place I cannot pardon.
  ⌜*To Lucio.*⌝ You, sirrah, that knew me for a fool, a
    coward,
  One all of luxury, an ass, a madman.   575
  Wherein have I so deserved of you
  That you extol me thus?

LUCIO Faith, my lord, I spoke it but according to the
    trick. If you will hang me for it, you may, but I had
    rather it would please you I might be whipped.   580

593. **therewithal:** moreover

594. **Remit . . . forfeits:** i.e., I cancel your other penalties; or, I forgive your other crimes

595. **our . . . herein:** i.e., my will in this

596. **punk:** prostitute; **pressing to death:** torture in which the body of an accused person who refused to speak was crushed under a mass of stones (See page 192.)

599. **look you:** i.e., see that you; **restore:** reinstate her dignity

602. **much:** great

603. **behind:** still to come; **gratulate:** gratifying, pleasing (than the mere thanks I have given you)

605. **place:** position, office

609. **motion:** suggestion, proposal; **imports:** concerns

610. **Whereto:** to which

611. **What's . . . mine:** proverbial

612. **bring:** accompany

613. **yet behind:** i.e., still to come; **meet:** appropriate, fitting

DUKE   Whipped first, sir, and hanged after.—
  Proclaim it, provost, round about the city,
  If any woman wronged by this lewd fellow—
  As I have heard him swear himself there's one
  Whom he begot with child—let her appear,   585
  And he shall marry her. The nuptial finished,
  Let him be whipped and hanged.
LUCIO   I beseech your Highness do not marry me to a
    whore. Your Highness said even now I made you a
    duke. Good my lord, do not recompense me in   590
    making me a cuckold.
DUKE
  Upon mine honor, thou shalt marry her.
  Thy slanders I forgive and therewithal
  Remit thy other forfeits.—Take him to prison,
  And see our pleasure herein executed.   595
LUCIO   Marrying a punk, my lord, is pressing to death,
    whipping, and hanging.
DUKE   Slandering a prince deserves it.
                         ⌜*Officers take Lucio away.*⌝
  She, Claudio, that you wronged, look you restore.—
  Joy to you, Mariana.—Love her, Angelo.   600
  I have confessed her, and I know her virtue.—
  Thanks, good friend Escalus, for thy much goodness.
  There's more behind that is more gratulate.—
  Thanks, provost, for thy care and secrecy.
  We shall employ thee in a worthier place.—   605
  Forgive him, Angelo, that brought you home
  The head of Ragozine for Claudio's.
  Th' offense pardons itself.—Dear Isabel,
  I have a motion much imports your good,
  Whereto if you'll a willing ear incline,   610
  What's mine is yours, and what is yours is mine.—
  So, bring us to our palace, where we'll show
  What's yet behind ⌜that's⌝ meet you all should know.
                                   ⌜*They exit.*⌝

A sweating tub used to treat venereal disease. (3.2.56–57)
From Thomas Randolph, *Cornelianum dolium . . .* (1638).

Longer Notes

1.1.45. Hold: Many editors believe that this marks the duke's first attempt to hand Angelo his commission, arguing that "hold," in Shakespeare, often means "Here, take it." At line 50 the duke says "Take thy commission" and again at line 57 he says "Therefore, take your honors." We have chosen to place our stage direction for the handing over of the commission at line 50, but in production Angelo sometimes continues to hesitate past this point and accepts the commission only at line 57.

1.2.4–5. Heaven grant us its peace, but not the King of Hungary's: This statement includes several allusions and much wordplay. "Heaven's peace" is the **peace** asked for in the familiar prayer, *Dona nobis pacem,* "grant us thy peace." The Geneva Bible (1560), in its marginal comment on Philippians 4.7: "the peace of God, which passeth all understanding," calls this the "peace of conscience." The **King of Hungary's** peace plays on the contemporary pun on "Hungary/hungry" and on "Hungarians" as "hungry people." The suggestion is that if **peace** between warring dukedoms and kingdoms is achieved, the soldiers will go hungry.

1.2.29–30. between the lists and the velvet: Lucio claims that, while shears can simply cut a piece of fabric in two, as the proverb in lines 27–28 implies, they can also cut between the fine velvet (himself) and the fabric's cloth border (his companion).

1.2.33–34. piled . . . for a French velvet: Besides the wordplay on "piles" and "pilled," and the general reference to "the French disease," there may also be allusions to the practice of wearing velvet patches to cover the lesions produced by syphilis. (Such velvet patches are discussed in Shakespeare's *All's Well That Ends Well*, 4.5). The word **piece** (line 32) can mean a fragment of cloth used as a patch. There may also be wordplay on **velvet**, in that one play of the period refers to an amateur prostitute as a "velvet woman."

1.2.83–111. **Yonder . . . Juliet:** Readers and some editors have been struck by the way this dialogue between Pompey and the bawd Mistress Overdone seems to repeat the news of Claudio's arrest. Perhaps even more striking is that, in talking to Pompey, Mistress Overdone seems not to know news that she has just brought to Lucio in lines 59–70, where she announced that Claudio, whom she initially described as "one yonder," had been arrested and was soon to be executed, and that his "crime" is impregnating Julietta. Now, when Pompey announces "Yonder man is carried to prison," Mistress Overdone asks the man's identity and his crime, both of which she has been represented before as already knowing. Such discontinuity and repetition as we find here are at odds with our more modern standards of consistency and economy of dramatic representation. But these standards do not always apply to the plays of Shakespeare's day, in which it is not uncommon for a play's plot development suddenly to grind to a halt with the entrance of a Clown (as Pompey is called in the Folio), who engages another character in a question-and-answer session that capitalizes on, and thereby repeats with comic differences, details of the plot that have already been presented to the audience in other ways.

1.2.117–19.
     pay down for our offense, by weight,
The words of heaven: on whom it will, it will;
On whom it will not, so . . .

The suggestion of earlier editors that a line is missing (after line 117) is attractive. As the lines now stand, the phrase "The words of heaven" seems elliptical. It may mean "as it says in the Bible," and may refer to what follows ("on whom it will . . ."), which scholars have traced to Romans 9.18, where Paul speaks of God as follows: "Therefore hath he mercy on whom he will have mercy, and whom he will he hardeneth."

2.1.43. **Some run from brakes of ice:** Many changes have been proposed in editorial attempts to give meaning to these words. The most frequent alterations are from "ice" to "vice" and from "brakes" to "breaks." None of the changes helps significantly. The clause stands in parallel with "some rise by sin" (line 42) and in contrast to "some condemnèd for a fault alone" (line 44). It may therefore be meant to suggest "some escape punishment for major crimes," though no emendation thus far proposed captures that meaning. Editors have pointed out an interesting parallel with Claudio's description of hell as a "thrilling region of thick-ribbèd ice" (3.1.138) and have quoted *The Three Voyages of William Barents to the Arctic Regions, (1594, 1595, 1596):* "the ice whereon we lay . . . brake and ran one peece upon another . . . the ice brake under our owne feet." Other editors have noted that *brakes* could be "tortures, traps, or thorny hedges," as well as "engines of punishment," "snaffles," or "sharp bits."

2.2.97–99.
Why all the souls that were were forfeit once,
And He that might the vantage best have took
Found out the remedy.

The reference in line 97 is to Adam's sin, which, in Christian thought, caused all souls to be lost unless redeemed by Christ. (See Romans 3.23: "For all have sinned, and come short of the glory of God.") Lines

98–99 refer to John 3.16 ("For God so loved the world, that he gave his only begotten Son, that whosoever believeth in him should not perish but have everlasting life"). The words **He that might the vantage best have took / Found out the remedy** present God as a creditor who could have profited from the losses of his debtors (i.e., **all the souls that were**), but who instead, through the death of his son, found a **remedy** for their loss.

2.2.176. **I will bethink me. Come again tomorrow:** These words, said in the presence of the provost, are, in effect, an informal order to delay Claudio's execution. The formal order to the provost had been that Claudio must be killed before "nine tomorrow morning" (2.1.38). The order to delay is again implied when, after Isabella asks, at 2.2.194–95, "At what hour tomorrow / Shall I attend your Lordship?" Angelo replies, "At any time 'fore noon."

2.2.193. **Where prayers cross:** These words might also mean: i.e., where our daily prayer that we be not led "into temptation, but deliver[ed] . . . from evil" is at cross-purposes with my desires. Angelo's words at 2.4.1–4 ("When I would pray and think, I think and pray / To several subjects. Heaven hath my empty words, / Whilst my invention, hearing not my tongue, / Anchors on Isabel") suggest that "where prayers cross" could also mean "where my prayers are at cross-purposes with each other."

2.2.206–9. **Having waste ground . . . there:** The contrast implied here is between "light women" (prostitutes, "waste ground") and the religious Isabella (the "sanctuary"). Why, he asks, destroy the sanctuary to make room for our evil purposes when there is plenty of spare land: in other words, why defile Isabella when prostitutes may be easily had? Some editors have suggested that "evils" is not an abstraction in this passage, but that it refers to "privies." If so, Angelo would be comparing his sensual attraction toward Isabella to destroying the sanctuary of a church in order to build a privy on church property.

2.3.31. **Then was your sin of heavier kind than his:** This charge expresses one point of view in a debate about relative responsibility for sexual sin. The other view held that, since men were more rational than women, they had less excuse for succumbing to sexual temptation. Certainly Juliet's sin had more visible consequences.

2.4.4–7. **God . . . conception:** The Folio reads "heauen in my mouth," but editors generally agree that "God" was replaced with "heauen" by a censor. This belief is supported by the phrase "His name" (line 5) and by the allusion to Isaiah 29.13 ("Wherefore the Lord said, . . . this people draw near me with their mouth . . . but have removed their heart far from me"), a familiar passage quoted by Jesus at Matthew 15.8.

2.4.16–17.
Let's write "good angel" on the devil's horn.
'Tis not the devil's crest.

In this complicated wordplay on Angelo's name (in **angel**), on the **horn** as the **devil's** insignia, and on the **crest** (an identifying figure worn atop a knight's helmet), Angelo may be saying that writing "good angel" on the devil's horn does not change the devil's nature, any more than Angelo's name is a proper **crest** for Angelo himself.

2.4.19. **sister:** That the servant identifies Isabella as a **sister**, i.e., a nun, makes clear that the actor playing the part is costumed as a religious. At 1.2.175–76, we are told that Isabella "This day . . . should the cloister enter / And there receive her approbation" (i.e., begin her novitiate or probationary period). And 1.4 stresses the fact that Isabella is not yet a nun: she begins the scene by asking Francisca "And have you nuns no farther privileges?" Francisca says to her (at line 10) "You are yet unsworn," and Lucio asks for "Isabella, a novice of this place" (lines 19–20).

"The Rewle of Sustris Menouresses Enclosid" (described in Historical Background 3, "Isabella and the Order of Poor Clares," pages 232–35) makes a distinction between the clothing appropriate to Poor Clares and to the Order's novices: "Each sister shall be clothed in woolen fabric or hair and . . . she may . . . have a mantle or two suitably long and broad. These robes shall be of coarse cloth and low price and of poor color. And she shall not use her overst coat all white nor all black. These sisters, after they been professed, they shall use before girdle cords which shall be curiously made. . . . And also that they have a black veil spread above her head so large and so long that it may stretch from each part to the shoulders and behind at the back. . . . But other servants and novices shall have girdles of wool and white veils on their heads."

2.4.47–48. coin God's image / In stamps that are forbid: The analogy here is between procreating illegitimately and counterfeiting money. **God's image** refers both to humankind (as in Genesis 1.27: "So God created man in his own image, in the image of God created he him") and to the **image** of the king stamped on legitimate coins. **Stamps** are the designs on coins and also the tools that make such designs. The analogy between creating bastards and making counterfeit coins continues in lines 50–51.

2.4.108. Th' impression of keen whips I'd wear as rubies: The image here of the woman's body, whipped and covered with drops of blood like rubies, suggests both the public whipping of prostitutes and the torture of virgin martyrs. The possible sexual suggestiveness of lines 108–10 is increasingly noted by Shakespeare scholars and editors who find in the words reflections of Isabella's repressed sexuality and see her as, perhaps unintentionally, inflaming Angelo's lust.

Scholars whose expertise is in the history of the religious life find this psychosexual reading of the lines rather uninformed. Jo Ann McNamara, author of *Sisters in Arms: Catholic Nuns Through Two Millennia* (Harvard University Press, 1996), responded to our question to her about this passage: "The language is reasonably typical of martyrs in hagiographical sources, both male and female. No student of religious writing would call this sexually repressed or sexually aggressive. It is an extremely mild form of the bridal language which monastics customarily drew from the Song of Songs. It's also the sort of thing any respectable virgin might say with a little leaning toward the hagiographic willingness to be a martyr."

2.4.140. credulous to false prints: Several metaphors are conflated here. **Credulous** means "too ready to believe"; **false prints** could refer to counterfeiting or to false impressions more generally. Isabella seems to be saying, simultaneously, "we are too gullible" and "we are too easily stamped or shaped."

2.4.146. If you be more, you're none: This can be interpreted in several ways. It probably means "if you are stronger than the frail creature you have described woman as being, then you are no woman." It could, however, mean "if you remain a virgin, you are no woman." If one accepts this second reading, then the reference in line 149 to "putting on the destined livery" would mean "losing your virginity."

3.1.7–40. If I do lose thee . . . pleasant: Throughout this passage, **thee, thy,** and **thou** refer to **life.** Many of the statements, however, can also be read as if addressed to Claudio himself.

3.1.105, 108. **prenzie:** In F2, the second edition of the Folio (1632), this word is changed to "princely," both here and at line 108. This F2 reading was followed by many editors in the past. Others followed a nineteenth-century emendation that changed "prenzie" to "precise." Most editors today retain "prenzie." The fact that it appears twice argues against a simple scribal or compositorial error; it may instead be a Shakespearean coinage that we simply don't understand.

3.1.113. **So to offend him still:** This is usually interpreted as referring to Claudio: i.e., as a reward from the "rank offense" against Isabella, Claudio will be empowered to keep offending Angelo through continued fornication. It is possible, though (as Mark Eccles points out in his Variorum edition of the play), that "So to offend him still" might instead refer to Angelo, who, "from this rank offense," would inevitably spend the rest of his life in perpetual offense against the "heaven" invoked in Claudio's "O heavens," line 111. Eccles points out that "O heavens" might well have originally read "O God." (See longer note to 2.4.4–7.)

3.1.142–43. **that lawless and incertain thought / Imagine howling:** That the lines refer to souls being tormented in hell is supported by a comment of Romeo's that links "the damned," "hell," and "howling" (". . . the damnèd use that word in hell. / Howling attends it" [*Romeo and Juliet*, 3.3.50–51]) and by Laertes' attack on the priest who refuses Ophelia proper funeral rites: "A minist'ring angel shall my sister be / When thou liest howling" (*Hamlet* 5.1.251–52).

3.1.203–4. **goodness . . . goodness:** These words of the duke sacrifice clarity for patterning of words and sounds. The scheme employed is called chiasmus (which, in Greek, means "crossing"). In chiasmus, words exchange places with or cross over each other: **goodness . . . beauty . . . beauty . . . goodness.** As a further contribution to the patterning, the words **cheap** and **brief,** the major words that intervene between **goodness** and **beauty,** are related through assonance (i.e., they share the same vowel sound).

3.1.274–75. **answer to convenience:** Some editors today transpose the words **time** (line 273) and **place** (line 274), arguing that "shadow and silence" are more in keeping with "place" and that Isabella could reasonably insist that the "time" she meets him "answer to [her] convenience." However, **the time may have all shadow and silence in it** can also make good sense. **Shadow** may refer to comparative darkness and **silence** to the cessation of activity at nightfall, **shadow and silence** thereby indicating a late hour.

3.2.45–48. **What, is there none of Pygmalion's images, newly made woman, to be had now, for putting the hand in the pocket and extracting it clutched?:** This seems to mean, loosely, "where are all your prostitutes?" "Pygmalion's images" would be statues of lovely women, like the sculpture made by Pygmalion which was so beautiful that he prayed that it be brought to life. (The story is in Ovid's *Metamorphoses*.) As a pimp, Pompey may have described his prostitutes as lovely, chaste creatures "newly made woman" like Pygmalion's statue when it came to life. The prostitutes, before the new laws in Vienna, could "be had" for money "clutched" in the fist.

3.2.203. **come Philip and Jacob:** Dating the child's age not by its birthday but by when it will be "a year and a quarter old" points to the anniversary of its conception rather than its birth. Lucio's child was thus conceived on May 1, not only the feast of Philip and James but also May Day, a time of revelry and sexual license.

3.2.223–31. None . . . news: The duke's response to Escalus's "What news abroad i' th' world?" takes the form of a series of paradoxes, some built on wordplay (e.g., in line 228 "secure" means "safe" while "security" means "excessive self-confidence") and some on figures of speech from the tradition of "the world turned upside down" (alluded to by the duke at 1.3.30–32: "liberty plucks justice by the nose, / The baby beats the nurse, and quite athwart / Goes all decorum"). Each sentence is in the form of what the duke calls a "riddle" (3.2.230), and the tone is cynical and worldly.

3.2.261–82. He who . . . contracting: This long set of couplets allows the duke to meditate on the present situation and to give the rationale for the solution he plans. The first three couplets generalize about a ruler's proper conduct; the next two couplets focus on Angelo's behavior in particular. The next three couplets once again generalize, this time on the deceptiveness of external appearances. The final set of three couplets describes the duke's plan to apply "craft against vice." Many of the lines are quite cryptic, and parts of the speech are so hard to understand that editors suggest that some lines are missing.

4.1.39–40. In action . . . o'er: The phrase "in action all of precept" (with **precept** meaning "detailed directions") may indicate that Angelo did not physically **show,** but rather told Isabella, **twice o'er,** how to find the garden. However, it is also possible that "in action all of precept" means, instead, teaching by demonstration, conveying his directions in action and gestures.

4.2.190. tie the beard: Editors have debated just what this instruction would involve and how it would promote disguise. One nineteenth-century editor proposed that the word "tie" was a compositor's mistaken insertion that should be deleted. The attraction of this suggestion is that the resulting "Shave the head and the beard" fits well with lines 191–92: "say it was the desire of the penitent to be so bared before his death." There is, however, a reference in another play of the period to tying "up [a beard] shorter."

4.3.2. house of profession: Pompey is probably playing here on a variety of meanings of these words. The word "profession," for example, may suggest that the brothel where he worked as a pimp was an acknowledged, or "professed," bawdy house; it may also allude to line 2.1.71, where we were told that Mistress Overdone "professes a hothouse." The primary association with the phrase, however, was with religious houses, or nunneries. There is considerable evidence that nunneries were frequently likened to brothels, and vice versa, so that Pompey's line might have been a familiar joke.

4.3.5–7. commodity . . . money: These lines describe a money-lending practice in which the borrower agrees to pay back a set amount (here, **ninescore and seventeen pounds**) having been given a **commodity** (here, **brown paper** and **ginger**) that he is to sell for **ready money** (here, **five marks**). Master Rash, in other words, owes £197, though he received only about £3 for the goods he sold.

4.3.14. Copper-spur: Copper was often used to simulate gold, and gilt spurs were associated with knights. Master Copper-spur perhaps pretends to wealth by wearing spurs coated with copper.

4.3.15–16. Drop-heir ... Pudding: The name **Drop-heir** has not been satisfactorily explained. Editors have linked it to various methods of destroying young heirs and to the effects of syphilis (through the pun on "heir" and "hair"). They have also found allegorical explanations in which Drop-heir becomes the usurer who destroys hospitality, since **pudding** could mean "sausages."

4.6.4. He says: The word **He** is ambiguous, and some editors think that it refers to Friar Lodowick (i.e., the duke in disguise). Our reason for believing that the man of whom Isabella and Mariana are speaking in lines 4–9 is, instead, Friar Peter rests entirely on Isabella's statement that the man in question has told her he may "speak against" her (line 7) in the trial scene that follows (5.1). There, it is Friar Peter who charges Isabella and Mariana with conspiring against Angelo, while Friar Lodowick supports Isabella and Mariana.

5.1.460–62. Being criminal in double violation / Of sacred chastity and of promise-breach / Thereon dependent for your brother's life: This description of Angelo's double crime is syntactically confused, so that, for example, Angelo is accused of "violation of ... promise-breach," when what is clearly required is either "violation of promise" or "promise-breach." Editors agree that the duke must be saying that Angelo is doubly criminal: he has violated Isabella's "sacred chastity," if only in imagination, and has broken his promise to save Claudio's life in exchange for Isabella's chastity, an exchange on which her "brother's life" was "dependent."

Historical Background

1. King James

For more than two centuries, readers and critics have argued for connections between King James I, who became King of England in 1603, and *Measure for Measure*, which was performed for James's court in Whitehall on December 26, 1604. A record of this performance survives among the accounts of the Office of the Revels, which was responsible for providing the king with entertainment. However, there is no documentary evidence to indicate that the play was specially written or even adapted for court performance, and it was the rare play that is known to have been written specifically for performance at court or that is known to have had its first performance there.

Nevertheless, critics have repeatedly argued that *Measure for Measure*'s duke was created by Shakespeare as a flattering representation or an idealization of King James or as a vehicle for Shakespeare to instruct the new king in just rulership. They argue, first, that lines 1.1.73–76 reflect James's dislike for crowds: "I love the people, / But do not like to stage me to their eyes. / Though it do well, I do not relish well / [The people's] loud applause and aves vehement," says the duke; and then he goes on in a way that has been read as Shakespeare's flattery of the king: "Nor do I think the man of safe discretion / That does affect it." King James was reported by his contemporaries to be a good deal less polite than the duke in dismissing his counselors' urging that he display himself to his subjects: "'God's wounds!'" James would reportedly "cry out in Scottish,

225

'I will pull down my breeches and they shall also see my arse.' "

Shakespeare's duke is also supposed to have mirrored James I by disguising himself and spying on his subjects, and by his display of mercy at the play's end. Like the argument about the shared dislike of crowds, however, these similarities have little substance. Shakespeare's duke is not consistent in avoiding crowds, since he appears to go out of his way to attract one when he formally returns to power in the play's last act. James I never did disguise himself; it was his grandfather, James V of Scotland, who sometimes went among his people in disguise. Further, stories of rulers going around incognito date back to classical times, and there is nothing specific to link the duke to James V. And, while it is true that once in the winter of 1603–4 James I did arrange to have delivery of pardons for some prisoners delayed until the men had actually mounted the scaffold on which they were to be executed, it is hard to find much resemblance between this incident and the end of *Measure for Measure*.

Critics have also searched King James's published writings for statements analogous to the dialogue of the play. The favorite source is James's *Basilicon Doron*, a book of advice about kingship that James wrote for his son Prince Henry. Published in England in 1603, the year of James's accession to the English throne, it was reportedly widely read. Full of Renaissance commonplaces about the duties of a ruler, *Basilicon Doron* cannot be shown to have provided Shakespeare anything that he could not have read or heard in many other places. So the several passages in it that are more or less analogous to passages in *Measure for Measure*—passages, for example, about the ruler's obligation to exercise self-control or about the calumny that rulers unjustly suffer—do not demonstrate that Shakespeare sought to reflect back to King James the monarch's own prescriptions on rulership.

Thus the search for connections between James I and Shakespeare's duke must rest, at least for now, with a handful of tempting but unsubstantiated resemblances.

2. Betrothal and Marriage

Measure for Measure is in large part a play about betrothal and marriage. Thus readers and audiences of the play can understand and enjoy it better if they are acquainted with the social customs and religious rituals concerning marriage in Shakespeare's England. (Even though the play is set in Vienna, the customs, if not the laws, are those of England.) The best source for a survey of these customs is Victoria Hayne's article listed among the "Further Readings"; the present discussion is greatly indebted to her work.

As Hayne demonstrates, the passage from being single to being married in Shakespeare's England was a complex and often extended one, not like our practice today when one is single until the wedding and then married after it. Rather, English custom of Shakespeare's day enjoined upon a couple a series of steps, some of which they took privately, some publicly; some steps they took as a couple, others as members of their families. Marriage began in courtship, which was usually brief in Shakespeare's day. The extent of family involvement in this early stage depended on the class to which the couple belonged; the higher the class, the greater the family involvement. Then would come a private exchange of a promise to marry, followed by a more or less public betrothal in a ceremony called "handfasting," in which the couple joined hands and exchanged vows, usually before witnesses.

Many couples appear to have regarded themselves as, at this point, actually married and free to begin their sexual relationship. But in the eyes of the church, the couple were not yet married and would not be until banns were read on three successive Sundays in their parish church, the marriage then solemnized in a church wedding, the couple formally bedded after their wedding feast, and, finally, they consummated their marriage.

Entwined among these social and religious practices was the legal process of negotiating a dowry, a process that had no fixed place in the passage from courtship toward marriage. Again class came into play: the higher the class of the couple, the bigger the dowry and the more important the negotiation of it, and therefore the earlier in the courtship the dowry needed to be settled. If the couple were from families that enjoyed less social importance or less wealth, the romantic development of their relationship might outstrip the legal process of negotiation of the dowry. Because of the complexity of the interaction that preceded the church wedding, it was customary in England for the church to be lenient to its members who began their sexual relations rather too far in advance of other steps they needed to take in their passage toward marriage. To sum up: between courtship and marriage, one had to accept the indeterminate status of being neither single nor married, and of being both single and married. While one was enduring the passage toward marriage, one was therefore subject to being represented in different ways depending on the point of view from which one was being judged.

It is the conflict among these diverse viewpoints that *Measure for Measure* dramatizes. Three couples in the play are on the way to marriage, and none of them has quite made it even by the end of the play. The first couple are Claudio and Juliet. Claudio narrates the impasse they have reached in seeking to marry:

> upon a true contract
> I got possession of Julietta's bed.
> You know the lady. She is fast my wife,
> Save that we do the denunciation lack
> Of outward order. This we came not to
> Only for propagation of a dower
> Remaining in the coffer of her friends,
> From whom we thought it meet to hide our love
> Till time had made them for us. But it chances
> The stealth of our most mutual entertainment
> With character too gross is writ on Juliet.
>
> (1.2.142–52)

Claudio's account makes it clear that he and Juliet have passed through courtship and made private promises to marry each other. There is even a suggestion in Claudio's language that they have progressed as far as "handfasting"—"She is fast my wife"—but it seems that if such a ceremony took place it was none too public, for the couple were concerned to keep their relationship secret from Juliet's relatives ("her friends") because the matter of the dowry was as yet an unresolved concern. Nevertheless, Claudio and Juliet have begun their sexual relationship, as has become all too evident in Juliet's visible pregnancy. From Claudio's viewpoint, he and Juliet have some justification for thinking they are married; again, as he says, "She is fast my wife." (As Hayne shows, this view was widely shared in Shakespeare's England by the many couples who thought of themselves as married before completing all the steps toward wedlock and who therefore engaged in sexual relations before solemnizing their marriage in church.) Most of the other characters in the play who voice an opinion take Claudio's viewpoint, even though those in the play who figure human conduct in religious terms all regard Claudio and Juliet as having sinned, as do the couple themselves. Only Angelo, who alone seems to have the power to enforce his viewpoint, regards Claudio as a criminal deserving of death for fornication, or pre-marital sex. Angelo's judgment and Viennese law appear extremely harsh—far harsher than English church law or social custom of the period—but Angelo's charge that Claudio engaged in pre-marital sex has some basis: from one contemporary viewpoint, the church's, Claudio and Juliet are not yet married.

And, it later becomes clear, Angelo himself and his betrothed, Mariana, are in a comparable situation. Indeed, this couple have proceeded through many more of the steps toward marriage than have Juliet and Claudio, even though Angelo now reserves to himself the state of a single man. The duke describes the situation of Angelo and Mariana:

[Mariana] should this Angelo have married, was affianced to her oath, and the nuptial appointed. Between which time of the contract and limit of the solemnity, her brother Frederick was wracked at sea, having in that perished vessel the dowry of his sister. But mark how heavily this befell to the poor gentlewoman. There she lost a noble and renowned brother, in his love toward her ever most kind and natural; with him, the portion and sinew of her fortune, her marriage dowry; with both, her combinate husband, this well-seeming Angelo . . . [who] left her in her tears and dried not one of them with his comfort, swallowed his vows whole, pretending in her discoveries of dishonor; in few, bestowed her on her own lamentation, which she

yet wears for his sake; and he, a marble to her tears,
is washed with them but relents not.   (3.1.238–56)

From the duke's account it would seem that Angelo and
Mariana had taken all the steps toward marriage, including successful dowry negotiations, up to the wedding itself, and that Angelo had backed out when the
promised dowry vanished in a shipwreck just before the
date set for the wedding. Because, in Shakespeare's
England, the commitment to marriage became stronger
the more steps the couple took toward their wedding,
Angelo is much closer to being married to Mariana than
Claudio is to Juliet. Claudio publicly honors his vows to
Juliet in accepting responsibility for her pregnancy,
while Angelo abandons Mariana to her grief, defaming
her reputation to justify his act. Perhaps this difference
in the number of steps taken goes part of the way toward
explaining why the duke, in disguise as friar, can assure
Mariana that because Angelo "is your husband on a
precontract [a pre-existing contract of marriage]. / To
bring you . . . together [sexually] 'tis no sin" (4.1.79–80).
(Strictly speaking, the duke is in error; the church
regarded sex before the wedding as a sin. Indeed, the
duke acknowledges the church's viewpoint when he
insists that Angelo's last act be to marry Mariana in
order to remove from her reputation any possible stain
for pre-marital sex.) Thus Angelo and Mariana, like
Claudio and Juliet, are, as Christy Desmet also notes,
both married and not married, depending on whether
one takes the duke's viewpoint expressed in 4.1 or
Angelo's expressed in 5.1, but the duke's claim that
Angelo is Mariana's "husband" has more legal and
social support. (For a different interpretation of the
Angelo-Mariana relationship, see the "Modern Perspective," pages 249–51.)
    The last couple whose progress toward marriage has

been halted prematurely are Lucio and Kate Keepdown. The play gives us little information about them; they seem to have been at a very early stage on the way to marriage when their sexual relationship began. According to Mistress Overdone, Lucio promised Kate marriage and impregnated her (3.2.200–2); Lucio foolishly confides to the friar (who is the duke in disguise) that he fathered a child upon a woman and then denied paternity under oath (4.3.184–87). It would seem then that Lucio and Kate got no further than a private promise to marry, rather than a handfasting before witnesses, because there were no witnesses to contradict Lucio's perjury. Yet, this private promise binds Lucio to marry Kate when the duke enforces the law.

The complex rituals and customs associated with marriage in Shakespeare's day and the variety of perspectives available for the assessment of people's marital states provide a rich mine of subject matter for *Measure for Measure*, a play that explores ethics, morality, and the law in ways generations of readers have continued to find fascinating long after the customs and rituals have changed.

3: Isabella and the Order of Poor Clares

When Shakespeare made Isabella a "votarist of Saint Clare"—that is, a member of the religious community of enclosed nuns known as the Order of Saint Clare—such religious orders had been gone from England for many decades. Despite this fact, both the dialogue of *Measure for Measure* and Isabella's and Francisca's names appropriately reflect the Order of Saint Clare.

The Order of Poor Clares, as it is popularly known, was founded by St. Clare in 1212 as a kind of sister order to the Franciscans, an order of friars devoted to the extraordinarily difficult task of living the lives of monks *in the secular world*. The first Clares were brought to England in the late thirteenth century, where a convent was established just outside the walls of the City of London near Aldgate. This convent was turned over to Henry VIII in 1539, when Roman Catholic monastic establishments in England were dissolved; Henry in turn gave the convent to a Church of England bishop.

We do not know how Shakespeare obtained his information about Poor Clares or about life in enclosed convents, but the conversation between Sister Francisca and Isabella is remarkably in line with the "rule" under which the London convent of Poor Clares functioned. While most convents of Poor Clares operated under the Hugoline Constitutions, the London convent lived in accord with a rule popularly (and interestingly) known as "the Isabella Rule," developed by the Blessed Isabella, sister of King Louis IX of France. Critics are now beginning to suggest that it is no coincidence that Shakespeare named his heroine "Isabella" and named the nun whom we meet "Francisca," since the Clares are a Franciscan order.

A fifteenth-century manuscript, "The Rewle of Sustris Menouresses Enclosid," gives the details of the Isabella Rule as it was practiced in the London convent. There are several points of similarity between this rule and the convent life described in *Measure for Measure*. For example, Isabella and Sister Francisca enter in 1.4 in the middle of the nun's instructions to Isabella about the "restraints" upon the "sisterhood, the votarists of Saint Clare." Such a conversation is in line with "The Rewle of Sustris Menouresses Enclosid," which instructs that "All those which this religious life shall take . . . before that they . . . shall enter into religious life, that it be well declared to them the hardnesses and the sharpnesses by which they come to joy of paradise and these which they shall be bound to after [i.e., in conformity with] this religious life."

To take a second example: At the sound of Lucio's voice, Francisca says to Isabella,

> Turn you the key and know his business of him.
> You may; I may not. You are yet unsworn.
> When you have vowed, you must not speak with men
> But in the presence of the Prioress.
>
> (1.4.9–12)

In "The Rewle" are several paragraphs delineating who should control the key to the convent and explaining that "When anybody to any of the sisters shall speak, first shall the abbess be warned thereof . . . , and if she grant, then shall the sister speak with the stranger so that she have two other sisters at the least with her, that they must see and hear what that they do or speak. . . . The sisters [should] take good heed . . . that none of them . . . speak to no man that is entered but in the manner and by the ordinance foresaid. . . ." (There is no parallel in "The Rewle" to Francisca's instructions in lines 13–14: "Then, if you speak, you must not show your face; / Or if you show your face, you must not speak.")

The relevance of this fifteenth-century manuscript to *Measure for Measure* was first pointed out by G. K. Hunter ("Six Notes on *Measure for Measure*," *Shakespeare Quarterly* 15:3 [1964]: 167–72). Darryl J. Gless seems to have been the first to note that it was, in fact, possible for Shakespeare to have seen the manuscript, since it was owned by Charles Howard, earl of Nottingham and patron of the acting company known as the Admiral's Men. Howard donated the manuscript to Oxford University's Bodleian Library in 1604, the year that *Measure for Measure* was probably written. (See Gless in the "Further Reading," page 262.) The manuscript of "The Rewle of Sustris Menouresses Enclosid" was published in *A Fifteenth Century Courtesy Book and Two Franciscan Rules*, "edited from a xv century ms. in the Bodleian Library, with an introduction, notes, and glossary by Walter W. Seton" (London: Early English Text Society, 1914, rpt. 1937, pages 63–119). We found Seton's introduction particularly helpful in drafting this part of the Historical Background. We have modernized the language quoted from "The Rewle."

4: Measure for Measure

Measure for Measure has as its title a biblical allusion that is also a highly suggestive part of the play's dialogue. The duke embeds the play's title in a context that alludes to more than one biblical passage:

> The very mercy of the law cries out
> Most audible, even from his proper tongue,
> "An Angelo for Claudio, death for death."
> Haste still pays haste, and leisure answers leisure;
> Like doth quit like, and measure still for measure.
> (5.1.463–68)

Several of the biblical allusions in this passage would suggest that the words **"measure . . . for measure"** are drawn from the Old Testament, which often develops the theme of retribution found in the duke's speech just quoted. Compare the speech to Leviticus 24.19–21, for example:

> And if a man cause a blemish in his neighbor as he hath done, so shall it be done to him; breach for

breach, eye for eye, tooth for tooth: as he hath caused a blemish in a man, so shall it be done to him again. And he that killeth a beast, he shall restore it: and he that killeth a man, he shall be put to death.

Closely similar language is also to be found in Exodus 21:23–25, "And if any mischief follow, then thou shalt give life for life, eye for eye, tooth for tooth, hand for hand, foot for foot, burning for burning, wound for wound, stripe for stripe," and in Deuteronomy 19:19–21, "Then shall ye do unto him as he had thought to have done unto his brother. . . . And thine eye shall not pity, but life shall go for life, eye for eye, tooth for tooth, hand for hand, foot for foot." The duke's speech thus creates a strong impression that "measure for measure" belongs to a class of Old Testament texts that authorize and even seem to require a merciless imposition of penalties for wrongs that are precisely equal in severity to the wrongs.

However, the phrase "measure for measure" can also be associated with biblical passages from the New Testament's Sermon on the Mount, which develops a theme of mercy that explicitly contradicts the Old Testament's emphasis on retribution: "Ye have heard that it hath been said, An eye for an eye, and a tooth for a tooth: but I say unto you that ye resist not evil: but whosoever shall smite thee on thy right cheek, turn to him the other also. . . . Judge not, that ye be not judged. For with what judgment ye judge, ye shall be judged: and with what measure ye mete, it shall be measured to you again" (Matthew 5.38–39, 7.1–2). (One finds comparable language in Luke 6:38: "Give, and it shall be given unto you; good measure, pressed down, and shaken together, and running over, shall men give into your bosom. For with the same measure that ye mete withal it shall be measured to you again.") The action in the play that may be most in harmony with this New Testament context of the play's title is Isabella's renunciation of any desire for revenge against Angelo and her plea to the duke to spare Angelo's life, even though she is still laboring under the misinformation that Angelo has put Claudio to death. Critics have suggested that the duke uses the phrase "measure for measure" in his speech to Isabella as a hint to her about her Christian obligation to mercy.

Whether or not we read the duke's speech in this way, implications of the New Testament passages associated with the phrase "measure for measure" may seem to resonate throughout this play. These New Testament passages remind all judges not to impose penalties on those within their power without reflecting on their own faults and their own dependence on divine mercy. In trying to persuade Angelo to revoke the death penalty for Claudio, Escalus encourages Angelo to engage in such reflection:

> Let but your Honor know,
> Whom I believe to be most strait in virtue,
> That, in the working of your own affections,
> Had time cohered with place, or place with wishing,
> Or that the resolute acting of your blood
> Could have attained th' effect of your own purpose,
> Whether you had not sometime in your life
> Erred in this point which now you censure him,
> And pulled the law upon you.
>
> (2.1.9–17)

Later, the duke, disguised as a friar, twice refers to the obligations that the New Testament imposes on Angelo to require of others a moral standard no higher than the one that Angelo himself has achieved in his own life. On one occasion, speaking to Escalus, the duke seems to threaten Angelo:

> If [Angelo's] own life answer the straitness of his proceeding, it shall become him well; wherein if he chance to fail, he hath sentenced himself.
> (3.2.256–58)

On another occasion the duke pretends to defend Angelo's harshness on the grounds that Angelo's own life is the very model of perfect rectitude requisite for such judgmental harshness:

> His life is paralleled
> Even with the stroke and line of his great justice.
> He doth with holy abstinence subdue
> That in himself which he spurs on his power
> To qualify in others. Were he mealed with that
> Which he corrects, then were he tyrannous,
> But this being so, he's just.
>
> (4.2.86–92)

This sample of passages from *Measure for Measure* indicates the importance, without exhausting the implications, of the biblical allusion in the play's suggestive title.

Textual Notes

The reading of the present text appears to the left of the square bracket. Unless otherwise noted, the reading to the left of the bracket is from **F**, the First Folio text (upon which this edition is based). The earliest sources of readings not in **F** are indicated as follows: **F2** is the Second Folio of 1632; **F3** is the Third Folio of 1663–64; **F4** is the Fourth Folio of 1685; **Ed.** is an earlier editor of Shakespeare, beginning with Rowe in 1709. No sources are given for emendations of punctuation or for corrections of obvious typographical errors, like turned letters that produce no known word. **SD** means stage direction; **SP** means speech prefix; **uncorr.** means the first or uncorrected state of the First Folio; **corr.** means the second or corrected state of the First Folio; ~ stands in place of a word already quoted before the square bracket; ∧ indicates the omission of a punctuation mark.

1.1	38. touched] tonch'd F
	81. SD *He exits.*] *1 line earlier in* F
1.2	12. Why,] ~? F
	15. relish] rallish F
	21. meter] meeter F
	49. dolors] Dollours F
	78. SD *Exit.* F
	81 *and hereafter.* SD *Pompey*] Ed.; *Clowne* F, *1 line later in* F
	83 *and hereafter.* SP POMPEY] Ed.; *Clo.* F
	107. SD *4 lines later in* F (*Enter Prouost, Claudio, Iuliet, Officers, Lucio, & 2. Gent.*)
	111. F *adds* "Scena Tertia."

119. SD *Entrance at line 111 in* F
122. liberty.] ~∧ F
160. straight] F (strait)
182. Besides] F (beside)

1.3 Ed.; *Scena Quarta* F
3. Why ∧]~, F
7 *and hereafter in this scene.* SP FRIAR THOMAS] Ed.; *Fri.* F
15. traveled] F (trauaild)
58. SD *Exit.* F

1.4 Ed.; *Scena Quinta* F
5. sisterhood] sisterstood F
6. SP LUCIO, *within*] Ed.; *Lucio within | Luc.* F
18. stead] F (steed)
26. you,] ~; F
35. heart,] ~: F
37. renouncement ∧] ~, F
45. teeming] teemlug F
58. givings-out] Ed.; giuing-out F
65. fast.] ~∧ F

2.1 0. SD *Enter Angelo, Escalus, and seruants, Iustice.* F
8. father.] ~, F
13. your] Ed.; our F
44. SD F (*Enter Elbow, Froth, Clowne, Officers.*)
145. SD *1 line earlier in* F
168. right, constable.] ~∧ (~) ∧ F
220, 221. Master] F (Mr.)
276. Faith] F ('Faith)
284. o'] a F

2.2 3. Pray] F ('Pray)
35. Save] F ('Saue)
39. Please] F ('Please)

78. back] F2; *omit* F
78. Well ∧ . . . this:] ~, . . . ~∧ F
117. slept.] ~∧ F
124. hatched] hatc'hd F
126. ere] Ed.; here F
181. sicles] F (Sickles)
186. dedicate] dediaate F
197. Save] F ('Saue)

2.3 22. conscience] F (consciēce)
28. offenseful] F (offence full)

2.4 4. God] Ed.; heauen F
9. sere] Ed.; feard F
31. SD *1/2 line later in* F
47. God's] Ed.; heauens F
50. metal] F (mettle)
55. or] Ed.; and F
82. so,] ~∧ F
83. me] F2; *omit* F
95–97. life | As . . . other— | But, . . . question,]
        ~∧ | (~ . . . ~, | ~∧ . . . ~) F
101. binding] Ed.; building F
172. report] reporr F
184. can,] ~; F
191. brother.] ~, F

3.1 10. doth] Ed.; dost F
30. thee sire,] F4; thee, fire∧ F
50. SD *4 lines earlier in* F
56. me . . . them] Ed.; them . . . me F
76. Though] Ed.; Through F
101. enew] Ed.; emmew F
107. damned'st] F2; damnest F
145. penury] F2; periury F
221–22. advisings. To . . . good,] ~, ~ . . . ~; F
277. stead] F (steed)
289. Angelo.] ~, F
291. Saint] F (S.)

3.2   0. SD *Enter Elbow, Clowne, Officers.* F
     8. law∧] ~; F
   12. Bless] F ('blesse)
   26. eat, array] Ed.; eate away F
   41. SD *1 line earlier in* F
   48. it] Ed.; *omit* F
74–75. bondage.] ~∧ F
   75. patiently,] ~: F
 153. dearer] Ed.; deare F
 220. See] F (Sea)
 225. and it] F3; and as it F
 237. merry] merrrie F

4.1   51. SD *1 line earlier in* F
   60. haste.] ~∧ F
   62. Will 't] F (Wilt)
   62. SD *Isabella . . . exit.*] Ed.; *Exit.* F
   68. SD *1/2 line later in* F

4.2   0. SD *Enter Prouost and Clowne.* F
    4. wife's] F (wiues)
   43. If] Ed.; *Clo.* If F
   58. yare] Ed.; y'are F
   59. SD *Exit.* F
   75. SD *1/2 line later in* F
 112. This] Ed.; *Duke.* This F
 112. Lordship's] Ed.; Lords F
 113. SP DUKE] Ed.; *Pro.* F
 132. SD F (*The Letter.*)
 191. bared] F (bar'de)
 227. SD *Exit* F

4.3   4, 9, 13 (2), 14, 16, 17, 22, 23.
     Master] F (Mr)
    7. Marry, then∧] ~∧~, F
   25. SP *Centered as SD in* F
   25. A pox] Ed.; *Bar.* A pox F
   40. SD *2 lines earlier in* F

69. SD *Enter Provost*] *2 lines earlier in* F
94. Claudio.] ∼, F
96. yonder] Ed.; yond F
99. Angelo.] ∼∧ F
99. SD *1 line earlier in* F
107. well-balanced] F (weale-ballanc'd); form,]
     ∼. F
114. SP ISABELLA *within*] Ed.; *Isabell within.*
     | *Isa.* F
139. convent] F (Couent)
143. can,] ∼∧ F
169. brother.] ∼, F
193. we'll] we'el F

4.4   3. manner.] ∼, F
6. deliver] F2; reliuer F
16. proclaimed.] ∼∧ F
21. SD *1 line earlier in* F

4.5   2. plot.] ∼, F
6. Flavius'] Ed.; Flauia's F
11 *and hereafter.* SP FRIAR PETER] Ed.;
   Peter F

4.6   10. SD *1 line earlier in* F
5.1   4. your] yonr F
15. me] F3; we F
42. speak.] ∼, F
62. absolute∧] ∼: F
83. Angelo.] ∼, F
95. then.] ∼, F
149. belike.] ∼: F
192. SD *1/2 line later in* F
194. her] F2; your F
243. Enough] Enoug F
248. promisèd] promis'd F
297. SD *1 line earlier in* F
317. SD *2 lines earlier in* F

349–50. touse him] Ed.; towze you F
370. voice.] ~, F
429. SD *Exit.* F
454. SD *1 line earlier in* F (*Enter Angelo, Maria, Peter, Prouost.*)
464. tongue,] ~. F
477. husband.] ~, F
483. confiscation] F2; confutation F
496. her.] ~, F
570. yours.] ~∧ F
613. that's] F2; that F
613. *The Scene Vienna.* | The names of all the Actors. (*See page 2.*)

Measure for Measure:
A Modern Perspective
Christy Desmet

Measure for Measure concludes with an elaborate mock trial, in which the duke passes judgment on a series of characters whose faults vary widely in severity. Angelo, having restored Mariana's reputation by marrying her, is condemned for Claudio's supposed death. Lucio is forced to marry the mother of his child, a fate he considers worse than "pressing to death, whipping, and hanging" (5.1.596–97). Both men richly deserve their sentences. But Isabella must also seek pardon for having unknowingly taken liberties with her sovereign, a transgression that her ignorance and the duke's enjoyment of his own disguise should certainly mitigate. Even less comprehensible is the duke's judgment of the provost, who is made to give up his keys of office for executing Claudio without a special warrant, a deed that the provost valiantly strove to prevent and that, in the end, never took place. Nevertheless, the provost readily confesses his fault and asks the duke's pardon before producing Claudio, the missing piece in the duke's puzzle that allows him to pardon in turn each of the characters' transgressions. Lucio's pardon is conditional, since he still must marry Kate Keepdown, but his life is safe, and the duke implies that marriage to a "punk," as Lucio calls her, is a small price for slandering a duke.

Under the duke's "just but severe law" (2.2.58), there is no mercy without prior justice. The biblical logic of the play's title, *Measure for Measure*, requires "An

Angelo for Claudio, death for death" (5.1.465). Every fault is condemned as soon as it is done, if not before, as Angelo tells Isabella; it therefore follows, as the duke says, that "Haste still pays haste, and leisure answers leisure" (466). The duke's ritual enactment of "measure for measure" assumes that the distinction between good and evil is both absolute and readily apparent. Yet the parody of judicial process over which Escalus presides, in which Elbow (as Justice) accuses Pompey (as Iniquity) of uncertain crimes, demonstrates the impossibility of clear moral divisions. Not only does Elbow confuse *benefactors* with *malefactors*, but the sexual crime also remains undefined (2.1.54–56). Nothing was done to Elbow's wife "once," is all that Pompey will admit. "Which is the wiser here, Justice or Iniquity?" Escalus asks, throwing up his hands in exasperation (2.1.180).

The world of *Measure for Measure* cannot be reduced to a morality play that pits Justice against Iniquity because human behavior is more varied than the scriptural model of judicial exchange—"An Angelo for Claudio, death for death"—would allow. A simple moral mathematics, one that divides the world into angels and devils, governs the notion that an unjust judge must pay with his life for his innocent prisoner's "death." Paradoxically, the logic of "measure for measure" depends as well on a contrary assumption, that Angelo and Claudio are indistinguishable from one another. Angelo's death may require Claudio's precisely because they have committed the same sexual crime: fornication. (For an examination of alternative biblical implications of the phrase "measure for measure," see Historical Background 4: "Measure for Measure," pages 235–38.)

At the lower ranks of Vienna's legal system, the line between innocence and guilt is even less clear. The comic tie between the executioner Abhorson (whose name suggests an unsavory appearance) and his apprentice Pompey Bum (whose "bum" is the "greatest thing" about him [2.1.225]) demonstrates that a thin line divides criminals from their masters within the judicial system. A "feather will turn the scale" (4.2.30–31) between them. Furthermore, despite the law's attempt to label malefactors according to their deeds, the relationship between intention and action is often uncertain. The host of allegorical characters who inhabit Abhorson's prison (Master Rash, young Dizzy, and the rest of Mistress Overdone's customers) are humors characters, shaped and driven by a single, obvious, and exaggerated trait. Because their crimes have a behavioral rather than moral origin, the terms "guilt" and "innocence" hardly apply to them. Barnardine, by contrast, positively flouts civic and religious law, drinking and sleeping around the clock despite the fact that, for him, the day of judgment is near. The duke calls him "gravel heart" (4.3.68), appalled by the lack of conscience that bolsters Barnardine's willful refusal to "rise and be hanged" (4.3.22–23).

In Shakespeare's Vienna, the equivocal nature of authority itself complicates the relation between law and morality. Both the play's biblical subtext and early modern political theory support the duke's characterization of the sovereign as God's secular arm. The duke says that "He who the sword of heaven will bear / Should be as holy as severe" (3.2.261–62). Angelo, being only an "angel on the outward side" (272), cannot fulfill the ideal of justice to which he has committed himself. But the mere fact that he can fill the duke's place contradicts the symbolic equation between secular and religious authority. In appointing Angelo as his deputy, the duke has created a counterfeit, the political equivalent of the illegitimate children produced by Vienna's sexual counterfeiters, who "coin God's image / In stamps that are forbid" (2.4.47–48).

Not only the duke's abdication of his authority, but
also his adoption of another identity as a friar, is
problematic. In drama from the period, the conventional figure of the disguised duke is morally unambiguous.
Passing unrecognized through his realm, he observes
the true nature of his subjects and learns important
lessons about them and himself. Shakespeare's duke,
however, usurps the function as well as the form of a
religious figure. He prepares Claudio for death and
attempts to perform the same function for Barnardine.
He also acts as confessor and spiritual guide to Juliet,
Isabella, and Mariana. The duke's assumption of religious authority is legally and theologically suspect.

Furthermore, his disguise seems to be a device for
political surveillance rather than enlightenment and
self-knowledge. The duke often is, as Lucio calls him,
the "fantastical duke of dark corners" (4.3.170). He
watches Angelo's failed stewardship as an interesting
experiment in the effect of power on human nature. He
eavesdrops on Isabella's private conference with her
condemned brother and establishes himself as Mariana's confidant. Even Lucio might object that the duke,
by virtue of his disguise and a strategic reticence,
encourages the slanders that he later punishes with
such rigor. Finally, the duke's wanderings throughout
Vienna seem to produce not knowledge, but doubt and
confusion, for the duke must turn to Escalus for confir-
mation of his own character. He praises the death of
Ragozine the pirate (whose severed head conveniently
replaces that of Claudio) as "an accident that heaven
provides" (4.3.82), but in this case, the substitution of
one head for another smacks more of desperate improvisation than of divine providence. In the play's concluding scene, Escalus orders that the "Friar" be sent to
prison for slander to the state, so that the duke seems
momentarily to become the victim of his own disguise.

The relationship between Iniquity and Justice is most complicated in the play's exploration of marriage as a legal institution. There are two, perhaps three, married couples in *Measure for Measure*: Claudio and Juliet, Angelo and Mariana, and, less obviously, Lucio and Kate Keepdown. The status of all three is uncertain. In Shakespeare's England, a series of rituals marked the stages of a couple's legal commitment to one another. The formality of courtship and the place of dowry negotiations in this process varied according to social class and geography. In general, however, after a period of courtship and a financial agreement negotiated between the families, the couple exchanged a promise to marry, which in most cases was quickly followed by a public betrothal.[1] After the public contract came the announcement of the banns in the parish church, a church ceremony, wedding feast, and the bedding of the couple.

Claudio and Juliet have engaged in a *sponsalia per verba de praesenti*, or public "handfast" marriage, a declaration that they are husband and wife made before witnesses and symbolized by the pair's clasped hands. Although Claudio confirms that Juliet is "fast" his wife (1.2.144), the secrecy surrounding that ceremony complicates the legality of their marriage. While Claudio and Juliet have reached the second stage in their commitment to one another, according to Angelo's account he and Mariana engaged only in a *sponsalia de futuro*, a private promise to marry in the future that went no further when dowry negotiations broke down. In this case, Angelo's abandonment of Mariana after her dowry was lost at sea might violate common decency, but it would not be illegal. Nevertheless, when the duke solicits Isabella's participation in the bed-trick, he assures her that Mariana was "affianced" to Angelo by oath and that the date was set for their nuptial ceremony, suggesting that the negotiations had proceeded much further than Angelo himself admits (3.1.238–40). To complicate matters even more, in the trial scene Mariana refers to "the hand which, with a vowed contract, / Was fast belocked in thine" (5.1.235–36). Situated between Mariana's memory of the deep past (when Angelo found her beautiful) and the recent past (when she substituted for Isabella in Angelo's bed), this statement might refer to a formal vow between Angelo and Mariana or a spur-of-the-moment betrothal between Angelo and the woman he thought was Isabella. Mariana's statement that she took away the "match" from Isabel (5.1.237) leaves the truth in doubt. Lucio and Mistress Kate Keepdown are involved in the most irregular of all the marriages. Mistress Overdone claims that Lucio promised to marry Kate Keepdown, which would probably suggest a private contract followed quickly by sexual consummation, especially since the child was apparently conceived on May Day, a holiday traditionally associated with courtship and sexual freedom. Lucio's marriage may be not only incomplete, but also irregular. Like other young women whose impromptu courtships and vows were conducted in the spirit of holiday license—women whose cases sometimes came before the ecclesiastical courts—Kate Keepdown may have discovered that she and Lucio understood their union in very different terms.[2] Thus they, like the other characters in this play, are at once married and not married.

In *Measure for Measure*'s representation of marriage as a legal institution, Shakespeare's audience would have recognized a social situation that was at once familiar and frighteningly strange. While waiting for Juliet's dowry or marriage portion to be finalized, Claudio and Juliet have prematurely consummated their relationship, and the signs of pregnancy are now obvious on Juliet's body. While the English church clearly considered sex before the wedding ceremony a sin, it was also common practice. Varieties of fornication were punished with degrees of penance by the ecclesiastical courts, but members of the play's audience, like the denizens of Shakespeare's Vienna, probably would have been horrified to see Claudio condemned to death for premarital sexual relations. They would have been equally confused by the duke's confident assurance to Mariana that her "precontract" to Angelo (4.1.79) prevents her substitution for Isabella in Angelo's bed from being a sin. Only Lucio's ability to evade his marital and parental responsibilities might have seemed sadly commonplace.

The inhabitants of Shakespearean Vienna evaluate Claudio's dilemma in different ways. Condemned by civil and ecclesiastical law, both Claudio and Juliet are penitent. Claudio, loathe to name his crime, philosophizes about how human nature seeks its own destruction as a rat consumes poison. Juliet not only acknowledges her sin in theological terms, but she is also willing to shoulder more than her fair share of guilt for the child's illegitimacy. Less scrupulous observers of the social scene, such as Lucio, regard Claudio's slip as a natural consequence of human nature, a mere "rebellion of a codpiece" hardly worth consideration, much less severe punishment (3.2.116). Pompey voices a widespread belief that the only way to eradicate fornication and bawdy houses in Vienna would be to "geld and splay all the youth of the city" (2.1.238–39). Even the provost, whose job it is to uphold the law, argues that Claudio committed his offense unknowingly, as if in a "dream" (2.2.6).

The fact that Lucio, the least penitent sexual transgressor in this play, has successfully evaded the law for so long suggests that the law itself, not just the imperfect state of human nature, is to blame for Vienna's sexual crisis. Escalus imagines the wheels of justice in Vienna turning erratically and unfairly, so that "some rise by sin and some by virtue fall" (2.1.42). Claudio, who does not exactly belong to either group, is "condemnèd for a fault alone" (44). The word "fault," which designates a moral failing somewhere between neglect and active transgression, often of a specifically sexual nature, is the term used most frequently to designate the culpable behavior of characters in *Measure for Measure*. The fact that a "fault" can be treated variously as a vice or personal habit, a civic crime, and a religious sin signals that the law in Vienna has failed to establish clear distinctions between Justice and Iniquity.

What is missing from Escalus's parodic vision of Viennese society, in which Justice and Iniquity spar ineffectually with one another, is a concept of positive virtue to counter the excesses of sexual vice and soften the corrective lash of public justice. Isabella and Angelo are the characters most committed to achieving a virtuous life. Angelo's virtue is in many ways a negative one, an abstinence and evasion of temptation that make him vulnerable to Lucio's satire and, eventually, to Isabella's beauty and eloquence. Isabella, as a religious novice seeking admittance to the strict Order of St. Clare, also yearns for a life removed from ordinary temptation. Some critics find Isabella's preference for her chastity over her brother's life to be cold, unnatural, and utterly reprehensible. But Isabella's rejection of Angelo's proposition is probably prudent. In some versions of this story, when the sister yields her virginity in exchange for her brother's life, the corrupt deputy quickly executes the brother to prevent him from avenging his sister's honor. More important, Isabella has intellectual and spiritual reasons for refusing Angelo's bargain. As an aspiring saint, she declares her willingness to throw down her life for Claudio within the terms of a Christian martyrdom. Isabella demonstrates the power of choice and commitment in a society that seeks to correct a culture of irresponsibility with tyrannical repression. Angelo's devilish bargain, by contrast, offers

Isabella an ignominious ransom for Claudio's life rather than a "free pardon" (2.4.119).

Ironically, Isabella's ability to articulate a strong ethical position arouses Angelo's dormant sexual appetite. She speaks "such sense" that Angelo's sexual "sense breeds with it" (2.2.172–73). Thus Angelo, who easily resists the strumpet's superficial arts, succumbs to the eloquence of Isabella's argument. Her plea for Claudio's life rests solidly on an analogy between divine and human authority, the same analogy that authorizes the duke and his deputy to enforce the law. God's willingness to look mercifully on human transgressions demands an equally unconditional mercy from human agents of justice. By the logic of analogy, Angelo must put himself in Claudio's place, imagine himself as "slipping" into sexual transgression, and show mercy to Claudio. By a perverse twist, the intellectual and emotional power of Isabella's rhetoric, her persuasive speech, allows Angelo to experience unlawful sexual desire and to demand, almost blasphemously, that Isabella put herself in the sexual position of ordinary women.

Isabella's ethics, based on putting oneself in the place of another person, becomes the grounds for *Measure for Measure*'s comic resolution, but the play is darkened by its insistence on silencing Isabella's female eloquence. Angelo, feeling the sting of sexual desire, is impelled to "raze the sanctuary" of Isabella's virginity (2.2.208). He can imagine feminine virtue only as an object, a monument to be either venerated or destroyed by male sexuality. Isabella's powerful speech challenges this division of women into virgins and whores by demonstrating her active commitment to virtue. Nevertheless, the duke himself contains and controls Isabella's ethical vision by dramatizing a kinship between feminine virtue and vice, first in the execution of the bed-trick and then in the elaborate trial scene that concludes the play. The duke represents the bed-trick, in which Mariana takes Isabella's place, as morally neutral and even as virtuous. Through this expedient device, Angelo will be judged and Mariana's long and lonely vigil concluded. "The doubleness of the benefit," the duke argues, "defends the deceit from reproof" (3.1.284–85). Here the duke conveniently ignores the church's requirement that a marriage be solemnized before sexual relations begin when he puts Mariana in the position already occupied by Juliet and Kate Keepdown.

Measure for Measure's concluding trial scene challenges further the role of feminine virtue in the public sphere. In this scene, the duke subjects Isabella and Mariana to his secular authority, completing Angelo's attempt to raze the sanctuary of female virtue by forcing each, in turn, to put on in public the "destined livery" of female sexuality (2.4.149). Jonathan Dollimore argues that the duke's strategy is political. He stages this elaborate trial of Angelo to demonstrate his own power and integrity as a ruler.[3] In this case, his ritual humiliation of the women is gratuitous. Isabella, noted both for her virginity and her truthful tongue, is forced to commit perjury, presenting herself as a victim of Angelo's lust. That Angelo is "a virgin-violator, / Is it not strange?" (5.1.46–47), she cries out to a public audience. Mariana, who has long been sequestered in her moated grange, now offers herself to public view as a sexual riddle, the woman who is neither "maid, widow, nor wife" (5.1.203–4), and easily becomes the object of Lucio's joke: "My lord, she may be a punk, for many of them are neither maid, widow, nor wife" (5.1.205–6). In the duke's didactic drama, Mariana and Isabella are collapsed into one figure, then relegated to an anomalous and sexually suspect category of "giglets" (5.1.391).

While the duke reestablishes law and order in Vienna,

he seems uninterested in cultivating among his subjects the kind of active virtue that would make "strict statutes and most biting laws" unnecessary (1.3.20). In a world governed by Isabella's ethics, based on identification with others and a sympathetic understanding of their faults, the laws that bolster the duke's power and confirm his identity as God's secular representative would wither away. The containment of Isabella's power is therefore politically expedient, even necessary.

The duke may demystify Isabella's ethics by making her an object of common curiosity, but he cannot silence her altogether. When the duke offers to sacrifice Mariana's new husband for the supposed death of Claudio, employing the logic of "like doth quit like," Mariana and Isabella join forces on Angelo's behalf. Mariana argues that "best men are molded out of faults" (5.1.503). Isabella bends her knee in solidarity with both Mariana and Angelo himself. She recognizes not only the other woman's feelings, but also the sincerity that governed Angelo's strict adherence to law before he encountered Isabella. Establishing an imaginative kinship with a man who has "slipped" in exactly the same way as her brother, she distinguishes between Angelo's bad thoughts and his deeds and pleads for mercy. In the debate between Justice and Mercy, Isabella and Mariana hold the day.

The ending of *Measure for Measure*, however, calls into question this triumph of female speech and ethics. The duke's final gesture, an apparent offer of marriage to Isabella, absorbs the aspiring nun into a traditional marriage plot and, at last, silences her altogether. Once the duke makes his proposal, Isabella never speaks another word. In the bed-trick and in the trial scene, the women enact a script provided for them by the duke. In their plea for Angelo, perhaps, they speak their minds. But what can be made of Isabella's silence in the face of the duke's marriage proposal? Our experience with the legal complexity of the various marriages in this play might make us regard skeptically the duke's evasion of all forms of ceremony attached to normal marriages of the period.

Contemporary productions of the play vary in their interpretation of Isabella's silence. In some, Isabella is swept up willingly in the marriage celebrations. In others, she resists the duke's offer or rejects him altogether. As *Measure for Measure*'s anatomy of marriage suggests, without the imposition of strict statutes and biting laws, marriage vows are valid only as long as two people agree on their validity. The theater, as another kind of social ritual, also depends on a consensus between audience and actors in the absence of strict laws of verisimilitude. To the duke's suggestion that "what's mine is yours, and what is yours is mine" (5.1.611), Isabella and the actor who played her offer no response. Throughout the play Isabella consistently resists the logic of measure for measure. She refuses to sacrifice Angelo's life for Claudio's death. Perhaps more important, she refuses to exchange her body for Claudio's life. To Angelo's offer, Isabella had pledged to wear the "impression of keen whips" as rubies rather than yield her "body up to shame" (2.4.108, 111). In light of this vow, her silence in the face of the duke's proposal may be very eloquent indeed.

---

1. For a detailed discussion of the stages of marriage in this period and their significance to *Measure for Measure*, see Victoria Hayne, "Performing Social Practice: The Example of *Measure for Measure*," *Shakespeare Quarterly* 44 (1993): 1–29. For an analysis that differs in some respects from my own, see Historical Background 2: "Betrothal and Marriage," pages 227–32.

2. John Ingram discusses a type of case that frequently came before the ecclesiastical courts, in which a male

defendant made "some kind of promise of marriage" to a gullible woman, but acted "insincerely or with fraudulent intention." For instance, Cecily Chisleton, a servant, allowed Robert Maundrell to have sex with her after he had promised marriage and had given her presents or love-tokens, including a letter with a pair of gloves. Robert, however, changed his mind when Cecily became pregnant. Although the master of the house attempted to force Robert to marry Cecily, in court Robert insisted that he had merely kissed her "as he did other of my lady's maids" (John Ingram, *Church Courts, Sex and Marriage in England, 1570–1640* [Cambridge: Cambridge University Press, 1987], p. 199). By contrast, at the end of a festival day another, wiser young woman named Alice Gidlowe was asked by John Cotgreve, a Cheshire clergyman, to enter an abandoned house and make love to him. She did, but only after the two had made the appropriate vows before their friends (John R. Gillis, *For Better, For Worse: British Marriages, 1600 to the Present* [Oxford: Clarendon Press, 1985], p. 38).

3. Jonathan Dollimore, "Transgression and Surveillance in *Measure for Measure*," in *Political Shakespeare*, ed. Dollimore and Alan Sinfield (Ithaca: Cornell University Press, 1985), pp. 72–87.

Further Reading

Measure for Measure

Adelman, Janet. "Bed Tricks: On Marriage as the End of Comedy in *All's Well That Ends Well* and *Measure for Measure*." In *Shakespeare's Personality*, edited by Norman Holland, Sidney Homan, and Bernard Paris, pp. 151–74. Berkeley, Los Angeles, and London: University of California Press, 1989.

Adelman maintains that the bed trick in *All's Well* and *Measure* serves "to legitimize sexual desire" by allowing Bertram and Angelo, respectively, to direct their illicit desires "back toward their socially sanctioned mates," thereby effecting the "conventional festive ending in marriage." The similarities end there, however, since marriage functions as a "cure" in *All's Well* but as a "punishment" in *Measure*. The duke's marriage proposal to Isabella, moreover, is shocking and unsettling because by the end of the play the duke has become for Isabella the "embodiment of the fantasied asexual father."

Baines, Barbara J. "Assaying the Power of Chastity in *Measure for Measure*." *Studies in English Literature* **30** (1990): 283–301.

Baines takes issue with Reifer's focus on Isabella's "powerlessness" (see below) to argue that Isabella's choice of chastity both empowers her and establishes her identity in the social structure of Vienna, so that "its forfeiture would constitute for her a form of social and psychological suicide." Chastity is the "definitive virtue" in the world of *Measure for Measure*, not for theological or religious reasons but "precisely because it is a site and mode of secular power": i.e., the State appropriates chastity to further its own ends—social health and patriarchy. The duke's proposal to Isabella at the end shows the extent to which "authority privileges chastity," which in turn (by virtue of its political and secular imperatives) "authorizes authority."

Desmet, Christy. " 'Who Is't Can Read a Woman?': Rhetoric and Gender in *Venus and Adonis*, *Measure for Measure*, and *All's Well That Ends Well*." In *Reading Shakespeare's Characters: Rhetoric, Ethics, and Identity*, pages 134–63, esp. pages 144–54. Amherst: University of Massachusetts Press, 1992.

The Renaissance ambivalence toward rhetoric as either decorative entrapment or a means to promote the civic good was often personified in terms of a woman's virtues or vices: rhetoric as noble lady (judicial public debate) vs. rhetoric as whore (ornate dissembling). It is within this ambivalence about rhetoric and its relation to truth that Desmet locates the moral ambiguity of Isabella, a skilled orator who flatters and lies for a good cause. By appropriating male argumentative strategies and analogies, Isabella illustrates "cross-identification"—the verbal equivalent of cross-dressing. In the final scene, where she is given a prominent voice in the debate surrounding Angelo's case, Isabella in her role as seductive sophist "trespasses into the male domain of judicial debate and for this reason threatens both masculine rhetoric and the masculine political prerogative." Her ultimate silence in the face of the duke's marriage proposal reveals Shakespeare's own unease about the power of rhetoric, particularly feminine rhetoric.

Dollimore, Jonathan. "Transgression and Surveillance in *Measure for Measure*." In *Political Shakespeare: New*

Essays in Cultural Materialism, edited by Jonathan Dollimore and Alan Sinfield, pp. 72–87. Ithaca: Cornell University Press, 1985.

In this materialist reading of *Measure for Measure,* Dollimore observes that the play's overriding concern with sexual transgression is rooted in political rather than ethical considerations: "Signify[ing] neither the unregeneracy of the flesh, nor the ludic subversive carnivalesque," sexual license provides the means for the state to legitimate its own authority because authority must control deviant behavior. In *Measure for Measure* "the more we attend to the supposed subversiveness of sexual license, and the authoritarian response to it, the more we are led away from the vice itself toward social tensions which intersect with it." Dollimore includes among the tensions prominent in the winter of 1604 the following: fear of a war with Spain, the plague, treason trials, and economic difficulties in London.

Friedman, Michael D. " 'O, let him marry her!': Matrimony and Recompense in *Measure for Measure.*" *Shakespeare Quarterly* 46 (1995): 454–64.

Intrigued by the ambiguity surrounding the duke's sudden marriage proposal to Isabella, Friedman proposes that a production of *Measure for Measure* "need not strive to make the play conform to conventions of romantic comedy in which marriage represents the culmination of erotic desire. If a production avoids importing the modern notion that a proposal of matrimony presupposes love," the audience may still derive comic pleasure from seeing the male characters, including the duke, accept responsibility for their own actions. All of the marriages that conclude *Measure for Measure* "are equally rooted in a Renaissance belief in recompense for sexual crimes, even where reciprocal affection also exists." The essay includes discussion of the following productions: Adrian Noble's 1983 and Trevor Nunn's 1991 Royal Shakespeare Company revivals; Michael Bogdanov's 1985 and Michael Langham's 1992 stagings at Stratford, Ontario; and Michael Kahn's 1992 interpretation for The Shakespeare Theatre in Washington, D.C.

Gless, Darryl J. *Measure for Measure: The Law and the Convent.* Princeton: Princeton University Press, 1979.

Concerned with the intellectual context of the play, Gless draws upon contemporary legal and religious documents to probe *Measure for Measure*'s depiction of flawed characters who wrestle with the ambiguities of morality in a journey toward forgiveness, reconciliation, and renewal. Shakespeare "appears consistently to have selected and dramatized doctrines that are especially flexible and tolerant of adjustment to particular circumstances." The play's thematic core centers on the Sermon on the Mount passage in Matthew, which does not forbid judgment but exhorts "proper judgment"—that which conforms with the laws of charity and with recognition of one's own sinfulness. Lucio, Isabella, Angelo, and Claudio all fail to judge with charity. In Gless's view, the duke functions as the instrument of a benign Providence that oversees the characters' ultimate redemption.

Hawkes, Terence. "Take Me to Your Leda." *Shakespeare Survey* 40 (1988): 21–32. Reprinted in *Meaning by Shakespeare,* pages 61–78. London and New York: Routledge, 1992.

Hawkes uses contrasting readings of *Measure for Measure* provided by G. Wilson Knight and William Empson in 1930 (and a similar clash between the interpretations of F. R. Leavis and L. C. Knights in 1942) to reveal how the play "periodically functions as a cultural arena in which significant ideological conflict takes place." The diametrically opposed readings offer a model for the critical divisions that have developed since the 1930s in determining where the critical emphasis should lie—with the author (Zeus) or with the reader/audience (Leda). Hawkes finds it appropriate that the "divide" between fixity of meaning (Knight and Leavis) vs. ambiguity (Empson and Knights) is centered on a play that is a "study of system, trial, and breakdown," in which any communication of "prepackaged, coherent, and unified 'meaning' seem[s] an impossible project."

Hayne, Victoria. "Performing Social Practice: The Example of *Measure for Measure*." *Shakespeare Quarterly* 44 (1993): 1–29.

Hayne argues that *Measure for Measure* participates in a cultural debate aired in books, sermons, and parliamentary bills of Tudor-Stuart England, the terms of which "centered not on *whether* sexual behavior should be regulated but on *how:* the alternatives were penance or death." The play exploits the ambiguities inherent in the fluid state of Elizabethan/Jacobean marriage formation. Just as the practice in the courts of the day often "winked" at sexual transgressions, opting for mediation and modification of "draconian" laws, so by way of comic conventions Shakespeare modifies the puritanical retribution of Angelo. By mingling social and literary conventions, *Measure for Measure* "takes up, and implicates its audience's theatrical responses in, its position in the contemporary debate over sexual regulation."

Kaplan, M. Lindsay. "Slander for Slander in *Measure for Measure*." *Renaissance Drama*, New Series 21 (1990): 23–54.

Kaplan applies her findings on "how slander figured as theater" in political and dramatic practice in late sixteenth- and early seventeenth-century England to an analysis of *Measure for Measure*. The English legal system as a whole operated "as a type of institutionalized slander" in that punishment, by making a criminal infamous, "essentially functioned as defamation." Focusing on the relation between the privately delivered slanders of Lucio against the duke and the duke's own publicly articulated criticism of the corrupt state of Vienna (5.1.356–62), Kaplan observes how the duke's punishment of Lucio indicates the former's greater concern with enforcing laws banning the "slandering" of princes than with laws against fornication. Lucio's unpardonable offense lies not in criticizing the duke's authority but in "competing with it." Kaplan concludes that *Measure for Measure* "employs the state's own methods of exposure to criticize the arbitrariness of its response to theater, and to warn that the greater peril of theatrical slander lies in the ruler's, not the theater's, abuse of it."

Leonard, Nancy S. "Substitutions in Shakespeare's Problem Comedies." *English Literary Renaissance* 9 (1979): 281–301.

Leonard focuses on the act of substitution as the dramatic means by which Shakespeare makes theatrically coherent the ambiguity of judgment that is central to the problem comedies. Where impersonation of a fictive character yields delight and manifests versatility in the romantic comedies, substitution of one character for another in plays like *Measure for Measure* compels

testing of character against role and other characters—
a process that beneficially engages both principal agents
(the duke and Isabella) and the ones substituted for
them (Angelo and Mariana).

Machiavelli, Niccolo. *The Prince*, trans. Robert M. Ad-
ams. New York: W. W. Norton, 1992.
  In this famous 16th-century political treatise, Machiavelli draws upon his experience as a member of the
Florentine government in order to present his conception of the kind of strong leader and tactics required to
impose political order for the good of the unified Italy
he envisioned. Because Machiavelli separates politics
from ethics and is more concerned with ends than with
means, his name has become identified with all that is
cynical and even diabolical in state affairs. In Shakespeare's England, this exaggeratedly negative reputation
gave rise to the conventional villain known as the
Machiavel. *Measure for Measure*'s "duke of dark corners" is not a Machiavel in the vein of Richard III, but
some critics argue for an affinity between his strategies
and policies and Machiavelli's political tenets.

Miles, Rosalind. *The Problem of Measure for Measure: A
Historical Investigation*. New York: Barnes & Noble,
1976.
  Miles's study falls into two parts. The first reviews
Measure for Measure's stage history from 1604 to the
early 1970s, tracing the peaks and valleys in its reception; *Measure for Measure* has been especially suscepti-
ble to shifts in taste and morality. The second part
provides a detailed analysis of the play's three main
characters (the duke, Angelo, and Isabella), overall
design, and plot mechanisms; Miles pays special attention to Shakespeare's use of such popular conventions
as disguise, stock character types, and the bed trick.

Mowat, Barbara A. "Shakespearean Tragicomedy." In *Renaissance Tragicomedy: Explorations in Genre and Politics,* edited by Nancy Klein Maguire, pp. 80–96. New York: AMS Press, 1987.

Mowat considers the problem plays *(All's Well, Measure for Measure,* and *Troilus and Cressida)* experiments in tragicomedy as defined by Guarini in his 1601 *Compendio della poesia tragicomica:* a story in which tragic and comic parts are mixed, with persons of high rank approaching death but ultimately avoiding it, and a miraculously achieved "happy ending" that purges melancholy. While *Measure for Measure* may deviate from the model in some respects (e.g., its "happy ending" lacks a sense of the "miraculous"), it conforms to Guarini's essential requirement: the blending of "action, grave or comic, and speech 'tending toward commiseration or toward laughter.'" In *Measure for Measure* Shakespeare "selects and shapes a story in which the events themselves are blends of the conventionally comic and the conventionally tragic. Lust and death are so intermingled . . . that the language of the play swings from the deeply serious to the sardonic to the genuinely amusing, with the tragicomic balance being maintained throughout." Even in the multiple marriages that conclude the play, the emotional response is mixed: marriage is a punishment for Lucio, "a fate less-bad-than-death" for Angelo, "an after-the-fact rite" for Claudio, and finally a "joyous celebration" for the duke and Isabella—provided she accepts his proposal.

Pope, Elizabeth. "The Renaissance Background of *Measure for Measure.*" *Shakespeare Survey* 2 (1949):66–82. Reprinted in George Geckle, ed., *Twentieth-Century Interpretations of Measure for Measure,* pp. 50–72. Englewood Cliffs, N.J.: Prentice-Hall, 1970.

Pope interprets *Measure for Measure* as being "very largely concerned with the 'Prince's duty,' particularly in regard to the administration of justice." Interest in the privileges and duties of a ruler was especially keen in 1603–4 with the accession of James I, who had written on the subject of kingship in *Basilicon Doron*. Pope examines contemporary thinking on equity, forgiveness, and the subject of rule as expounded in Renaissance sermons, tracts, and biblical commentaries. Divine Right theory, which posits the ruler as God's substitute on earth, explains why the duke moves so easily through the play—"like an embodied Providence." In *Measure for Measure* Shakespeare strengthens, clarifies, and attempts to resolve the "disturbing discrepancy between the concepts of religious mercy and secular justice" found in the commentaries on the "measure-for-measure" passage from *Matthew* and *Luke* as it relates to matters of rule. The doctrinal teaching on the passage is of "primary importance, since it covers most—if not all—of the major ethical issues that appear in *Measure for Measure*."

Riefer, Marcia. " 'Instruments of Some More Mightier Member': The Constriction of Female Power in *Measure for Measure*." *Shakespeare Quarterly* 35 (1984): 157–69.
More than any other previous Shakespearean play, *Measure for Measure* "exposes the dehumanizing effects on women of living in a world dominated by powerful men who would like to recreate womanhood according to their fantasies." Riefer rejects the typical ways of viewing Isabella as either "idealized saint" or "denigrated vixen," seeing her instead as a victim of sexual subjugation who dwindles from "an articulate, compassionate woman" during her first encounter with Angelo "to a stunned, angry, defensive woman" in her later confrontations with him and Claudio and "to finally a

shadow of her former articulate self, on her knees before male authority in Act 5." Her final speech urging mercy for Angelo—filled with "casuistical legalisms"— is the "opposite" of moral growth and provides further proof of her loss of a personal voice—a loss that makes *Measure for Measure* "Isabella's tragedy."

Rossiter, A.P. *"Measure for Measure."* In *Angel with Horns and Other Shakespeare Lectures,* edited by Graham Storey, pp. 152–70. New York: Theatre Arts Books, 1961.

Rejecting neatly imposed Christian allegorical solutions to *Measure for Measure,* Rossiter finds the play riddled with ambiguities which are essential to its dramatic structure and which, therefore, cannot be easily resolved. Shakespeare may have intended a "higher" Christian ethic in *Measure for Measure,* but he fails to achieve it because of flawed character development and because the texture of the writing after 3.1 "goes thin," thus revealing a lack of "inner conviction." Instead of functioning as "an image of Providence," the duke, who holds the key to the way we interpret the ending, is a "shadowy figure." For Rossiter, the two confrontations between Angelo and Isabella are unique in the Shakespeare canon, few scenes matching their power on the modern stage.

Schleiner, Louise. "Providential Improvisation in *Measure for Measure." PMLA* 97 (1982): 227–36.

Schleiner agrees with those who find in the play's many biblical allusions a parallel between the duke and God (as testing master, redeemer, and judge), but she interprets the parallel within a comic, not didactic, context. The duke is not God but a ruler whose "quixotic attempts" to imitate God (as a good ruler should, according to the political/religious thinking of the time) yield "mixed and humorous results." The key to *Measure for Measure*'s delicate balance between laughter and darkness lies in the duke's function as moral tester, a role he performs throughout this "chameleon" play. The duke is "fallible, meddling, and laughable but beneficent, inventive, and in large measure successful in helping his subjects."

Stevenson, David L. *The Achievement of Shakespeare's Measure for Measure*. Ithaca: Cornell University Press, 1966.
    Stevenson classifies *Measure for Measure* as an intellectual comedy on "moral obtuseness" constructed around "the twin themes of mercy and justice" in a schematic design of interrelated ironies and reversals that are finally resolved through the "balancing out of paradox." In addition to a discussion of the play's overall dramatic design, the volume includes a scene-by-scene analysis, a survey of critical resistance to the play, and a refutation of readings that derive from theological interpretation. The "stuff" of *Measure for Measure* is "the tantalizing excitement, the fear, the shame of man's sexuality, his shared common denominator of sexual desire." For Stevenson, the play is Shakespeare's "most ingeniously constructed comedy."

Summers, Joseph H. "Comedy of Justice: *Measure for Measure*." In *Dreams of Love and Power: On Shakespeare's Plays*, pp. 68–94. London and New York: Oxford University Press, 1984.
    Summers points out that, while the dramaturgy of most of Shakespeare's plays allows us to know the characters and their world by Act 2 and thus anticipate likely developments, in *Measure for Measure* we cannot at all predict what will happen. Proceeding through the play scene by scene, Summers shows how "we are

reduced to a state of childlike waiting for the revelations of wonders by a secretive duke and a mysterious playwright." The last scene presents a masque of judgment in which we "are invited to be baffled by and then to rejoice in a complicated, limited . . . working out of a happy ending" that suggests the "unimaginable dream" of "justice fully satisfied and yet everyone forgiven."

Watson, Robert N. "False Immortality in *Measure for Measure:* Comic Means, Tragic Ends." *Shakespeare Quarterly* 41 (1990): 411–32.

Watson classifies *Measure for Measure* as tragicomedy because it persistently subverts comedy's promise of immortality (whether in the form of fame, salvation, or procreation) and replaces it "with an emphasis on the destruction of the individual, an emphasis that is typical of tragedy." Instead of dispelling the pervasive darkness of this "death-filled" play, the marriages that conclude the action, by virtue of their abrupt and formulaic nature, "encourage . . . a suspicion that the aftermath of marriage and death alike is merely a biological process with no regard for human consciousness." Watson speculates that *Measure for Measure* is a product of the plague year 1603 "not only in its emphasis on the replenishment of the population but also in its portrayal of a city abandoned by its benevolent but exasperated Lord to an agency of deadly retribution."

Wheeler, Richard P. "Vincentio and the Sins of Others: The Expense of Spirit in *Measure for Measure.*" In *Shakespeare's Development and the Problem Comedies: Turn and Counter-Turn*, pp. 92–153. Berkeley, Los Angeles, and London: University of California Press, 1981.

Wheeler makes extensive use of Freudian and contemporary psychoanalysis in his study of the problem comedies and where they fit in Shakespeare's development. The chapter on *Measure for Measure* discusses the play under the headings "Angelo's Brief Authority," "Sexuality, Life and Death," "Deputation and the Sins of Others," and "Ghostly Fathers and Spectral Women." Wheeler relates the conflicts in *Measure for Measure* to those that Shakespeare "masters more fully" in his tragedies; *Measure for Measure* is, in fact, disturbing as a comedy because it depicts the kind of psychological complexity we associate more with tragic drama. A play dominated by "mistrust of sexuality" and informed by an attitude that views sexuality as debased, *Measure for Measure* is "guided to its comic conclusion by a character whose essence is the denial of family ties and sexuality, the denial, that is to say, of the essence of comedy." While the marriage of Kate Keepdown and Lucio is "an appropriately debased culmination of the play's unpurged tension between sexuality and the moral order," the marriage proposal of the duke (ghostly father) to Isabella (aspiring nun) is, Wheeler concludes, "the appropriately barren culmination of the play's moralized comic design."

Shakespeare's Language

Abbott, E. A. *A Shakespearian Grammar.* New York: Haskell House, 1972.

This compact reference book, first published in 1870, helps with many difficulties in Shakespeare's language. It systematically accounts for a host of differences between Shakespeare's usage and sentence structure and our own.

Blake, Norman. *Shakespeare's Language: An Introduction.* New York: St. Martin's Press, 1983.

This general introduction to Elizabethan English discusses various aspects of the language of Shakespeare and his contemporaries, offering possible meanings for hundreds of ambiguous constructions.

Dobson, E. J. *English Pronunciation, 1500–1700.* 2 vols. Oxford: Clarendon Press, 1968.
This long and technical work includes chapters on spelling (and its reformation), phonetics, stressed vowels, and consonants in early modern English.

Houston, John. *Shakespearean Sentences: A Study in Style and Syntax.* Baton Rouge: Louisiana State University Press, 1988.
Houston studies Shakespeare's stylistic choices, considering matters such as sentence length and the relative positions of subject, verb, and direct object. Examining plays throughout the canon in a roughly chronological, developmental order, he analyzes how sentence structure is used in setting tone, in characterization, and for other dramatic purposes.

Onions, C.T. *A Shakespeare Glossary.* Oxford: Clarendon Press, 1986.
This revised edition updates Onions's standard, selective glossary of words and phrases in Shakespeare's plays that are now obsolete, archaic, or obscure.

Robinson, Randal. *Unlocking Shakespeare's Language: Help for the Teacher and Student.* Urbana, Ill.: National Council of Teachers of English and the ERIC Clearinghouse on Reading and Communication Skills, 1989.
Specifically designed for the high-school and undergraduate college teacher and student, Robinson's book addresses the problems that most often hinder present-day readers of Shakespeare. Through work with his own

students, Robinson found that many readers today are particularly puzzled by such stylistic devices as subject-verb inversion, interrupted structures, and compression. He shows how our own colloquial language contains comparable structures, and thus helps students recognize such structures when they find them in Shakespeare's plays. This book supplies worksheets—with examples from major plays—to illuminate and remedy such problems as unusual sequences of words and the separation of related parts of sentences.

Williams, Gordon. *A Dictionary of Sexual Language and Imagery in Shakespearean and Stuart Literature.* 3 vols. London: Athlone Press, 1994.

Williams provides a comprehensive list of the words to which Shakespeare, his contemporaries, and later Stuart writers gave sexual meanings. He supports his identification of these meanings by extensive quotations.

Shakespeare's Life

Baldwin, T. W. *William Shakspere's Petty School.* Urbana: University of Illinois Press, 1943.

Baldwin here investigates the theory and practice of the petty school, the first level of education in Elizabethan England. He focuses on that educational system primarily as it is reflected in Shakespeare's art.

Baldwin, T. W. *William Shakspere's Small Latine and Lesse Greeke.* 2 vols. Urbana: University of Illinois Press, 1944.

Baldwin attacks the view that Shakespeare was an uneducated genius—a view that had been dominant among Shakespeareans since the eighteenth century. Instead, Baldwin shows, the educational system of

Shakespeare's time would have given the playwright a strong background in the classics, and there is much in the plays that shows how Shakespeare benefited from such an education.

Beier, A. L., and Roger Finlay, eds. *London 1500–1800: The Making of the Metropolis*. New York: Longman, 1986.

Focusing on the economic and social history of early modern London, these collected essays probe aspects of metropolitan life, including "Population and Disease," "Commerce and Manufacture," and "Society and Change."

Bentley, G. E. *Shakespeare's Life: A Biographical Handbook*. New Haven: Yale University Press, 1961.

This "just-the-facts" account presents the surviving documents of Shakespeare's life against an Elizabethan background.

Chambers, E. K. *William Shakespeare: A Study of Facts and Problems*. 2 vols. Oxford: Clarendon Press, 1930.

Analyzing in great detail the scant historical data, Chambers's complex, scholarly study considers the nature of the texts in which Shakespeare's work is preserved.

Cressy, David. *Education in Tudor and Stuart England*. London: Edward Arnold, 1975.

This volume collects sixteenth-, seventeenth-, and early-eighteenth-century documents detailing aspects of formal education in England, such as the curriculum, the control and organization of education, and the education of women.

Dutton, Richard. *William Shakespeare: A Literary Life*. New York: St. Martin's Press, 1989.

Not a biography in the traditional sense, Dutton's very readable work nevertheless "follows the contours of Shakespeare's life" as he examines Shakespeare's career as playwright and poet, with consideration of his patrons, theatrical associations, and audience.

Fraser, Russell. *Young Shakespeare*. New York: Columbia University Press, 1988.

Fraser focuses on Shakespeare's first thirty years, paying attention simultaneously to his life and art.

De Grazia, Margreta. *Shakespeare Verbatim: The Reproduction of Authenticity and the Apparatus of 1790*. Oxford: Clarendon Press, 1991.

De Grazia traces and discusses the development of such editorial criteria as authenticity, historical periodization, factual biography, chronological development, and close reading, locating as the point of origin Edmond Malone's 1790 edition of Shakespeare's works. There are interesting chapters on the First Folio and on the "legendary" versus the "documented" Shakespeare.

Schoenbaum, S. *William Shakespeare: A Compact Documentary Life*. New York: Oxford University Press, 1977.

This standard biography economically presents the essential documents from Shakespeare's time in an accessible narrative account of the playwright's life.

Shakespeare's Theater

Bentley, G. E. *The Profession of Player in Shakespeare's Time, 1590–1642*. Princeton: Princeton University Press, 1984.

Bentley readably sets forth a wealth of evidence about

performance in Shakespeare's time, with special attention to the relations between player and company, and the business of casting, managing, and touring.

Berry, Herbert. *Shakespeare's Playhouses.* New York: AMS Press, 1987.
Berry's six essays collected here discuss (with illustrations) varying aspects of the four playhouses in which Shakespeare had a financial stake: the Theatre in Shoreditch, the Blackfriars, and the first and second Globe.

Cook, Ann Jennalie. *The Privileged Playgoers of Shakespeare's London.* Princeton: Princeton University Press, 1981.
Cook's work argues, on the basis of sociological, economic, and documentary evidence, that Shakespeare's audience—and the audience for English Renaissance drama generally—consisted mainly of the "privileged."

Greg, W. W. *Dramatic Documents from the Elizabethan Playhouses.* 2 vols. Oxford: Clarendon Press, 1931.
Greg itemizes and briefly describes many of the play manuscripts that survive from the period 1590 to around 1660, including, among other things, players' parts. His second volume offers facsimiles of selected manuscripts.

Gurr, Andrew. *Playgoing in Shakespeare's London.* Cambridge: Cambridge University Press, 1987.
Gurr charts how the theatrical enterprise developed from its modest beginnings in the late 1560s to become a thriving institution in the 1600s. He argues that there were important changes over the period 1567–1644 in the playhouses, the audience, and the plays.

Harbage, Alfred. *Shakespeare's Audience*. New York: Columbia University Press, 1941.

Harbage investigates the fragmentary surviving evidence to interpret the size, composition, and behavior of Shakespeare's audience.

Hattaway, Michael. *Elizabethan Popular Theatre: Plays in Performance*. London: Routledge & Kegan Paul, 1982.

Beginning with a study of the popular drama of the late Elizabethan age—a description of the stages, performance conditions, and acting of the period—this volume concludes with an analysis of five well-known plays of the 1590s, one of them (*Titus Andronicus*) by Shakespeare.

Shapiro, Michael. *Children of the Revels: The Boy Companies of Shakespeare's Time and Their Plays*. New York: Columbia University Press, 1977.

Shapiro chronicles the history of the amateur and quasi-professional child companies that flourished in London at the end of Elizabeth's reign and the beginning of James's.

The Publication of Shakespeare's Plays

Blayney, Peter. *The First Folio of Shakespeare*. Hanover, Md.: Folger, 1991.

Blayney's accessible account of the printing and later life of the First Folio—an amply illustrated catalog to a 1991 Folger Shakespeare Library exhibition—analyzes the mechanical production of the First Folio, describing how the Folio was made, by whom and for whom, how much it cost, and its ups and downs (or, rather, downs and ups) since its printing in 1623.

Hinman, Charlton. *The Printing and Proof-Reading of the First Folio of Shakespeare*. 2 vols. Oxford: Clarendon Press, 1963.

In the most arduous study of a single book ever undertaken, Hinman attempts to reconstruct how the Shakespeare First Folio of 1623 was set into type and run off the press, sheet by sheet. He also provides almost all the known variations in readings from copy to copy.

Hinman, Charlton. *The Norton Facsimile: The First Folio of Shakespeare*. Second Edition. New York: W. W. Norton, 1996.

This facsimile presents a photographic reproduction of an "ideal" copy of the First Folio of Shakespeare; Hinman attempts to represent each page in its most fully corrected state. The second edition includes an important new introduction by Peter Blayney.

Key to
Famous Lines and Phrases

. . . Spirits are not finely touched
But to fine issues . . .   [*Duke*—1.1.38–39]

Thus can the demigod Authority
Make us pay down for our offense, by weight,
The words of heaven: on whom it will, it will;
On whom it will not, so; yet still 'tis just.
                                   [*Claudio*—1.2.116–19]

As surfeit is the father of much fast,
So every scope by the immoderate use
Turns to restraint. Our natures do pursue,
Like rats that raven down their proper bane,
A thirsty evil, and when we drink, we die.
                                   [*Claudio*—1.2.123–27]

. . . liberty plucks justice by the nose,
The baby beats the nurse, and quite athwart
Goes all decorum.   [*Duke*—1.3.30–32]

. . . Lord Angelo is precise,
Stands at a guard with envy, scarce confesses
That his blood flows or that his appetite
Is more to bread than stone.   [*Duke*—1.3.54–57]

I'll be supposed upon a book, his face is the worst thing
about him.   [*Pompey*—2.1.163–64]

No ceremony that to great ones longs,
Not the king's crown, nor the deputed sword,
The marshal's truncheon, nor the judge's robe,
Become them with one half so good a grace
As mercy does.   [*Isabella*—2.2.79–83]

Why all the souls that were were forfeit once,
And He that might the vantage best have took
Found out the remedy. How would you be
If He which is the top of judgment should
But judge you as you are? O, think on that,
And mercy then will breathe within your lips
Like man new-made.   [*Isabella*—2.2.97–103]

. . . man, proud man,
Dressed in a little brief authority,
Most ignorant of what he's most assured,
His glassy essence, like an angry ape
Plays such fantastic tricks before high heaven
As makes the angels weep . . .
                                  [*Isabella*—2.2.146–51]

O cunning enemy that, to catch a saint,
With saints dost bait thy hook.
                                  [*Angelo*—2.2.217–18]

. . . Thou hast nor youth nor
    age,
But as it were an after-dinner's sleep
Dreaming on both . . .   [*Duke*—3.1.33–36]

                    If I must die,
I will encounter darkness as a bride,
And hug it in mine arms.   [*Claudio*—3.1.93–95]

Ay, but to die, and go we know not where,
To lie in cold obstruction and to rot,

This sensible warm motion to become
A kneaded clod; and the delighted spirit
To bathe in fiery floods, or to reside
In thrilling region of thick-ribbèd ice,
To be imprisoned in the viewless winds
And blown with restless violence round about
The pendent world; . . .
The weariest and most loathèd worldly life
That age, ache, penury, and imprisonment
Can lay on nature is a paradise
To what we fear of death.   [*Claudio*—3.1.133–47]

Take, O take those lips away,
  That so sweetly were forsworn . . .
                                    [*Song*—4.1.1–2]

Haste still pays haste, and leisure answers leisure;
Like doth quit like, and measure still for
  measure.
                                    [*Duke*—5.1.466–68]